BIBLE COMMENTARY

ROMANS

PAUL'S MASTERPIECE ON GRACE

ANDREW WOMMACK

Published by Harrison House Publishers
Shippensburg, PA 17257

ISBN 13 HC: 978-1-6803-1865-4

ISBN 13 eBook: 978-1-6803-1866-1

For Worldwide Distribution, Printed in the U.S.A.

3 4 5 6 7 8 / 25 24 23 22

CONTENTS

INTRODUCTION

The book of Romans is the Apostle Paul's scholarly explanation of the New Covenant, where he reveals how God deals with us through His mercy and grace instead of through our works of performance. It's what Scripture calls the Gospel!

We use the word "Gospel" to refer to anything related to Christianity. But when Paul used this word, he was describing the good news of everything Jesus did for us in His death and resurrection. It countered a lot of Old Testament ideas that many people hold even to this day. The Gospel had such a radical connotation that it seemed too good to be true. So, people were offended when this word had any association with God. To them, good news like this could never come from Him.

Paul constantly encountered this religious mindset. The people were so legalistic that they had a limit on how many steps you could take on a Sabbath Day! One group, the Essenes, had it in their writings that you couldn't have a bowel movement on a Sabbath. I mean, it was oppressive! These people had such strict religious practices that it makes you wonder how anyone could live under it. Then Paul comes along and says he's not ashamed of the nearly-too-good-to-be-true news that Jesus paid for everything and it's not based on his performance. I'm sure you can see how this boggled the religious minds of his day.

When Paul explained why he wasn't ashamed of the Gospel, he wrote that it's because it's the power of God unto salvation (Rom.

1:16). This includes the forgiveness of sins but is not limited to only being forgiven. It's also talking about healing, deliverance, prosperity, joy, and peace! Paul said that the Gospel releases the power for everything you need. All you have to do is believe and receive. There's no better place to understand these things than the book of Romans. It's one of my favorite books. I believe I can say that if Romans isn't one of your favorite books, then you do not have a revelation of the true Gospel. Romans is where you really get a solid foundation and begin to mature in these things.

In the summer of 1968, after I first got really turned onto the Lord, I was at a meeting where I heard a man say, "If you could understand the first eight or nine chapters of the book of Romans, it would cause you to be a mature Christian." I remember that stuck out to me, and so I started seriously studying the book of Romans. I would venture to say it was at least ten or maybe fifteen years before I felt like I got a revelation of it. Up until that time, I had knowledge, but it just didn't really impart the truth that Paul was trying to get across. I'm still learning. I'm not saying that I've got it all figured out yet, but this has become one of the most important things that God has spoken to me. I tell you, if it affects you the way that it has affected me, I believe this could be just totally life-transforming for you.

So, I pray that as you read the pages that follow, God will give you a supernatural understanding of the book of Romans. You'll find hundreds of my personal notes and commentary for nearly every verse, taken from my Life for Today and Living Commentary materials. These are the result of thousands of hours of study, as I have spent decades poring over these scriptures and meditating on the things God was revealing to me. It's a tremendous resource! Countless lives all around the world have been changed by these truths, so I'm excited to be sharing them with you. You are going to be so blessed!

NOTE:

Romans: Paul's Masterpiece on Grace is a combination of Andrew's *Life for Today* commentary, written between 1983 and 1990, and the newer *Living Commentary*, which Andrew regularly updates. The shaded portions of the pages are pulled from *Living Commentary*, and the non-shaded notes are the original *Life for Today* content. Additionally, if the references at the ends of some of the notes are not straightforward, it's because this book is a merging of the old and new works. For a clearer picture of how this commentary on Romans relates to other biblical passages, we encourage you to explore *Living Commentary*, which contains more than 25,000 notes (as of 2021) and is available at www.awmi.net/LC.

LIVING COMMENTARY ON ROMANS

Introduction to Romans

The book of Romans is the longest and the clearest exposition by the Apostle Paul on the Gospel. This book contains the doctrinal foundation for the Christian faith, and it is for this reason that it was arranged first in order among the New Testament epistles. The truths presented here must be understood before proceeding to other doctrinal matters.

In this letter, Paul dealt with a larger number of doctrinal issues than in any other of his epistles. His treatment of the doctrine of salvation by grace through faith was so masterfully done that its divine inspiration cannot be questioned. The depth with which Paul treated these great subjects shows that this knowledge was truly given to him by the direct revelation of God (Galatians 1:12).

An understanding of the truths in Romans 3 transformed Martin Luther's personal life and ignited the fires of the Reformation that shook the world. Indeed, an understanding of the truths expressed in this book are essential not only to the salvation of every individual but also to the maturing and success of every Christian.

Authorship

Paul is undoubtedly the author of the letter to the Romans. The first verse of this epistle clearly states so (Romans 1:1). There is no dissenting opinion of this among the early writings of the church. The writer also sent greetings to Priscilla and Aquila (Romans 16:3, see note 2 at Acts 18:2), his helpers, and also to Timotheus, his workfellow (Romans 16:21). The book of Acts confirms these people worked closely with Paul.

The Recipients of Paul's Epistle "Romans"

Paul addressed this letter to all the Christians that were in Rome (Romans 1:7). There is no scriptural account of any apostolic mission taking the Gospel to Rome, so it may therefore be supposed that these Christians were converts from the Day of Pentecost when the Holy Spirit was given (Acts 2:10) and from the personal witness of believers as they traversed the empire.

These saints in Rome were a diverse group: Gentiles who had come from pagan worship to trust in Jesus as their Savior, and devout Jews who had believed in Jesus as the Jewish Messiah. This gave rise to many problems among the believers, and these were aggravated, no doubt, by the fact that no apostle had been to Rome to settle disputes and provide doctrinal teaching and guidance.

The Jewish Christians were adamant that the Gentiles had to convert to Judaism through the rite of circumcision. They lacked proper teaching in the revelation of grace that was given to Paul. Therefore, Paul felt an obligation, as the apostle to the Gentiles (Romans 11:13), to instruct them in these matters and hence this letter.

Date and Place of Writing

This letter to the Romans was probably written during Paul's third missionary trip, around A.D. 57-58, when Paul was in Corinth or that vicinity (Acts 20:2-3).

The date can be deduced from some of Paul's statements in Romans 15:25-28 about how he was headed to Jerusalem to take the offering from the saints in Macedonia (see note 1 at Acts 16:9) and Achaia (see note 11 at Acts 18:12) to the poor saints in Judea (see note 1 at John 4:3). This places the writing of this book toward the end of Paul's third missionary trip (see note 2 at Acts 18:23) as he headed for Jerusalem.

Phebe, a servant of the church in Cenchrea (see note 1 at Acts 18:18), was the one who carried this epistle to the church in Rome (Romans 16:1, subscript at Romans 16:27). So it can be supposed that Paul was in Phebe's hometown of Cenchrea or in Corinth (see note 1 at Acts 18:1) when he wrote this letter.

About the Author

Some facts about Paul's persecution of the church, his conversion, and the intervening time until the beginning of his ministry have been dealt with in note 4 at Acts 7:58, note 1 at Acts 9:1, and note 1 at Acts

9:26. Information about Paul's life after the close of the book of Acts is included in note 1 at Acts 28:30. Many notes about Paul's exploits, character, and hardships are found throughout the book of Acts.

ROMANS

CHAPTER ONE

Romans 1:1

Paul, a servant of Jesus Christ, called to be an apostle, separated unto the gospel of God,

Note 1

Out of the six Greek words for "servant" used in the New Testament, Paul used one of the most slavish terms possible. The word used in this verse is "DOULOS" and comes from the root word "DEO." DEO means "to bind" (Strong's Concordance). So Paul is literally speaking of himself as being a bondman or slave of Jesus Christ—a slave by free choice yet owned and purchased by Jesus Christ (1 Corinthians 6:19-20). The idea of being a love-slave by choice comes from Old Testament passages such as Exodus 21:2-6 and Deuteronomy 15:12-17. When Israelites bought Hebrew slaves, they had to set them free in the seventh year. However, if the slaves loved their masters and didn't want to go free, then holes were bored through the lobes of their ears, pronouncing them bond-slaves forever. By the use of this word, Paul was declaring Jesus as his absolute Master yet indicating the idea of his expression of love and free choice to the one whom he served.

Note 2

Notice that Paul spoke of his servitude to Christ before he mentioned his apostleship. This reveals Paul's priorities and humility. These were key factors in his success.

Romans 1:2

(Which he had promised afore by his prophets in the holy scriptures,)

Note 3

The concept of the Gospel (see note 5 at Acts 20:24) was not new. Galatians 3:8 says that the Lord preached the Gospel unto Abraham. Also, Moses gave the conditions of the Gospel in Deuteronomy 30:11-14. Paul quoted this passage in Romans 10:6-8 as he explained faith as the only condition to receiving God's grace. Jesus Himself said that the Law of Moses, the prophets, and the psalms were full of prophecies concerning Him (Luke 24:44). The Gospel was woven throughout the Old Testament scriptures. Indeed, the job of the Old Testament Law was to "shut us up" or constrain us toward the Gospel (Galatians 3:23). In this sense, there is no conflict between the Old Testament Law and the New Testament grace. The Old Testament ministry of Law was only temporary (Galatians 3:19) until the Gospel could be put into effect by the sacrifice of Jesus. The conflict between Law and grace comes when people try to mix the two. As Jesus described in His parables about the new wine in the old wineskin and the new patch on the old garment (see note 1 at Luke 5:36), the two covenants are not compatible. The Old Testament Law paved the way for the Gospel and pointed people toward the Gospel. If the Law is used to point out people's need and bring them to their knees through hopelessness of self-salvation, then the Gospel is used to provide salvation and relationship; there is no conflict. Conflict arises only when people refuse to use faith in God's grace as the only means of salvation and insist that some degree of adherence to Law is required for justification (see note 2 at Luke 9:55 and note 1 at Luke 16:16).

Romans 1:3

Concerning his Son Jesus Christ our Lord, which was made of the seed of David according to the flesh;

LIVING COMMENTARY

This verse makes special mention of Jesus' flesh being according to the seed of David. This is saying His physical body was directly descended of David, but in His spirit, He was Lord at His birth (see my note at Luke 2:11).

Romans 1:4

And declared to be the Son of God with power, according to the spirit of holiness, by the resurrection from the dead:

LIVING COMMENTARY

Just as Romans 1:3 pointed out that Jesus' physical attributes made Him the son of David, so the miraculous resurrection of Jesus from the dead proved to all that He was the Son of God in His spirit.

Note 4

The resurrection of Jesus from the dead is the greatest witness of all to the validity of Jesus' claims (see note 1 at Acts 1:3).

Romans 1:5

By whom we have received grace and apostleship, for obedience to the faith among all nations, for his name:

LIVING COMMENTARY

Notice there is a comma between the words "apostleship" and "for" in this verse. That means Paul wasn't saying he received grace and apostleship in exchange for his obedience to the faith; he received grace and apostleship—COMMA—in order to produce or bring people to obedience to the faith. Other translations bear this out. The Amplified Bible says, "It is through Him that we have received grace (God's unmerited favor) and [our] apostleship to promote obedience to the faith and make disciples for His name's sake among all the nations." The New International Version says, "Through him and for his name's sake, we received grace and apostleship to call people from among all the Gentiles to the obedience that comes from faith."

Note 5

This is the first of 24 times the term "grace" is used in Paul's epistle to the Romans. The Greek word for "grace" is "CHARIS," and CHARIS is translated many different ways throughout the New Testament. It is translated in the following ways: "acceptable, benefit, favour, gift, grace(-ious), joy, liberality, pleasure, thank(-s, -worthy)" (Strong's Concordance). The most common way it is translated is as "grace," used 130 times in the New Testament. According to Thayer's Greek-English Lexicon, "the word 'charis' contains the idea of 'kindness which bestows upon one what he has not deserved'...the N.T. writers use 'charis' pre-eminently of that kindness by which God bestows favors even upon the ill-deserving." Another form of the Greek word CHARIS is "CHARISMA," and CHARISMA is translated "(free) gift" (Strong's Concordance). Vine's Expository Dictionary defines CHARISMA as "a gift of grace, a gift involving grace (charis) on the part of God as the Donor." In other words, CHARISMA is a specific form or manifestation of the grace of God. It is used to describe as free gifts the following: righteousness (Romans 5:16-17), spiritual gifts (1 Corinthians 12:28-31 and Romans 12:6-8), eternal life (Romans 6:23), the five ministry gifts (Ephesians 4:11), celibacy (1 Corinthians 7:7), healings (1 Corinthians 12:9, 28, and 30), and miraculous intervention (2 Corinthians 1:11).

Note 6

The Greek word used here for "obedience" is "HUPAKOE," and it means "attentive hearkening, i.e. (by implication) compliance or submission" (Strong's Concordance). Many times in the New Testament, faith and obedience are linked together (Acts 6:7, Romans 16:26, James 2:14-22, and 1 Peter 1:21). This is because the origin and historical development of the words "believe" and "obey" are closely related. What you believe is what you will do. If you really believed that the building you were in was on fire, you would do something. Different people might do different things, but it is inconceivable that anyone who really believed the building was on fire would do nothing. The New Testament calls this a "work of faith" (1 Thessalonians 1:2-3 and 2 Thessalonians 1:11). This is an action corresponding to and induced by what a person believes. This differs from a work of the Law in that works of the Law require no faith and are works of one's own resources without any reference to, reliance on, or trust in God (Galatians 2:16, 3:12, 5:4; Romans 3:28, 4:15-16, and 9:30-32).

Romans 1:6

Among whom are ye also the called of Jesus Christ:

Note 7

This verse states that we are "the called of Jesus Christ." The next verse (Romans 1:7) states to what Jesus has called us: He called us to be saints (see note 5 at Acts 9:13). God's grace has extended the call (or invitation) to every person to become a saint through salvation (Titus 2:11), but not everyone chooses to respond positively to this call. If a person rejects God's call, then God chooses to reject that person (Luke 12:9 and 1 John 2:23), therefore the statement of Matthew 22:14, "For many are called, but few are chosen."

Romans 1:7

To all that be in Rome, beloved of God, called to be saints: Grace to you and peace from God our Father, and the Lord Jesus Christ.

LIVING COMMENTARY

Every true believer in Jesus is a saint. The Catholic Church's elevation of some believers to sainthood isn't scriptural.

Note 8

It is one of the greatest truths of the Bible, and also one of the hardest to comprehend, that we are the objects of God's love. God didn't just pity us or feel some sense of moral obligation to save us; He saved us because of His infinite love for us (John 3:16). An experiential under-standing of God's love is the key to being filled with all the fullness of God (Ephesians 3:19).

Romans 1:8

First, I thank my God through Jesus Christ for you all, that your faith is spoken of throughout the whole world.

LIVING COMMENTARY

Everything, including our thanks, has to go through Jesus Christ. There is no way to approach the Father without going through Him (John 14:6).

Note 9

This is quite a statement! It is to be understood that this is speaking of the Roman Empire, but this is still an astounding fact. These believ-ers—who had never had an apostolic visit and, as far as we know, had very little teaching—had such a strong faith in the Lord that stories of that faith had spread throughout the world. This is quite a contrast with many churches today that haven't even impacted their neighborhoods with the Gospel of Christ.

Romans 1:9

For God is my witness, whom I serve with my spirit in the gospel of his Son, that without ceasing I make mention of you always in my prayers;

LIVING COMMENTARY

Paul made an astounding statement here that he prayed for the Roman Christians without ceasing. Very few Christians pray for anything or anyone without ceasing, but that was Paul's claim. And he said God was his witness that what he was saying was true. Notice that Paul said he served God with his spirit. It's the spirit part of us that is born again and full of God (see my note at 2 Corinthians 5:17). The only acceptable way of serving God is to walk in the Spirit (see my note at Galatians 5:16).

Romans 1:10

Making request, if by any means now at length I might have a prosperous journey by the will of God to come unto you.

LIVING COMMENTARY

Paul did make it to Rome but probably not the way he had hoped. He was arrested in Jerusalem (Acts 21:30-36) and remained in prison in Judea for two whole years (Acts 24:27). Then Paul was transported by ship to

Rome where he remained in prison for two more years
(Acts 28:30).

Romans 1:11

*For I long to see you, that I may impart unto you some spiritual
gift, to the end ye may be established;*

Note 10

Two things are very significant in Paul's statement here: First, we
see that spiritual gifts can be imparted or passed from one person to
another. This is the whole purpose of the presbytery laying hands on an
individual during ordination, as Paul reminded Timothy (1 Timothy
4:14). Second, spiritual gifts help establish or strengthen an individual.
This is in stark contrast to what some critics of the gifts of the Holy
Spirit claim. As Paul said in 1 Corinthians 14:3-4, the gifts of the Spirit
operating in the church produce edification, exhortation, and comfort.
In private use, they edify the individual.

Romans 1:12

*That is, that I may be comforted together with you by the mutual
faith both of you and me.*

LIVING COMMENTARY

Those who share our faith are a comfort to us. This is
very important. Those who are not in fellowship with
other believers are missing a lot.

Romans 1:13

Now I would not have you ignorant, brethren, that oftentimes I purposed to come unto you, (but was let hitherto,) that I might have some fruit among you also, even as among other Gentiles.

Note 11

The word "let" that was used here is an old English word that means hindered. It is still used in that sense in the sports of tennis and table tennis. Paul was saying that he had purposed many times to travel to Rome, but he had been hindered up to that point. In Romans 15:21-22, Paul clearly stated what his hindrance was—that others, closer to where he was, had not heard the Gospel yet. In other words, he was hindered from taking the Gospel to Rome because there were so many other places that needed him just as much. However, in Romans 15:23, Paul said he had presented the Gospel to every region in those parts (probably the area of Corinth - see Life for Today Study Bible Notes, Introduction to Romans, Date and Place of Writing), and he was now ready to begin his journey to Rome.

Romans 1:14

I am debtor both to the Greeks, and to the Barbarians; both to the wise, and to the unwise.

Note 12

Paul was making this statement in a spiritual sense. He was expressing his sense of obligation to share the Gospel of Jesus Christ with all. This was one of Paul's attitudes that motivated him to travel to the ends of the known world and constantly lay his life on the line for the sake of

Christ. Likewise, those who seek to be used of God today need to recognize that their duty to share Christ with a dying world is not optional.

Note 13

In Paul's day, the term "barbarian" was not an offensive one. It was simply used to distinguish anyone who did not speak the Greek language or, later, to identify anyone who was not of the Hellenic race.

Romans 1:15

So, as much as in me is, I am ready to preach the gospel to you that are at Rome also.

Note 14

Paul had now dispensed with the preliminaries and was beginning to present his defense of the Gospel, his primary purpose of writing.

Romans 1:16

For I am not ashamed of the gospel of Christ: for it is the power of God unto salvation to every one that believeth; to the Jew first, and also to the Greek.

LIVING COMMENTARY

The Greek word "EUAGGELION," which was translated "gospel" in this verse, was used seventy-seven times in the New Testament in seventy-four verses. It was translated "gospel" seventy-four times and "gospel's" three times. It means "good message" or "good news" (Vine's Expository Dictionary). But it actually means more than that. This Greek word was so seldom used that I only found two examples of its usage outside of the Bible. The reason for that was because it really means the nearly-too-good-to-be-true news. And there is precious little outside of the news of what Jesus did for us that is nearly-too-good-to-be-true news. But when Jesus took all of our sin and paid the debt we owed and then gave us new life, that was nearly too good to be true. So, this word became correctly associated with the salvation Jesus provided for us. This Greek word, as used in the Bible, also stresses the means by which we appropriate the great benefits of our salvation. This all comes by faith in God's grace (see my note at Ephesians 2:8). Galatians 1:6 and Acts 20:24 use the words "grace" and "gospel" interchangeably. This is very important. Any teaching that doesn't emphasize grace as the way of receiving what Jesus provided isn't the true Gospel. As Paul phrased it in Galatians 1:7, trying to receive from God by our own effort is a perversion of the Gospel. That's often harder to deal with than out-and-out rejection, because it's more subtle. That's the condition of the church today. The Greek word "PROTON," which was translated "first" in this verse, means "firstly (in time, place, order, or importance)" (Strong's Concordance). It was translated "beginning" in John 2:10 and "before" in John 15:18. In those verses, it is clearly speaking of being the first in a sequence. Therefore, this verse is speaking of the Jews being the first to receive the Gospel, before

> the Gentiles—not being ahead in importance or closer
> to salvation.

Note 1

The Gospel is the power of God that releases the effects of salvation in our lives. Salvation is much more than just being born again. This refers to every benefit that the believer is entitled to through Jesus. Therefore, if we are not experiencing the abundance that Jesus provided for us—in any area of our lives—then we are having a problem understanding and/or believing the Gospel. The term "Gospel" has become so familiar to Christians that the true meaning and understanding have been lost. As discussed in note 5 at Acts 20:24 and note 7 at Matthew 24:14, the truths of the Gospel are not commonly preached or understood in many churches. This is the reason that so many Christians are not walking in all the benefits of their salvation. They don't have the power of the Gospel working in them. If a person needs healing, it's in the Gospel. If deliverance is needed, it's in the Gospel. Prosperity, answered prayer, joy, peace, love—they are all found through understanding and believing the Gospel.

Note 2

In the Bible, most English words that end with the suffix "-eth" carry the idea of an act or process that continues. So, the person that "believeth" is a person who has believed and is continuing to believe. In the Greek language, the word that was translated "believeth" here is a present participle that expresses the idea of a continuous and repeated action. Therefore, the faith that results in salvation cannot be abandoned and still produce its results (Hebrews 6:4-6, 10:29; and Colossians 1:21-23). It may appear to be abandoned, as in the case of Peter when he denied the Lord (Luke 22:57-62), but Jesus had prayed that his "faith fail not" (see note 2 at Luke 22:32). The Scriptures present true Bible faith as an ongoing experience, not a one-time action.

Romans 1:17

For therein is the righteousness of God revealed from faith to faith: as it is written, The just shall live by faith.

LIVING COMMENTARY

Notice that the righteousness of God has to be revealed. The Holy Spirit is the one who reveals God's righteousness (1 Corinthians 2:9-16), and He does that through understanding the Gospel of grace.

Note 3

The expression "from faith to faith" describes the means whereby righteousness is given and retained. God's righteousness cannot be earned; it can only be acquired through faith. As proof that righteousness received by faith is not a new idea or concept, Paul quoted Habakkuk 2:4, "The just shall live by his faith" (also quoted in Galatians 3:11 and Hebrews 10:38).

Note 4

The just shall **live** by faith. They don't just visit faith every once in a while or vacation there once a year; they live in and by faith.

Romans 1:18

For the wrath of God is revealed from heaven against all ungod-liness and unrighteousness of men, who hold the truth in unrighteousness;

Note 1

Paul's purpose in writing Romans 1:18-20 was to explain why the Gospel is the power of God unto salvation (Romans 1:16). The problem was that then, just as now, most people felt the way to get others to come to God was to condemn them and scare them out of hell. People doubted that Paul's good news of the love of God would be enough to cause repentance. Therefore, Paul began to prove that every person already has an instinctive knowledge of God's wrath against their sin. We don't need to prove God's wrath; God has already done that. What people need to know is the good news that God placed His wrath for our sins upon His own Son so that we could be completely forgiven. This good news will draw people to God more than the bad news will ever drive people to God.

Note 2

In Romans 1:18-20, Paul was declaring that God has revealed Himself to all mankind. Old Testament scriptures proclaim that God has revealed Himself to everyone through nature (Psalm 19:1-3), but Paul was stating here that there is an intuitive revelation of God within every person. There are five words used in these three verses to describe the extent to which God has revealed Himself to mankind, and they are worth special note. Any one of these five words used by itself would have made a strong argument for Paul's case.

However, the combination of these words in just two sentences empha-sizes the certainty of Paul's claims. The use of the word "all" in Romans 1:18 shows the extent to which God has revealed Himself. God has placed a witness within every person against **all** ungodliness and unrighteous-ness. In Romans 1:19, the Greek word that was translated "manifest" is the Greek word "PHANEROS," and it means "shining, i.e. apparent" (Strong's Concordance). The Greek word translated "shewed" in this verse is "PHANEROO," which is derived from PHANEROS. PHA-NEROO means "to render apparent (literally or figuratively)" (Strong's Concordance). These words make it very clear that this instinctive or intuitive knowledge is not so subtle that it can be overlooked. God gives every individual the right to choose, but there can be no doubt that every person has, at one time, clearly seen and understood (Romans 1:20) the basic truths of God's existence. In Romans 1:20, Paul said this inner witness of God causes the individual to clearly see the invisible things of God and even understand the Godhead. The Greek word that was translated "clearly seen" is the word "KATHORAO," and it means "to behold fully, i.e. (figuratively) distinctly apprehend" (Strong's Con-cordance). This leaves no doubt that every person who has ever walked the earth has had a clear revelation of God. The use of the word "under-stood" emphatically states that God gave man not only knowledge but also the understanding to use that knowledge. Therefore, no one will be able to stand before God on the Day of Judgment and say, "God is not fair." He has given all people who have ever lived, regardless of how remote or isolated they may have been, the opportunity to know Him. They are without excuse. Someone might say, "If all this is true, then why can't we observe more of this intuitive knowledge of God in the lives of those who have not heard the Gospel?" Paul gave the answer to this in Romans 1:21-23 (see note 1 at Romans 1:21).

Romans 1:19

Because that which may be known of God is manifest in them; for God hath shewed it unto them.

LIVING COMMENTARY

Notice this knowledge is in them. There is an intuitive knowledge of God's existence and man's transgression against Him within every person who has ever lived. We are without excuse (Romans 1:20).

Romans 1:20

For the invisible things of him from the creation of the world are clearly seen, being understood by the things that are made, even his eternal power and Godhead; so that they are without excuse:

LIVING COMMENTARY

Because God has revealed Himself in every person's heart (Romans 1:18-20), there will be no excuse for those who didn't respond positively to this inner witness. We are without excuse.

Note 3

The Easton's Bible Dictionary definition of the word "Godhead" is "the essential being or the divine nature of God." Therefore, Paul was stating that God has given every person an intuitive revelation of His divine nature. What a statement! And what a responsibility when people will have to stand before God and answer for the perversions they have perpetrated in the name of God. In their hearts, they knew better.

Romans 1:21

Because that, when they knew God, they glorified him not as God, neither were thankful; but became vain in their imaginations, and their foolish heart was darkened.

LIVING COMMENTARY

Romans 1:18-20 describes that everyone has an intuitive knowledge of the wrath of God on the inside of them. Beginning in Romans 1:21, Paul was describing the progressive steps that people take away from that God-breathed revelation. The fact that people depart from that revelation doesn't void the fact that God has placed it there. The steps described here in walking away from that revelation apply to anything the Lord has shown us or spoken to us. The first step that people take away from any revelation that God has given them is they fail to glorify Him as God. The word "glorified" means "to render (or esteem) glorious" (Strong's Concordance). The word "esteem" means "to place a high value on; respect; prize" and "to judge to be; consider" (Houghton Mifflin American Heritage Electronic Dictionary). Basically, people magnify, esteem, or place a greater value on something other than God. Moses esteemed reproach to be greater than riches (see my note at Hebrews 11:26). Jesus disesteemed the suffering of the cross and focused instead on those who would be freed through

His offering (Hebrews 12:2). Psalm 69:30 says that we "magnify" God (one of the definitions of glorify) with thanksgiving. The same Greek word that was translated "glorified" in Romans 1:21 was also translated "magnify" in Romans 11:13. Also, Jesus said the leper who returned and gave Him thanks for his healing had glorified Him (Luke 17:16-18). In Romans 4:19-21, Abraham "was strong in faith, giving glory to God." He esteemed God's promise more than he valued anything else. For instance, the doctor says you are going to die. That won't stop you from being healed unless you place a higher value on what the doctor says than on what God says. If you glorify God instead of the sickness, you will retain the revelation and sickness will have to flee, because "to be spiritually minded is life and peace" (Romans 8:6). So, you should begin to magnify the Lord instead of the negative report. You do that by controlling your heart through controlling your thinking. Your thoughts magnify whatever you focus your thinking upon. If you see marital problems, what should you do? You should go to God's Word and magnify what God says instead of what you see. In Mark 6:41, Jesus "looked up" and blessed the five loaves of bread and two fish before dividing them among the multitude. The Greek word that was translated "looked up" was translated "receive sight" (or some form of this) fifteen times. This is referring to Jesus seeing with His spiritual eyes into the supernatural realm of God instead of being bound to the natural realm, where the five loaves and two fish were not enough. He glorified God's ability beyond the limitations of the natural.

The spies who searched out the land of Canaan in Numbers 13 are classic examples of people who glorified the problem more than the Problem Solver. This took all thankfulness away, and their imaginations became vain. They had more to be thankful about than any of their ancestors, yet they forgot all that God had done for them and complained, glorifying the negative. The result was that they died in the wilderness and never saw the Promised Land. In Hebrews 12:2, Jesus set joy before Him and despised the shame of the cross. The Greek word that was translated "despising" there means to "disesteem" (Strong's Concordance). Jesus glorified the good and disesteemed the bad. That's why He was able to endure the cross. In Hebrews 12:3, we are told to consider Jesus and what He went through lest we be weary and faint in our minds. Our minds are where the battle is being fought. Those who rule in absolute victory don't usually have things different on the outside, but they think differently on the inside. The second step away from the revelation of God is not being thankful.

Thankfulness involves memory, humility, and reflection. Busy people are not usually thankful. They don't have time for reflection. Again, Psalm 69:30 says that thanksgiving magnifies God. It takes time and effort to remember and be thankful. Second Timothy 3:1-2 says that one of the signs of apostasy in the last days is that people will be unthankful. That characterizes our day and age. To be thankful, one has to remember. Psalm 103:2 says to "forget not all his benefits." The reason we were commanded not to forget is because it is our tendency to forget. We will forget if we don't make an effort to remember. Thankfulness helps us remember. The next thing mentioned in Romans 1:21 is imagination (see my note at 2 Corinthians 10:5). Imagination is the main part of our memory. If we don't glorify God and become thankful, our imagination just naturally begins to start picturing what we focus on. We picture and remember the negative. That's a vain imagination. The fourth and final progressive step away from God and/or any revelation we get from Him is that our foolish hearts becomes darkened. Ephesians 4:18 speaks both of the blindness of the heart and of the understanding being darkened. The foolish, darkened heart being spoken of here is the heart of a person whose understanding (imagination - see my note at Proverbs 15:28) is vain, or negative, and that makes them hardhearted (see my note at Mark 6:52).

Note 1

As Paul explained in Romans 1:18-20 (see note 2 at Romans 1:18), all people who have ever lived have had God reveal Himself to them, but this verse is explaining that revelation is not always received. Each individual has the freedom of choice. In Romans 1:21-23, Paul described different characteristics of those who reject God's revelation. These could also be descriptive of progressive steps that one takes away from the true revelation of God. The first step in rejecting God is not to glorify Him as the supreme, all-knowing, unquestionable God. This was what happened with Adam and Eve in the Garden of Eden. They questioned God's intent behind His command (Genesis 3:1-6). They ceased to magnify and honor God like they once did. Submission to God as supreme is always humbling, and therefore "self" rebels. This is very prevalent today. Second, they were not thankful. This is always a sign that self is exalting itself above God. A selfless person can be content with very little. A self-centered person cannot be satisfied. Thankfulness is a sign of humility, and cultivating a life of thankfulness will help keep "self" in its proper place. After these first two steps have been taken, then the individual's mind is free to begin imagining foolish, wicked, and idolatrous thoughts. This leads to a hardened heart ("foolish heart was darkened," see note 10 at Mark 6:52) and being reprobate (see note 6 at Romans 1:28).

Romans 1:22

Professing themselves to be wise, they became fools,

LIVING COMMENTARY

This is happening in epidemic proportions today. Most of the people who are considered the smartest and the elite are people who don't even believe in God (Psalms 14:1 and 53:1) or don't fear Him (Proverbs 1:7).

Romans 1:23

And changed the glory of the uncorruptible God into an image made like to corruptible man, and to birds, and fourfooted beasts, and creeping things.

LIVING COMMENTARY

Any person who believes that the God who created us is like an animal is a fool. It is obvious to any who pay attention that mankind is the smartest of all creatures and the crown of creation. So, why would the God who created us be less than us?

Romans 1:24

Wherefore God also gave them up to uncleanness through the lusts of their own hearts, to dishonour their own bodies between themselves:

LIVING COMMENTARY

Romans 1:18-20 shows that God reveals Himself against all our sin. But if we refuse His witness as Romans 1:21 speaks of, He will give us up to do what we want. That is a terrible thing. And this verse describes those who commit sexual sins as being given up to them. The phrase "give up" means "to surrender" (American Heritage Dictionary) So, when God gives up a person to sin, He is surrendering them to their lust. They want to go that way, so the Lord will let them. He doesn't force anyone to follow Him. Notice that sexual sin is dishonoring our bodies. God made us to be better than that. The context of this verse is speaking of homosexual acts (Romans 1:26-27). So, it's possible that "uncleanness" in other New Testament passages could be referring to the same (for example, Mark 5:2-13). Fritz Rienecker's "Linguistic Key to the Greek New Testament" says that "uncleanness" refers to "sexual aberration," which is any sexual act that is abnormal. This would certainly include homosexuality.

Note 2

This phrase "God gave them up" is used twice in this passage (here and in Romans 1:26), and the phrase "God gave them over" is used once (Romans 1:28). These phrases are drawing on the fact that there is a God-given, intuitive knowledge inside of all people that would prevent them from committing such depraved acts (see note 2 at Romans 1:18). However, because of our free choice, God will not continue to force that restraint upon us against our will. If people persist in their rebellion against this conviction of God, He will give those people up to their own hearts' lust. Therefore, those who are committing some of the terrible acts spoken of here (idolatry, homosexuality, etc.) and say that they have no conviction about it are either lying (Romans 1:18-20) or have been given over to a reprobate mind (see note 6 at Romans 1:28) by God.

Romans 1:25

Who changed the truth of God into a lie, and worshipped and served the creature more than the Creator, who is blessed for ever. Amen.

LIVING COMMENTARY

This verse says those who rebel change the truth into a lie. The hardest person to reach isn't the one who denies the truth but the one who perverts it (see my note at Galatians 1:7).

Romans 1:26

For this cause God gave them up unto vile affections: for even their women did change the natural use into that which is against nature:

LIVING COMMENTARY

Romans 1:24 speaks of God giving these people up to "uncleanness." This verse and Romans 1:27 speak of homosexuality. So, at least in this instance, "uncleanness" (see Mark 5:2-13) refers to homosexual acts.

Note 3

Romans 1:26-27 is speaking of lesbianism and homosexuality. If anyone could doubt the clear statements of the Old Testament scriptures that this is an abomination to God (Leviticus 18:22, 20:13; and Deuteronomy 23:17-18), then these scriptures should forever settle the question.

Romans 1:27

And likewise also the men, leaving the natural use of the woman, burned in their lust one toward another; men with men working

that which is unseemly, and receiving in themselves that recom-
pence of their error which was meet.

Note 4

This is speaking of the emotional and physical consequences of homosexuality. Paul here said these consequences are "meet." The word
that Paul used (Greek - "DEI") is found in 104 verses, but it is only
translated "meet" one other time (Luke 15:32). All other times the
translation clearly denotes something that is necessary ("behoved,
must (needs), (be) need(-ful), ought, should" [Strong's Concordance]).
This implies that these consequences (such as disease) are prescribed
payment for such acts. Add to this the use of the word "recompense"
(meaning payment or compensation for an act) in this same verse, and
it clearly looks as if physical and emotional scars are God's judgment
upon this sin. These natural consequences of sin are not necessarily
God's direct punishment on the individuals who commit these acts.
Those who participate in homosexuality, which is expressly forbidden
by God, are bringing punishment on themselves. It's like the law of
gravity. Many people are killed when they violate this God-given law,
but it is not accurate to say God killed them. They killed themselves.
There was no malice on God's part. Likewise, God established natural
laws governing sexual behavior. Marriage was given while man was still
in a perfect state (Genesis 2:21-24), and it is very possible that God
never imagined man perverting such a beautiful gift (Jeremiah 7:31).
When people violate God's sexual order, they are destroying themselves
just as surely as someone who tries to breathe underwater or walk off
a cliff. This verse is saying that the devastation that many homosexuals experience in their bodies is an appropriate payment for those who
have willfully perverted the perfect gift of marriage that God gave to us
before the Fall. But this does not mean that God hates all homosexuals

and is personally punishing them. If that were so, some of the diseases we see would not be selective. All homosexuals would contract these diseases. No, these maladies occur naturally when God's perfect order is perverted. God hates homosexuality, but loves the homosexuals. If homosexuals will turn to God and put faith in Jesus as their Savior, they can be saved just the same as anyone else.

Romans 1:28

And even as they did not like to retain God in their knowledge, God gave them over to a reprobate mind, to do those things which are not convenient;

LIVING COMMENTARY

This is the third time in five verses that Paul spoke of God giving the ungodly up or over to something. The first two mentions (Romans 1:24 and 26) were speaking of the Lord giving people up to vile sins. This verse speaks of God giving people up to a reprobate mind. That is a mind that no longer has the intuitive conviction that Romans 1:18-20 speaks of. A reprobate mind is a mind that has no restraints. There is no conviction. The conscience has been seared as with a hot iron (1 Timothy 4:2). Those who are reprobate know they are wrong and don't care. Anyone who still cares, regardless of what they have done, isn't reprobate. John 6:44 says, "No man can come to me, except the Father which hath sent me draw him." Without the drawing power of the Holy Spirit, none of us have any desire for God. Those who are reprobate are people who don't like God and the knowledge He is trying to impart to them, so He just leaves them alone to live as they please without any conscience. Second Thessalonians 2:10-12 describes God giving a strong delusion to people who don't love the truth. This is done to blind them to truth so they will be damned. This is what Isaiah prophesied in Isaiah 6:9-10 (see my note at Matthew 13:14).

Note 5

The reason they did not like to retain God in their knowledge is because the knowledge of God would have convicted them and restrained them from committing such acts. This is the same motivation behind the actions of those who oppose Christianity so strongly today. People want to sin without anyone convicting them.

Note 6

The Greek word translated "reprobate" is "ADOKIMOS," and it means undiscerning, not distinguishing, and void of judgment. In this text it may be understood as "an abominable mind, a mind to be abhorred by God and man" (The Hebrew-Greek KeyWord Study Bible by Dr. Spiros Zodhiates). This is describing the state of a person who has "passed the point of no return" with God. As the context explains, God has revealed Himself to every person who has ever walked the earth. But there comes a point when God's Spirit will not strive with man any longer (Genesis 6:3). When that happens, individuals are hopelessly damned because people cannot come to the Father except the Spirit draws them (see note 8 at John 6:44 and note 6 at Acts 24:25). Therefore, reprobate people are people whom God has abandoned, and there is no hope of salvation for them. Paul applied this term to Christians who had renounced their faith in Christ (2 Corinthians 13:5-7, 2 Timothy 3:8, and Titus 1:16; see note 5 at Acts 5:5). Some people may fear that they are reprobate because of some sin or blasphemy (see note 1 at Matthew 12:31) that they have uttered. However, as these verses describe, reprobate people are past feeling remorse or conviction. If people are repentant over some terrible action, then that itself is proof that the Spirit of God is still drawing them and they are not reprobate. Reprobate people wouldn't care.

Romans 1:29

Being filled with all unrighteousness, fornication, wickedness, covetousness, maliciousness; full of envy, murder, debate, deceit, malignity; whisperers,

LIVING COMMENTARY

Covetousness is the same as idolatry (Colossians 3:5). Envy is listed right next to murder (James 3:16).

Note 7

It is very interesting to see some of the things included in this list of abominations that many people would not consider sin, or certainly not a "bad" sin like others on the list. For instance, the word "debate" means "a quarrel, i.e. (by implication) wrangling" (Strong's Concordance). Some people think quarreling is perfectly okay, but Paul lists it right along with murder and sexual sins. The word "whisperers" means "a secret calumniator" (Strong's Concordance). A calumniator is a slanderer or maligner. A "backbiter" is someone who slanders the character or reputation of another when that person is not present. Pride is listed among these sins that are an abomination to God, as well as being disobedient to parents. A "covenantbreaker" is a person who cannot be trusted to keep his or her word. The truth is that there are no little sins or acceptable sins. All unrighteousness is sin (1 John 5:17) and should be rejected.

Romans 1:30

Backbiters, haters of God, despiteful, proud, boasters, inventors of evil things, disobedient to parents,

LIVING COMMENTARY

Notice that pride is listed as one of the signs of being reprobate. That's not to say that everyone who is proud is reprobate, but all reprobates are proud boasters. Children who are disobedient to parents are listed in the same verse as those who hate God. Obeying parents is one of the Ten Commandments (Exodus 20:12).

Romans 1:31

Without understanding, covenantbreakers, without natural affection, implacable, unmerciful:

LIVING COMMENTARY

The Greek word that was translated "without understanding" in this verse literally means "unintelligent" (Strong's Concordance). When the Lord stops dealing with people—these verses are describing how the Lord withdraws from a reprobate person—then intelligence leaves. God is the one who gave mankind intelligence. Without the influence of the Lord, we are all unintelligent. The fool says there is no God (Psalms 14:1 and 53:1). "Without natural affection" was translated from the Greek word "ASTORGOS," which means "hardhearted towards kindred" (Strong's Concordance). The Greek word translated "implacable" means "without libation (which usually accompanied a treaty), i.e. (by implication) truceless" (Strong's Concordance). A libation was a sacrificial liquid offering. This is speaking of a person who never makes peace or a truce. They are hardhearted.

Note 8

Although this phrase "without natural affection" has been interpreted by many to mean homosexual acts, the Greek word suggests something different. The Greek word used is "ASTORGOS," and it literally means "hard-hearted towards kindred" (Strong's Concordance). This describes someone who is unloving and without the natural tenderness that a mother would express toward a child. Therefore, Paul was describing a hardhearted person who is void of love and tenderness.

Romans 1:32

Who knowing the judgment of God, that they which commit such things are worthy of death, not only do the same, but have pleasure in them that do them.

LIVING COMMENTARY

Reprobate people (see my note at Romans 1:28) love those who live ungodly lives as they do. But righteous people hate evil (Proverbs 8:13).

Note 9

When God turns individuals over (see note 2 at Romans 1:24) to a reprobate mind (see note 6 at Romans 1:28), those people do not lose their knowledge of what's right and wrong; they just lose God's conviction about it. They still know they are wrong, but they don't care.

ROMANS

CHAPTER TWO

Romans 2:1

Therefore thou art inexcusable, O man, whosoever thou art that judgest: for wherein thou judgest another, thou condemnest thyself; for thou that judgest doest the same things.

Note 1

In the preceding chapter, Paul had conclusively proved that the Gentiles were guilty before God. They had no excuse for their vile actions (Romans 1:20). This, no doubt, pleased the Jews. That's exactly what they believed and what they had been arguing. They maintained that unless these Gentiles converted to Judaism and observed the Law of Moses (specifically the law of circumcision), they could not be saved. However, after Paul had taken full advantage of the Jews' prejudice, he turned his arguments to the Jews, showing them that they were just as guilty or even guiltier than the Gentiles. He ended this chapter with statements about the Gentiles' faith being superior to the Jews' circumcision and concluded a true Jew is born of faith, not of the flesh (Romans 2:28-29). Thus, the second chapter proves the Jews, or religious persons, are just as guilty before God as the heathen. Then in the third chapter, Paul drew this all together by proclaiming that since everyone—Jew and Gentile—was in "the same boat," then all could be saved by one method of salvation, through faith.

Note 2

From a human perspective, some people have obtained a level of holiness that gives them the right to judge others. However, when viewed from God's standpoint, we are all sinners, and one sinner has no justification for condemning a fellow sinner (see note 46 at Matthew 7:1). We may not be doing the exact same transgressions, but we are guilty of being lawbreakers (James 2:10) and are therefore disqualified from being the judge. Also, whenever people condemn one another, they are showing that they have a knowledge of right and wrong and therefore can no longer claim ignorance for their own offenses. As Romans 2:2 explains, we are better off to leave the judging to God.

Note 3

The Greek word that is rendered "judgest" three times in this verse and once in Romans 2:3 is the word "KRINO." It is speaking of a harsh, condemning type of judging that was warned against in Matthew 7:1. There is a Greek word, "ANAKRINO," that signifies discernment, which is encouraged in Scripture (see note 46 at Matthew 7:1).

Romans 2:2

But we are sure that the judgment of God is according to truth against them which commit such things.

LIVING COMMENTARY

God's judgment is always accurate. He doesn't have the ego and prejudices found in people.

Romans 2:3

And thinkest thou this, O man, that judgest them which do such things, and doest the same, that thou shalt escape the judgment of God?

Note 4

These pious Jews could have argued with Paul that they were not committing the same sins that these heathens were, but in reality they were. They may not have worshiped idols, but they were covetous.

Colossians 3:5 reveals that is idolatry. They may not have committed adultery, but they had lusted in their hearts. Jesus said that was equal to adultery (Matthew 5:28). They may not have murdered anyone, but they had hated. Those both come from the same root sin (Matthew 5:21-22). When viewed in this way, judgment for others disappears and mercy comes to light.

Romans 2:4

Or despisest thou the riches of his goodness and forbearance and longsuffering; not knowing that the goodness of God leadeth thee to repentance?

Note 5

This is a radical statement that the Jews of Paul's day and the religious legalists of our day reject. They refuse to accept that the goodness of God is sufficient motivation for people to turn from sin. They insist that fear of punishment is a superior motivator. It is true that fear is a more familiar motivator to most people. Even a lost person or carnal Christian can identify with fear and respond to it. But as 1 John 4:18

states, "Fear hath torment." Those who respond to God through fear will also be tormented with thoughts of doubt and condemnation as to whether they have done enough. Fear will move some toward God, but it is inferior to love. There is nothing that fear can do that love can't do better and without the side effect of torment. Those motivated to seek God because of fear if they didn't will cease to be motivated when things are going well.

They become the ones who only pray when they are in trouble. Those who come to God because of His goodness will see God as the source of their success and continue to serve God in the good and the bad times. The world, and especially religion, has used negative reasons to motivate us. The Gospel uses the positive reason of God's great love to draw us unto God. We need to renew our minds to line up with God's thinking.

Romans 2:5

But after thy hardness and impenitent heart treasurest up unto thyself wrath against the day of wrath and revelation of the righteous judgment of God;

Note 6

The Apostle James said, "For he shall have judgment without mercy, that hath shewed no mercy; and mercy rejoiceth against judgment" (James 2:13). Those who show mercy will be shown mercy, but those who are hardhearted and unmerciful will reap the same when they stand before the judgment seat of God.

Romans 2:6

Who will render to every man according to his deeds:

LIVING COMMENTARY

This doesn't negate faith in a Savior. In fact, putting faith in what Jesus did for us is a deed that will grant salvation. We will be granted eternal life based on that one deed.

Note 7

Romans 2:6-16 is speaking of the final judgment of God at the end of this world. The Lord will judge us and render a due reward according to every person's work. Although this is true, some have taken these scriptures to mean the opposite of what Paul was saying in context here. From the context, we see that Paul was preaching that Jews and Gentiles alike have sinned and come short of the glory of God (Romans 3:23).

Therefore, we cannot be saved by our actions (Romans 3:20). The only way to be saved is through faith in Jesus and what He did for us (Romans 3:24-28). Therefore, these verses cannot be contradicting everything else that Paul was saying by proclaiming that acceptance by God is based on performance. No, the action that will be rewarded with eternal life is the action of faith (John 3:16). Faith alone saves, but saving faith is never alone. True faith has actions (James 2:17-20). The Greek word that is translated "do not obey" in Romans 2:8 means "to disbelieve (willfully and perversely)" (Strong's Concordance). So it is faith that is the issue, even though actions are being spoken of. Therefore, those whose faith is causing them to patiently continue in well doing (Romans 2:7), they will receive eternal life. But those whose rejection of God's mercy causes them to disobey (disbelieve) the truth, they will receive indignation and wrath, tribulation and anguish (Romans 2:8-9).

Romans 2:7

To them who by patient continuance in well doing seek for glory and honour and immortality, eternal life:

LIVING COMMENTARY

Romans 3:23 says all have sinned and come short of the glory of God, and Romans 6:23 says the wages of sin is death. Therefore, if the only thing evaluated at the judgment was our actions, we would all be damned. But this verse (and hundreds of others) shows there will be mercy on those who are seeking to please God.

Romans 2:8

But unto them that are contentious, and do not obey the truth, but obey unrighteousness, indignation and wrath,

LIVING COMMENTARY

God's Word is truth (John 17:17). But no one has ever kept all the precepts of God's Word perfectly except Jesus (Hebrews 7:26). So, this cannot be interpreted in a way that removes Jesus and salvation by grace through faith. Therefore, I think a proper way to interpret this would be to say that those who refuse the great salvation offered freely through faith in Jesus will receive indignation and wrath.

Romans 2:9

Tribulation and anguish, upon every soul of man that doeth evil, of the Jew first, and also of the Gentile;

LIVING COMMENTARY

This is what all of us deserve because all of us have sinned (Romans 3:23). But praise God for His Son, Jesus. Through Him we are cleansed from all our sin (Acts 13:39 and Revelation 1:5).

Romans 2:10

But glory, honour, and peace, to every man that worketh good, to the Jew first, and also to the Gentile:

LIVING COMMENTARY

This isn't just saying that "good" people will make it to heaven and "bad" people will go to hell. The Scriptures reveal that "there is none righteous, no, not one" (Romans 3:10; see also Psalms 14:1-3, 53:1-3; and Romans 3:10-18). "All have sinned, and come short of the glory of God" (Romans 3:23), and the wages for our sin are death (Romans 6:23). But only through faith in the finished work of Christ can we be saved (Ephesians 2:8, Romans 5:2, and Titus 3:4-5). When that salvation takes place, our response is to live holy. Holiness is a fruit of salvation and not the root of it (see my note at

Romans 6:22). Therefore, this verse is dealing with those who have been saved by grace through faith and are now exhibiting that changed life in their actions.

Romans 2:11
For there is no respect of persons with God.

LIVING COMMENTARY

It is well established in Scripture that the Lord is not a respecter of persons (Deuteronomy 10:17, 2 Chronicles 19:7, Job 34:19, Proverbs 24:23, Acts 10:34, Galatians 2:6, Ephesians 6:9, Colossians 3:25, and 1 Peter 1:17).

Romans 2:12
For as many as have sinned without law shall also perish without law: and as many as have sinned in the law shall be judged by the law;

LIVING COMMENTARY

As Paul explained in Romans 1:18-20, everyone has an intuitive knowledge of God and their relative unworthiness on the inside of them. If that is all they have, that makes them guilty before God and without excuse (Romans 1:20). Those who have been exposed to the Law of God are doubly guilty. They have not only the conviction of their consciences but also the revealed Word of God that shows them their sin and their need for a Savior (Romans 3:19-20).

Romans 2:13

(For not the hearers of the law are just before God, but the doers of the law shall be justified.

LIVING COMMENTARY

The Jews prided themselves on the fact that the Lord had chosen them as His people and given them His Law. But Paul revealed that if they didn't keep the Law, then all the Law did was condemn them (2 Corinthians 3:7-9 and James 2:10). Just knowing what God's Word says is not enough. Faith without works is dead (James 2:20). We need to do the Word (James 1:22-25).

Romans 2:14

For when the Gentiles, which have not the law, do by nature the things contained in the law, these, having not the law, are a law unto themselves:

Note 8

This is speaking of the intuitive knowledge of God described in Romans 1 (see note 2 at Romans 1:18).

Romans 2:15

Which shew the work of the law written in their hearts, their con-
science also bearing witness, and their thoughts the mean while
accusing or else excusing one another;)

LIVING COMMENTARY

These verses were speaking about nonbelievers and their consciences bearing witness to the law written in their hearts. So, even people who haven't heard the Law have a law written in their hearts, which their consciences use to judge their actions and thoughts. But the conscience alone isn't a trustworthy guide. It can be seared (1 Timothy 4:2) and weakened (1 Corinthians 8:7, 10, and 12). We have to purge ourselves from dead works (Hebrews 9:14) and evil consciences (Hebrews 10:22). So, we can't ignore the conscience (1 Timothy 1:5, 19; and 1 John 3:20-21), but we can't rely on it exclusively. We have to let God's Word be the final authority in our lives.

Note 9

The conscience is the part of us that bears witness as to what is right and wrong. This happens through our thoughts either accusing or excusing us. The conscience is a part of the soul (see note 2 at Matthew 22:37). This can be deduced from the fact that even a Christian's conscience can be defiled (1 Corinthians 8:7), evil (Hebrews 10:22), and weak (1 Corinthians 8:7 and 10), but the born-again spirit cannot be (see note 3 at Matthew 26:41). A good conscience is essential to faith. Without a good conscience, our faith is made shipwrecked (1 Timothy 1:19). A good conscience produces confidence (1 John 3:21 and Hebrews 10:35).

An evil conscience condemns us (1 John 3:20). It is possible that God created man without a conscience and that the conscience was acquired through the Tree of the Knowledge of Good and Evil. The name of that tree is descriptive of the function of the conscience. The conscience is referred to by name thirty-one times in twenty-nine verses in the New Testament (John 8:9; Acts 23:1, 24:16; Romans 2:15, 9:1, 13:5; 1 Corinthians 8:7, 10, 12, 10:25, 27-29; 2 Corinthians 1:12, 4:2; 1 Timothy 1:5, 19, 3:9, 4:2; 2 Timothy 1:3; Titus 1:15; Hebrews 9:9, 14, 10:2, 22, 13:18; 1 Peter 2:19, 3:16, and 21).

Romans 2:16

In the day when God shall judge the secrets of men by Jesus Christ according to my gospel.

Note 10

This is quite a statement of authenticity for the Gospel Paul preached. God didn't get His understanding of the Gospel from Paul, but Paul received his revelation of the Gospel from God. He was so sure of this that he could make statements like this and like that of Galatians 1:8-12.

Romans 2:17

Behold, thou art called a Jew, and restest in the law, and makest thy boast of God,

Note 1

It is true that the Jews had been given the Word of God, and this gave them a superior knowledge of God. However, since they had not kept the Law, their superior knowledge had just made them more accountable than other people (see note 5 at Luke 12:48).

Romans 2:18

And knowest his will, and approvest the things that are more excellent, being instructed out of the law;

LIVING COMMENTARY

God's Word revealed His will and gives us a more excellent way of living.

Romans 2:19

And art confident that thou thyself art a guide of the blind, a light of them which are in darkness,

LIVING COMMENTARY

Paul was speaking against the Jews' spiritual pride. He ought to know. At one time, he was the Pharisee of the Pharisees (Philippians 3:4-5). It's true the Jewish nation was blessed by the Lord as no other nation, but it wasn't because they deserved it. It was only because of faith (Romans 4:1-5). Likewise, all New Covenant believers have been blessed with all spiritual blessings (Ephesians 1:3), but it's not because of our holiness.

God commended His love toward us while we were sinners (Romans 5:8). It wasn't because of any works of righteousness that we did (Titus 3:5). We are loved by God because He is love (1 John 4:8), not because we are lovely. Therefore, we have no reason to boast (Romans 3:27). All we should be is thankful (1 Corinthians 4:7).

Romans 2:20

An instructor of the foolish, a teacher of babes, which hast the form of knowledge and of the truth in the law.

LIVING COMMENTARY

In the few verses prior to this, Paul had been speaking to the Jews who had knowledge of God's Word and felt superior to those who didn't. They gloated in their superior knowledge. But in this verse, Paul revealed they only had the form of knowledge. The English word "form" was translated from the Greek word "MORPHOSIS," and this Greek word means "formation, i.e. (by implication), appearance (semblance or (concretely) formula)" (Strong's Concordance). They had the "appearance" and "formulas," but they had missed the true heart of God's Word. Likewise today, there are people who can quote the Bible but don't know it. As Paul said in 1 Corinthians 8:1-2, "Knowledge puffeth up, but charity edifieth. And if any man think that he knoweth any thing, he knoweth nothing yet as he ought to know." True understanding of the Word of God teaches us how much we don't know. It leaves no room for spiritual pride.

Romans 2:21

> *Thou therefore which teachest another, teachest thou not thyself?*
> *thou that preachest a man should not steal, dost thou steal?*

Note 2

The Jews took pride in their keeping of the Law, but no Jews could boast that they had kept the Law perfectly (see note 4 at Mark 10:20). "All have sinned, and come short of the glory of God" (Romans 3:23). Paul highlighted three areas where they boasted of their own holiness, but he revealed that they were actually sinners in these very things. They boasted that they didn't steal, but Paul revealed that they did steal. Jesus also rebuked the Pharisees for stealing. This was not the typical type of theft, but what we would call "white- collar crime." Paul said that they were adulterers, even though they prided themselves on not committing adultery. They were guilty of spiritual adultery if nothing else (James 4:4), and Jesus had revealed that adultery was also a sin of the heart, even if there was no action (Matthew 5:28). They also thought they were not idolatrous, but Paul convicted them on this count also. He used the word "sacrilege". This referred to them being temple robbers, thereby making direct reference to their covetousness, which is idolatry (Colossians 3:5). Therefore, even though they had a form of godliness, they were sinners just like the Gentiles, and their hypocrisy gave the Gentiles a reason to blaspheme God. This led Paul to proclaim that the Jews' claim to some kind of special covenant with God was made void through their breaking of the Law. In the third chapter of Romans, he went on to draw the conclusion that everyone, Jew and Gentile, is in the same condition of sin and needs the same salvation through Christ.

Romans 2:22

Thou that sayest a man should not commit adultery, dost thou commit adultery? thou that abhorrest idols, dost thou commit sacrilege?

LIVING COMMENTARY

Jesus revealed that if we lust in our hearts, it's adultery (Matthew 5:27-28). Paul revealed that covetousness is idolatry (Colossians 3:5). So, they were as guilty as the ones they were judging.

Romans 2:23

Thou that makest thy boast of the law, through breaking the law dishonourest thou God?

LIVING COMMENTARY

Legalists will always brag about their holiness. But if you were to ask them if they are perfect, they would have to admit that they have sinned too. And therein lies the problem with people approaching God on the basis of their goodness. A little bit of sin doesn't make people more acceptable to God than those who have a lot of sin. If we keep the whole Law and yet offend in one point, we become guilty of breaking all of the Law (James 2:10). We have all sinned and come short of God's standard (Romans 3:23). Everyone needs a Savior. Some don't need less saving than others. We are all in the same boat

(Galatians 3:22). So, those who boast of their relative holiness are deceived.

Romans 2:24

For the name of God is blasphemed among the Gentiles through you, as it is written.

LIVING COMMENTARY

This was true 2,000 years ago, and it's still true today. Many unbelievers are totally turned off to God because of the hypocrisy of religious people. Mahatma Gandhi said that he would have been a Christian if he hadn't met one. It's a shame that God's children don't represent His loving heart to the world as they should.

Romans 2:25

For circumcision verily profiteth, if thou keep the law: but if thou be a breaker of the law, thy circumcision is made uncircumcision.

Note 3

If Jews could keep the Law perfectly, then the Jewish covenant that was sealed with the sign of circumcision would give them an advantage over others. But that has never, and can never, happen. No one can keep the Law, and the Law was not given to provide a way to God (see note 2 at Matthew 19:17). Therefore, because Jews have never kept the Law perfectly, they are the same as uncircumcised in the sight of God.

Romans 2:26

Therefore if the uncircumcision keep the righteousness of the law, shall not his uncircumcision be counted for circumcision?

Note 4

Notice that Paul did not say that the uncircumcision kept the Law. Instead he mentioned them keeping the "righteousness" of the Law (this verse) and "fulfilling" the Law (Romans 2:27)—there is a difference. A person can fulfill the righteousness of the Law through faith in Jesus, but no one, Jew or Gentile, can keep the Law.

Romans 2:27

And shall not uncircumcision which is by nature, if it fulfil the law, judge thee, who by the letter and circumcision dost transgress the law?

LIVING COMMENTARY

The truth is that circumcision or uncircumcision doesn't really matter (Galatians 5:6). No one is able to receive salvation without faith in a Savior. So, holiness or lack of holiness doesn't make or break people when it comes to God. But in this discussion, Paul was showing that many who don't have any of the religious mannerisms are closer to what God wants than the religious hypocrites who look down their noses at those who aren't as pious as them.

Romans 2:28

*For he is not a Jew, which is one outwardly; neither is that circum-
cision, which is outward in the flesh:*

Note 1

As with so many commandments of the Old Testament, circumcision
was an outward sign of a greater inward reality. Paul used this term
"sign" in referring to the circumcision of Abraham in Romans 4:11.
The Jews of the first century had ignored the circumcision of the heart
and had focused all their attention on the flesh (1 Samuel 16:7). Paul
was clarifying that it is the condition of the heart—not the flesh—that
makes someone a child of God.

Romans 2:29

*But he is a Jew, which is one inwardly; and circumcision is that of
the heart, in the spirit, and not in the letter; whose praise is not of
men, but of God.*

LIVING COMMENTARY

A person can be a Jew by physical birth, but the true
children of Abraham are those who have the faith of
Abraham (Galatians 3:7). There are some promises to
physical Jews, but the spiritual blessings promised to
Abraham only come to those who are true children of
God by faith in Jesus as their Savior.

Note 2

This is a remarkable statement. Paul was saying that those who have been born again through faith in Jesus have been circumcised in their hearts (Colossians 2:11-12) and are the true Jews. They aren't Jews in nationality or religion, but they are the true people of God. Paul dealt with this in more detail in Romans 9 and clearly made a case that Gentiles who are united with Christ in the new birth are now God's people. Paul made the same point in Galatians 3, saying that those who are saved through faith in Jesus are now Abraham's seed and heirs according to the promise (Galatians 3:16, 22, and 26-29). This leaves no doubt that the church is now God's chosen people on earth. This does not mean that God has forsaken the Jews. Paul dealt with that issue in Romans 9. There are still prophecies that apply to the physical nation of Israel, and they will be fulfilled. However, the New Testament church, composed of Jews and Gentiles, is now God's kingdom on earth.

Note 3

Paul's statement here definitely places the spirit in the heart of man. This has led some to believe that the heart and spirit are the same. However, 1 Peter 3:4 refers to the spirit of man as the hidden man of the heart, implying that the spirit comprises only a part of the heart. The heart of man is actually made up of two parts: The soul and the spirit. This is the reason the Scripture speaks of having two minds in our hearts (James 4:8) and why we must believe with all our hearts (Acts 8:37), not just a part (see note 3 at Matthew 12:34).

Note 4

The Greek word that is used here for "letter" is "GRAMMA" and literally means "a writing, i.e. a letter, note, epistle, book, etc." (Strong's Concordance). Paul was saying that circumcision is spiritual rather than natural. True circumcision is a born-again nature and not a mark in the flesh.

ROMANS

CHAPTER THREE

Romans 3:1

What advantage then hath the Jew? or what profit is there of circumcision?

Note 1

Paul had just proven that the Jews were as guilty as the pagans whom they disdained (see note 1 at Romans 2:1). This led to the question, "What advantage is there in being a Jew?" Paul gave the most important answer to that question in Romans 3:2 (see note 2 at that verse) and then addressed the issue more in Romans 9:4-5.

Romans 3:2

Much every way: chiefly, because that unto them were committed the oracles of God.

Note 2

The main advantage that the Jews had over others was that God had committed His Word unto them. They not only had the intuitive knowledge of God (see note 2 at Romans 1:18), but they also had a written record of God's instructions that should have served as an added restraint from departing from God. They, however, had missed the true intent of God's Law and therefore were not taking advantage of the benefits God's Word afforded them.

Note 3

The Greek word for "oracles" is "LOGION," and it means "an utterance (of God)" (Strong's Concordance). Therefore, this is speaking of the Word of God that was committed to the Jews. In the Old Testament, the word "oracle" was also used to designate the innermost part of the temple, since the Ark of the Covenant was kept there (1 Kings 6:5, 16, 19-23, 31, 7:49, 8:6, 8; 2 Chronicles 3:16, 4:20, 5:7, 9; and Psalm 28:2). The word "oracles" is used four times in the New Testament (Acts 7:38, this verse, Hebrews 5:12, and 1 Peter 4:11). In each of these instances, the word is clearly referring to the Word of God.

Romans 3:3

For what if some did not believe? shall their unbelief make the faith of God without effect?

Note 4

Paul was using the phrase "the faith of God" in this verse interchangeably with the phrase "the oracles of God" in Romans 3:2. He was saying that the unbelief of the Jews did not make the Word of God, or the promises of God, without effect. Therefore, the Word of God is the faith of God. No wonder faith comes by hearing God's Word: God's Word contains His faith.

Note 5

Paul was asking the question, "If some of the Jews did not believe God's Word, does that make God's Word of no effect?" The answer to this question is a resounding "no" (Romans 3:4). However, Mark 7:13 says we make the Word of God of none effect through our traditions. What's the harmony between these two verses? People can make God's Word of no effect in their personal lives. Hebrews 4:2 says God's Word will not profit people unless they mix it with faith. So the Word will not profit anyone who doesn't believe it, but God's Word itself doesn't lose any power. That is what Paul was stating here. The unbelief of the Jewish nation as a whole did not void the promises of God concerning salvation through a savior. The promises of salvation were of no effect to the individuals who rejected Jesus, but to those who will put their faith in Jesus as Messiah, the Word of God still has its power to save.

Romans 3:4

God forbid: yea, let God be true, but every man a liar; as it is written, That thou mightest be justified in thy sayings, and mightest overcome when thou art judged.

Note 6

This is the first of ten times that Paul used the expression "God forbid" in the book of Romans (this verse, 3:6, 31; 6:2, 15; 7:7, 13; 9:14; 11:1, and 11). He also used this expression four other times in his other epistles (1 Corinthians 6:15; Galatians 2:17, 3:21, and 6:14). The Greek words that are used here for "God forbid" are "ME GINOMAI" meaning "let it not be...God forbid...far be it" (Vine's Expository Dictionary) and express emphatic denial of the false conclusion that someone might draw from his teaching.

Note 7

This phrase "let God be true, but every man a liar" is given in response to the question of Romans 3:3 (see note 5 at that verse). Paul was stating that God and His promises are always true even if people don't believe Him. However, other applications of this truth can benefit us greatly. When anyone or anything contradicts a promise made to us in God's Word, we need to reckon God to be true and that person or thing to be lying. We need to believe that what God's Word says about our prosperity is true (2 Corinthians 8:9 and 3 John 2), instead of what our checkbooks say. We need to believe that we were healed by His stripes (Isaiah 53:5, Matthew 8:17, and 1 Peter 2:24), instead of believing what the x-rays show. In every aspect of our lives, we need to believe God's Word above what we see or hear.

Note 8

This is a quotation from David out of Psalm 51:4 when he was repenting of his sin with Bathsheba and the murder of her husband. David was admitting his sinfulness and proclaiming God's complete justification in judging his sin in whatever way He saw fit. David's sin had not made God unholy; it made David unholy. In his sinfulness, David saw the holiness of God more clearly than ever. This is what Paul was drawing from this Old Testament passage. He was saying that in a similar manner, God retained His holiness even when His people were unholy. It was the Jews, not God, who suffered from not believing God's Word.

Romans 3:5

But if our unrighteousness commend the righteousness of God, what shall we say? Is God unrighteous who taketh vengeance? (I speak as a man)

Note 9

Paul had just explained that the Jews' faithlessness did not make God unfaithful to His Word (see note 5 at Romans 3:3). Therefore, when you consider how unfaithful we have been to God, it makes God's mercy and faithfulness appear even greater. So this brings up new questions: If our unrighteousness reveals God's righteousness or causes it to be seen in an even greater way, then are we actually helping God? Would it be right for God to judge us for something like that? Of course, Paul's answer to that is another "God forbid." It is true that we would never have seen the love and goodness of God as clearly if we had not sinned, but that does not mean our sins were a good thing. This is one piece of information that the Lord never wanted us to know by experience. None of us will be able to tell God on the Day of Judgment that our sins just helped Him reveal how great His mercy was. The Lord will be totally just in bringing His judgment on all those who refuse His offer of mercy given through Jesus, His Son.

Note 10

Paul was saying that the logic he had just been using was not from God but was carnal logic. He was not saying this as God's spokesman; he was expressing a thought held by opponents of the Gospel so that he could expose the error in it. Therefore, he gave a disclaimer in parentheses that this was not God's wisdom but man's.

Romans 3:6

God forbid: for then how shall God judge the world?

Note 11

Paul was saying that if this were true (Romans 3:5), God couldn't judge the world, and it is a well-established fact in Scripture that God will judge the world. Therefore, this argument has to be rejected.

Romans 3:7

For if the truth of God hath more abounded through my lie unto his glory; why yet am I also judged as a sinner?

LIVING COMMENTARY

Of course our lies, or rejection of God's truths, do not glorify the Lord. However, when we repent and receive the salvation offered through Jesus, that glorifies the Lord.

Romans 3:8

And not rather, (as we be slanderously reported, and as some affirm that we say,) Let us do evil, that good may come? whose damnation is just.

Note 12

Paul preached the grace of God as no one else recorded in Scripture (see note 2 at Acts 15:1). This led many people to slander him and his teaching by accusing him of encouraging people to sin. This was totally untrue. The grace of God teaches us to deny ungodliness and worldly lust (Titus 2:11-12). Here Paul showed his total rejection of those allegations by saying that the damnation of those people was just. He also "raised the stakes" for anyone who wants to criticize those who proclaim the grace of God. According to Paul, they will be damned.

Romans 3:9

What then? are we better than they? No, in no wise: for we have before proved both Jews and Gentiles, that they are all under sin;

Note 1

In Romans 1:18-32, Paul proved that the Gentiles were guilty before God for their actions because of an intuitive knowledge of God (see note 2 at Romans 1:18). In Romans 2, Paul proved that the Jews were even worse off than the Gentiles because they had been given the Word of God and yet had not kept it (see note 1 at Romans 2:1). Here in Romans 3, he brought all this together and concluded that every one (Jew or Gentile, religious or pagan, moral or immoral) is guilty before God. Paul cited many Old Testament scriptures to verify this claim and to show that this was not some new doctrine. Faith in the sacrificial death of a savior was God's plan of redemption all along. Paul's arguments in Romans 3:9-18 provide the reason for salvation by grace through faith (Ephesians 2:8) and refute the doctrines of every other religion. People are so destitute that they cannot save themselves; they have to have a savior. Therefore, all other religions are wrong, because they don't provide a savior. To some degree or another, the other religions of the world teach that the burden of salvation is upon people's own shoulders. In contrast, Christianity has a Savior, and not just some man: God Himself provided salvation for mankind. Within the ranks of those who claim Christianity, this is also the pivotal issue. Any deviation from trust in Jesus and His imputed righteousness, to reliance on our own holiness for right standing with God, is error. Therefore, the truth expressed in these verses is critical to understanding God's plan of salvation. Since people could never "make up" for their sins, God did what people could not do; He paid the price Himself. No other method of payment is acceptable.

Romans 3:10

As it is written, There is none righteous, no, not one:

LIVING COMMENTARY

This is a quotation from Psalms 14:1-3 and 53:1-3.

Romans 3:11

There is none that understandeth, there is none that seeketh after God.

LIVING COMMENTARY

Like Romans 3:10, this verse is also quoting Psalms 14:1-3, 53:1-3.

Romans 3:12

They are all gone out of the way, they are together become unprofitable; there is none that doeth good, no, not one.

LIVING COMMENTARY

This is continuing the quotation from Psalms 14:1-3, 53:1-3.

Romans 3:13

Their throat is an open sepulchre; with their tongues they have used deceit; the poison of asps is under their lips:

LIVING COMMENTARY

Paul was quoting from Psalm 5:9 in this verse. Jesus used similar reasoning in Matthew 23:27. A sepulcher is full of death and decay. Natural man's mouth is just like that. It spews out death (Proverbs 18:21). Notice that the tongue is likened to the venom of a snake.

Romans 3:14

Whose mouth is full of cursing and bitterness:

LIVING COMMENTARY

Paul gave a command to bless and not curse (Romans 12:14). Cursing people and having bitterness in our hearts is devilish. This is not how God intended us to live, but this is describing how carnal man is.

Romans 3:15

Their feet are swift to shed blood:

LIVING COMMENTARY

In this passage (Romans 3:10-18), Paul was describing how fallen human nature is. He listed these things to show the necessity of the Law to reveal our sin to us, and he concluded by saying that everyone has sinned (Romans 3:23).

Romans 3:16

Destruction and misery are in their ways:

LIVING COMMENTARY

It's amazing how far mankind has fallen. The Lord created us for His pleasure (Revelation 4:11). What's described here in Romans is not the way the Lord intended us to live (Genesis 6:5-6). Sadly, this is still descriptive of those who have not been transformed by the renewing of their minds (Romans 12:2).

Romans 3:17

And the way of peace have they not known:

LIVING COMMENTARY

This verse is describing fallen man apart from the redemptive power of Jesus. Jesus is our peace (Ephesians 2:14). Without faith in what Jesus did for us, there is no true peace (Romans 5:1). Peace is much more than the absence of problems. We have a peace that passes understanding (Philippians 4:7), and those who keep their minds stayed on the Lord will have perfect, continuous peace (Isaiah 26:3). Peace comes through the knowledge of God (2 Peter 1:2).

Romans 3:18

There is no fear of God before their eyes.

LIVING COMMENTARY

The fear of the Lord is to hate evil (Proverbs 8:13). Those who don't hate evil don't fear God. Psalm 36:1 says, "The transgression of the wicked saith within my heart, that there is no fear of God before his eyes."

Romans 3:19

Now we know that what things soever the law saith, it saith to them who are under the law: that every mouth may be stopped, and all the world may become guilty before God.

Note 2

Paul had conclusively proven that both Jews and Gentiles were sinners (see note 1 at Romans 3:9) and therefore incapable of saving themselves through their own works of righteousness. They both needed a savior. Here Paul began to reveal that the means of that salvation is through faith in Jesus the Messiah and not through people's moral goodness.

Note 3

This very clear statement by Paul comes as a complete shock to most Christians. Christianity as a whole has embraced the Old Testament Law, and most Christians have never thought that the Law was not intended for them. However, Paul was saying that the Law was given to the Jews. The purpose of that Law was to produce guilt (see note 4 at this verse); therefore, those who deny their guilt before God can profit from its condemning effect (2 Corinthians 3:9 and 1 Timothy 1:9). But Christians who embrace the Old Testament Law (not everything that is in the Old Testament is Law) as God's gift to them have misunderstood its purpose. That is not to say that we as Christians should reject the Old Testament as God's holy Word—God forbid. It certainly is God's Word and is, therefore, profitable for doctrine, reproof, etc. (2 Timothy 3:16).

However, it needs to be interpreted in light of the New Covenant. Jesus didn't only set us free from the curse of the Law (Galatians 3:13); He also set us free from the Law itself (Romans 4:16, 6:14-15, 7:4-6, 8:2; 2 Corinthians 3:7; Galatians 2:19, 3:24-25, 4:21, 5:18; Ephesians 2:14-15; Colossians 2:14; 1 Timothy 1:9; Hebrews 7:18-19, 8:7-13, and 10:8-9). A desire to live under the commands of the Old Testament Law is a return to bondage and a misunderstanding of our New Covenant in Jesus (see note 2 at Luke 9:55, note 1 at Luke 16:16, and note 6 at Luke 19:8).

Note 4

Here Paul began to make a series of radical statements. They were radical because the Jews of his day, just like many church people of our day, thought that the Law of God was given so that they could earn their salvation through keeping it. That wasn't its purpose. The Law was not given for the purpose of producing justification (Romans 3:20, 28, 4:13; Galatians 2:16, 3:11, 5:4; and Titus 3:5). The Law was given to kill (2 Corinthians 3:7) and condemn (2 Corinthians 3:9). The Law strengthened sin (1 Corinthians 15:56) and made sin come alive (Romans 7:9). The Law gave sin an occasion against us to deceive us and work all manner of lust in us (Romans 7:8 and 11). In short, the Law strengthened our enemy, sin, not us. Why would God give us something that strengthened our enemy? It's because sin had already beaten us, and we didn't know it.

Mankind was deceived into thinking that although we weren't perfect, surely our sins weren't that bad. We really were pretty good people, and the outcome would be "okay." The only thing wrong with that thinking is that God doesn't grade on a curve. It doesn't matter if we are better than someone else. All have sinned and come short of the glory of God (Romans 3:23), and the wages for sin (any sin) is death (Romans 6:23). James 2:10 says, "For whosoever shall keep the whole law, and yet offend in one point, he is guilty of all." If we commit any sin, we are guilty of them all. It's similar to breaking a window. It doesn't matter how big a hole is made in the window. If it's broken, the whole window has to be replaced. If we break even the slightest command, we are guilty of breaking them all. So God had to break the deception that people had fallen into, of thinking they were surely good enough to be accepted by God. The way He did this was to give the Law. It made sin and its lust come alive in people. To those who would receive it, it became obvious that if this holy perfection of the Law was what God demanded, people could not be saved by their own goodness. That was the point that God wanted to make, and that was the point that Paul was making here. No one can be saved by keeping the Law, because all have sinned and come short of the Law's perfection (Romans 3:23). Therefore, the Law stripped people of every excuse and made them guilty before God. The Law gave them knowledge of just how sinful they were and removed any deception of them ever being saved because they were such "nice guys" in comparison to others. As Paul said in Galatians 3:23, "But before faith came, we were kept under the law, shut up unto the faith which should afterwards be revealed." The Law took away every hope of salvation except faith in a savior. That was the purpose of the Law.

Romans 3:20

Therefore by the deeds of the law there shall no flesh be justified in his sight: for by the law is the knowledge of sin.

LIVING COMMENTARY

This is a very revealing passage of Scripture. The Law wasn't given to produce justification ("to render (i.e. show or regard as) just or innocent" [Strong's Concordance] or "just as if I'd never sinned" [Wommack]). That wasn't its purpose. What was its purpose then? It was given to give us the knowledge that we were sinners and needed salvation (see my note at Romans 3:31). If people would use the Law for that purpose, that would be fine (see my notes at 1 Timothy 1:7-8). If we use the Law for what it was intended to do, it is useful, but the problem comes when we use the Law for what it wasn't intended to do. It wasn't God's way of getting us saved (see my note at Galatians 3:11). The only way to obtain salvation is to put faith in Jesus and what He did for us as our Savior (see my note at Ephesians 2:8). We are justified by faith without the deeds of the Law (Romans 3:28).

Romans 3:21

But now the righteousness of God without the law is manifested, being witnessed by the law and the prophets;

Note 1

This was another one of Paul's radical statements (see note 4 at Romans 3:19) that was diametrically opposed to the Jewish thinking of his day. Mercy and grace were present in the Old Testament, but they were typified in the Old Testament sacrifices that were incorporated in the Law. Therefore, the Jews had come to think that the only way God would grant any forgiveness was through them fulfilling the Law as much as possible and then offering the appropriate sacrifice prescribed in the Law for any sins. For Paul to say that a person could be righteous apart from the Law was unthinkable. Paul didn't end there though; he went on to say that this method of receiving right standing with God was promised under the Old Testament Law and Prophets. This means Paul was not putting forth a new doctrine but expounding the true doctrine that the Old Testament Law and prophets had advocated all along. This left no doubt that the Jews' trust in the Old Testament Law for justification was never God's intent. They had misunderstood and misapplied the Law in this area. Likewise today, many religious people misunderstand the true intent of the Old Testament Law (see notes 3 and 4 at Romans 3:19).

Romans 3:22

Even the righteousness of God which is by faith of Jesus Christ unto all and upon all them that believe: for there is no difference:

Note 2

Paul made an even clearer presentation of this truth in Romans 9:30-10:9. The Jews were seeking to produce their own righteousness according to their holy actions that conformed to the Law. Paul was speaking of a different type of righteousness—not a human righteousness that was flawed but the perfect righteousness of God Himself. Through faith in Jesus, we can receive the very righteousness of God as a gift (2 Corinthians 5:21). God's righteousness is infinitely better in quality and quantity than man's puny righteousness (Isaiah 64:6). People can never be justified in the sight of God based on a righteousness that comes from their own acts of holiness. They must have God's righteousness, and that only comes through faith in the Lord Jesus Christ as Savior. Paul said in Philippians 3:9, "And be found in him, not having mine own righteousness, which is of the law, but that which is through the faith of Christ, the righteousness which is of God by faith." This is "the righteousness of God" that Paul was referring to here.

Note 3

Notice that Paul did not say that this righteousness of God came by faith **in** Jesus Christ. No, it comes by the faith **of** Jesus Christ. There is a big difference. Our faith does not produce our righteousness. Jesus obtained righteousness (the perfect righteousness of God) through His faith and offers it to everyone who will believe on Him as Lord. Therefore, our faith (which is also a gift from God, Ephesians 2:8) just receives what Jesus has already obtained for us through His faith. Jesus obtained our justification and righteousness through His faith (Galatians 2:16).

Note 4

The only difference between Jew and Gentile, or the moral and immoral, is in the sight of people. From God's point of view, there is no difference. All have sinned and come short of the glory of God (Romans 3:23 and James 2:10).

Romans 3:23

For all have sinned, and come short of the glory of God;

Note 5

As explained in note 1 at Romans 3:9, this is one of the pivotal doctrines of Scripture. Jesus only came to save sinners (1 Timothy 1:15). Unless people acknowledge that they are sinners, they cannot be saved.

Romans 4:5 says that God justifies the ungodly. Therefore, until people admit they are ungodly, they cannot be saved. People have to be stripped of all other means of salvation (John 14:6) before they can receive Jesus as their Savior. That was the purpose of the Old Testament Law (see note 4 at Romans 3:19), and that was the argument Paul gave in Romans 1:21-23. Therefore, the truth of universal guilt before God that is expressed in this verse is true in all its applications. However, in context, this verse is just a steppingstone to an even greater truth, expressed in Romans 3:24-26. Because the whole world is guilty before God, He has provided one way of salvation for everyone. In the same way that everyone is guilty, so everyone has already been justified freely by God's grace. That does not mean everyone is saved. All people have had the sacrificial offering of Jesus made for their sins by grace (1

Timothy 4:10 and 1 John 2:2), but grace alone doesn't save. They have to put faith in what God has provided for them by grace (Ephesians 2:8). Therefore, although the price has been paid for the sins of the whole world, only those who receive it by faith will benefit from the salvation that Jesus offers.

Note 6

The Greek word that was translated "glory" here is "DOXA," and according to Vine's Expository Dictionary, it means "the manifested perfection of His character, especially His righteousness, of which all men fall short." A simple way of saying this is that all people fall short of Jesus. Jesus is the glory of the Father (John 1:14, 2 Corinthians 4:6, Hebrews 1:3, and Revelation 21:23). A common mistake that people make is comparing themselves with other people (2 Corinthians 10:12). Nearly everyone has heard, "If the hypocrites down there at church make it, then I'll make it." The only thing wrong with that thinking is that the hypocrites down there at church aren't God's "measuring stick." Everyone is going to be compared to Jesus, the glory of God, and therefore everyone will come up short. We all need a savior.

Romans 3:24

Being justified freely by his grace through the redemption that is in Christ Jesus:

Note 7

Justification is not something to be earned but a gift to be received. Seeking to earn salvation is the only sin that will prevent people from being saved, because they cannot submit themselves to the righteousness of

God, which comes as a gift through faith, as long as they are seeking to establish their own righteousness (Romans 10:3).

Note 8

Grace is God's ability given to us on an unearned, undeserved basis. However, this grace comes through the redemption that Jesus provided. Therefore, there can be no grace in our lives apart from faith in Jesus.

Romans 5:2 says, "By whom also we have access by faith into this grace wherein we stand, and rejoice in hope of the glory of God."

Romans 3:25

Whom God hath set forth to be a propitiation through faith in his blood, to declare his righteousness for the remission of sins that are past, through the forbearance of God;

LIVING COMMENTARY

God doesn't declare us righteous because of anything we've done (Titus 3:5). God the Father put Jesus' righteousness to our account. We are the righteousness of God in Christ Jesus (2 Corinthians 5:21).

Note 9

This verse is speaking of the sins that were committed under the Old Covenant, before the sacrifice of Jesus was made. Those sins were also paid for by the blood of Jesus. The Old Testament sacrifices were only types and shadows of the true sin offering that Jesus made. It was impossible for the blood of bulls and of goats to ever take away sins (Hebrews

10:4). The Lord dealt with sins under the Old Testament through His forbearance. In a similar way that a person gives a check or credit card in exchange for the real currency desired, so the Lord gave the Old Testament sacrifices. However, just as these substitutes would be unacceptable if there was no reality to back them up, so the Old Testament sacrifices only served as a token of the real sacrifice of Jesus that would pay for sin (Hebrews 9:13-14).

Romans 3:26

To declare, I say, at this time his righteousness: that he might be just, and the justifier of him which believeth in Jesus.

LIVING COMMENTARY

The Lord repeats this amazing concept that it was the righteousness of Jesus that made us have relationship with the Father.

Note 10

Here Paul restated this amazing fact that it is the righteousness of Jesus that has been given to us (see note 2 at Romans 3:22). We don't just have enough righteousness to let us slip into heaven; we have been given Jesus' righteousness. First Corinthians 1:30 says, "But of him are ye in Christ Jesus, who of God is made unto us wisdom, and righteousness, and sanctification, and redemption." Jesus is our righteousness! Second Corinthians 5:21 says, "For he hath made him to be sin for us, who knew no sin; that we might be made the righteousness of God in him."

Romans 3:27

Where is boasting then? It is excluded. By what law? of works? Nay: but by the law of faith.

LIVING COMMENTARY

Faith is governed by law. That means it's universal and constant, just like gravity. If we ignore the laws of gravity, they can kill us. Likewise, if we ignore the laws of faith, even if it's through ignorance, we can die. Faith can be counted on more than any physical thing controlled by law, such as electricity. The Greek word "NOMOS," which was translated "law" twice in this verse, means "law (through the idea of prescriptive usage), genitive case (regulation), specially, (of Moses (including the volume); also of the Gospel), or figuratively (a principle)" (Strong's Concordance). It was derived from the Greek word meaning "to parcel out, especially food or grazing to animals" (Strong's Concordance). This is describing that faith is "parceled" out or can only be utilized according to "prescriptive usage." We have to learn how to use faith according to the prescription that is given us in the Word of God.

Note 11

Boasting, bragging, and pride about our holiness or spiritual accomplishments are sure signs that we don't understand justification by grace through faith like Paul was teaching it here. If we acknowledge that we are no better than anyone else regardless of our conduct and that the only way we obtained peace with God was through putting faith in what Jesus did for us, then there is no room for boasting about our achievements. It was the accomplishments of Jesus that saved us. Pride is the root of all divisions in the church today (see note 11 at Acts 20:30). Therefore, the prevalence of division in the church is a painful testimony to the lack of this foundational truth of justification by grace through faith.

Note 12

Notice that Paul referred to the **law** of faith. Faith is governed by law, just as gravity or electricity is. If we would view faith as a law, rather than as something that sometimes works and other times doesn't, we would begin to get very different results. The law of electricity has been here on earth since creation. Man has observed it in such things as lightning and static electricity, but it was not until someone believed that there were laws that governed the activity of electricity that progress began to be made in putting it to use.

Likewise, none deny the existence of faith, but it is only when people begin to understand that there are laws that govern faith and then begin to learn what those laws are that faith begins to work for them.

Romans 3:28
Therefore we conclude that a man is justified by faith without the deeds of the law.

LIVING COMMENTARY

What a radical statement! Faith is what justifies us. The word "justified" was translated from the Greek word "DIKAIOO," which means "to render (i.e. show or regard as) just or innocent" (Strong's Concordance). My simple layman's definition of justified is "just as if I'd never sinned." It means to declare us free from the guilt and penalty attached to our sins. All of this happens by grace through faith (see my note at Ephesians 2:8), without us keeping the Law. This is where most people have problems. They can accept that they aren't perfect and need help. But most people don't have the revelation that right standing with God comes solely through putting faith in Jesus as our Savior. They think we have to keep a minimum standard of the Law, and then God's grace will cover the rest. But grace mixed with any works isn't true grace (see my note at Romans 11:6). Therefore, the only thing that is needed to be right with God is faith in what Jesus did for us. Jesus + nothing = everything. Jesus + anything = nothing. This is the scripture that the Lord used to reveal this truth to Martin Luther, and it sparked the Reformation. We need a reformation of the church today just as much as in the days of Martin Luther.

Romans 3:29

Is he the God of the Jews only? is he not also of the Gentiles? Yes, of the Gentiles also:

LIVING COMMENTARY

In Christ, there is neither Jew nor Gentile (Galatians 3:28 and Colossians 3:11). We are all the children of

> God, with just one ailment (Romans 3:23) for which
> Jesus is the one Cure.

Romans 3:30

*Seeing it is one God, which shall justify the circumcision by faith,
and uncircumcision through faith.*

Note 13

There is no reason to believe that Paul was making any distinction
between the way the Jews and the Gentiles are justified by his use of the
words "by" and "through." The same end (justification) is achieved, and
faith is the way for both Jew and Gentile to receive it.

Romans 3:31

*Do we then make void the law through faith? God forbid: yea, we
establish the law.*

Note 14

Paul had just systematically taken away the Jews' trust in the Law for
the purpose of justification. This led to the question, "Is the Law useless?" Paul emphatically answered, "God forbid." The real purpose of
the Law was established by the Gospel (see note 5 at Acts 20:24). The
problem with the Jews was that they were using the Law for something
that God never intended. The Law was useless to produce justification.
God didn't give the Law so that they could keep it and thereby earn
justification. The Law was given to reveal to them that they could never

live up to such a holy standard and thereby drive them to God to call out for mercy (Galatians 3:22-24). The true purpose of the Law is still functional today (see note 4 at Romans 3:19). As 1 Timothy 1:8-9 say, "But we know that the law is good, if a man use it lawfully; Knowing this, that the law is not made for a righteous man." The Law is God's way of revealing to people their need. It is powerless to make provision for that need. It's the Gospel that provides the power to produce salvation (see note 1 at Romans 1:16). In Romans 4, Paul went on to use two great men of the Old Testament (Abraham and David) as examples of how justification came through faith, not through the Law.

ROMANS

CHAPTER FOUR

Romans 4:1

What shall we say then that Abraham our father, as pertaining to the flesh, hath found?

Note 1

The question is, "What good, then, were Abraham's works?" Paul answered this indirectly. He stated what Abraham's works were not good for. They were not good enough to grant him justification in the sight of God; that came by faith. He showed that Abraham's works, or efforts, didn't earn him anything from God. Abraham was justified by faith for over thirteen years (see note 3 at Romans 4:10) before he performed the act of circumcision that the Jews were insisting was necessary for right standing with God (Romans 4:10-11).

Romans 4:2

For if Abraham were justified by works, he hath whereof to glory; but not before God.

Note 2

Our own good works will only allow us to boast if we're comparing ourselves with other people (2 Corinthians 10:12). However, in the sight of God, not one of us has anything to brag about. We have all come short of the glory of God (see notes 5 and 6 at Romans 3:23).

Romans 4:3

> *For what saith the scripture? Abraham believed God, and it was counted unto him for righteousness.*

LIVING COMMENTARY

See my note at Romans 4:22.

Note 3

Paul was showing an inspired revelation of the Old Testament scriptures. All devout Jews knew the story of Abraham, but they had missed this simple truth that Paul brought out. In Genesis 15:6, the Scriptures clearly say that Abraham believed God and God counted Abraham's faith for righteousness. It can't get any clearer than that. Later in this same chapter, Paul referred to the interval of time (over thirteen years) between when the Scriptures state Abraham was counted righteous and the time when he was circumcised, as further proof that Abraham's righteousness was given to him before he performed the righteous acts of the Law (see note 3 at Romans 4:10).

Note 4

Paul had just made a series of radical statements (see note 4 at Romans 3:19 and note 1 at Romans 3:21) that were hard for these Jews to swallow. Here he went back to Old Testament scripture and the founder of the Jewish nation to prove his assertions. He skillfully used the very scriptures they had misunderstood to verify his Gospel of grace. He also quoted David to draw on two of the most revered men of the Old Testament as examples of salvation by grace through faith.

Note 5

Hebrews 11:6 says, "But without faith it is impossible to please him." It was Abraham's faith that pleased God. The Lord promised Abraham that his seed would be as numerous as the stars in the sky and the sand on the seashore, and Abraham believed God. That pleased God so much that He counted Abraham righteous right then, even though Abraham had not yet fulfilled the rite of circumcision and was not living such a holy life. According to Leviticus 18:9, it was an abomination (Leviticus 18:26) for a man to marry a half sister.

Sarah, Abraham's wife, was his half sister (Genesis 20:12). Therefore, Abraham's marriage to Sarah was not what pleased God. Abraham had already lied about Sarah being his wife so that he could save his own neck. He was willing to let a man commit adultery with his wife with no objections from him. Immediately after this instance where the Lord counted Abraham's faith for righteousness (Genesis 15:6), Abraham tried to accomplish God's will in the flesh with Hagar (Genesis 16) and then repeated this terrible sin with Sarah again (Genesis 20). Anyone who really looked at the life of Abraham and the favor that he found with God would have to conclude that it was Abraham's faith that pleased God. It's the same with any of us. The only thing that we can do to please God is put faith in Jesus as our Savior.

Note 6

The Greek word that was translated "counted" in this verse is "LOGI-ZOMAI," and it means "to take an inventory, i.e. estimate" (Strong's Concordance). It is an accounting term that means "to enter in the account book" ("Linguistic Key to the Greek New Testament" by Fritz Rienecker). This same word is used eleven times in this chapter. It was translated "counted" twice (Romans 4:3 and 5), "impute" once (Romans 4:8), "imputed" four times (Romans 4:11 and 22-24), "imputeth" once (Romans 4:6), and "reckoned" three times (Romans 4:4 and 9-10). By comparing the different ways this same Greek word was translated into English, it becomes very easy to discern an accurate meaning for it.

Romans 4:4

Now to him that worketh is the reward not reckoned of grace, but of debt.

Note 7

Paul was saying that if an individual could be saved by works, then God would be providing salvation as a payment to that person, and of course, that doesn't make sense. God is not under obligation or debt to save anyone. Trust in our own works voids grace, and likewise, trust in God's grace makes faith in our own efforts useless. This was repeated by Paul again in Romans 11:6—"And if by grace, then is it no more of works: otherwise grace is no more grace. But if it be of works, then is it no more grace: otherwise work is no more work."

Romans 4:5

But to him that worketh not, but believeth on him that justifieth the ungodly, his faith is counted for righteousness.

Note 8

What a statement! Paul had countered the false doctrine that acting righteous could make people righteous. Here he dropped the bomb that God justifies the ungodly! We might add from the context that this is the only kind of people whom He justifies. That's because He doesn't have any other kind of people to justify. All people have sinned and come short of the glory of God (see notes 5 and 6 at Romans 3:23). This verse should forever dispel any delusions that people might have of trying to earn God's favor by their performances.

Note 9

Faith in the atonement of Jesus grants us righteousness; our actions don't. However, true faith will produce actions (James 2:17-18), and these actions, or lack thereof, can be used by others to determine where we stand with the Lord (1 John 3:7-10). Although our actions are indications of our inner faith, they can be misinterpreted, and therefore any judgments made based on actions need to be for the purpose of discernment only and not condemnation (see note 46 at Matthew 7:1).

Romans 4:6

Even as David also describeth the blessedness of the man, unto whom God imputeth righteousness without works,

Note 10

King David (see note 8 at Acts 13:22) was living under the Old Covenant of Law (see note 3 at Romans 3:19). However, this scripture that Paul quoted (Romans 4:7-8) from Psalm 32, as well as the things David wrote in Psalm 51 when repenting for his sins against Uriah and

Bathsheba, shows that he had a tremendous revelation of the salvation by grace through faith that was coming with the Messiah.

Romans 4:7

Saying, Blessed are they whose iniquities are forgiven, and whose sins are covered.

LIVING COMMENTARY

This is a quotation from Psalm 32:1-2.

Romans 4:8

Blessed is the man to whom the Lord will not impute sin.

Note 11

The Greek words that are translated "will not" in this verse are what is called "a double negative, strongly expressing a negation" (Vine's Expository Dictionary). This is the strongest language possible stating that those who receive forgiveness will not ever have their sins held against them. He didn't just say "did not" or "does not" but "will not," implying that even future-tense sins have been dealt with through the sacrificial offering of Jesus, once for all (Hebrews 10:10 and 14). Most Christians have the concept that the sins they committed before they professed faith in Christ were forgiven at salvation, but any sins that are committed after that time are not forgiven until they are repented of and forgiveness is asked for. That is not the case. All of our sins—past, present, and future—were forgiven through the one offering of Jesus (see my notes at Hebrews 9:12, 15; 10:10, 14; and 12:23). If God can't forgive future-tense sins, then none of us can be saved, because Jesus only died once, nearly 2,000 years ago, before we had committed any sins. ALL of our sins have been forgiven. Why, then, 1 John 1:9? "If we confess our sins, he is faithful and just to forgive us our sins, and to cleanse us from all unrighteousness." This is not speaking of the eternal salvation of our spirits but, rather, the salvation of our souls (James 1:21 and 1 Peter 1:9). It's our spirits that become born again at salvation, and sin will never be imputed to our born-again spirits. They have been sanctified and perfected forever (Hebrews 10:10, 14; and 12:23) and cannot sin (1 John 3:9). However, we are still in the process of saving our souls (James 1:21 and 1 Peter 1:9). When we sin, the devil has a legal right to bring his forms of death into our soulish area (Romans 6:16). How do we get the devil out once he has gotten in? We confess it, and God brings out into the soulish realm that forgiveness that is already a reality in our born-again spirits, and the devil has no right to stay. If we had to confess every sin committed after our born-again experience in order to maintain our salvation, no one would ever make it. What if we forgot to confess some sin? That puts the burden of salvation back on us. We must remember that "God is a Spirit" (John 4:24), and we must worship Him through our new born-again spirits. Therefore, we truly are blessed because God will not hold any sin against our spirits. Our spirits are clean and pure (Ephesians 4:24, Hebrews 12:23, and 1 John 4:17) and will not change due to our performance.

Romans 4:9

Cometh this blessedness then upon the circumcision only, or upon the uncircumcision also? for we say that faith was reckoned to Abraham for righteousness.

Note 1

Paul had previously shown in this chapter that Abraham's faith was what granted him right standing with God (see notes 3 and 5 at Romans 4:3), and he used a quote from David to verify salvation by grace through faith (see note 10 at Romans 4:6). Here he returned to the story of Abraham and used the very religious act that the legalists were demanding compliance with (i.e., circumcision) to further certify that salvation is by grace through faith.

Romans 4:10

How was it then reckoned? when he was in circumcision, or in uncircumcision? Not in circumcision, but in uncircumcision.

Note 2

The time between when God counted Abraham's faith for righteousness and when Abraham was circumcised was over thirteen years. This can be deduced in the following way: The instance when God counted Abraham righteous took place in Genesis 15:6, before the birth of Ishmael (Genesis 16:15). Abraham circumcised Ishmael the same day that he was circumcised (Genesis 17:26), and Genesis 17:25 says that took place when Ishmael was thirteen years old. Therefore, the circumcision of Abraham was at least thirteen years and nine months after his justification by faith in Genesis 15:6.

Note 3

This truth is so simple and obvious that it is amazing that the legalistic Jews had missed it. Paul explained that God said Abraham was righteous (Genesis 15:6) over thirteen years (see note 2 at this verse) before he performed the rite of circumcision (see note 2 at Acts 15:1). Now if circumcision was necessary for justification with God, as some Jews were advocating, then Abraham could not have been righteous until after the performing of this act. But God Himself said Abraham was righteous. Therefore, the rite of circumcision (or any other act of obedience) cannot be a prerequisite for justification. In our day, religious people no longer contend that circumcision is essential for salvation; Paul conclusively disproved that.

However, many people are still making the same mistake. They have just substituted some other act of holiness for circumcision. They may have changed cars, but they are headed down the same road to the same destination. For instance, entire denominations are built around the doctrine that water baptism is essential for salvation. There is no disputing that water baptism is a command of Jesus' (Matthew 28:19-20), just as circumcision was a command under the Old Testament (Genesis 17:9-14). However, the same logic that Paul used here to disprove circumcision as a prerequisite to justification can be used to prove that water baptism is not required before a person can be saved (example - Cornelius; see note 9 at Mark 16:16, note 4 at John 3:5, and note 1 at Acts 10:44). Any condition that must be met for salvation, except faith in what Jesus did for us, is error (Romans 3:28). This is what Paul called "another gospel" or, more accurately, a perversion of the Gospel (Galatians 1:6-7).

Romans 4:11

And he received the sign of circumcision, a seal of the righteousness of the faith which he had yet being uncircumcised: that he might be the father of all them that believe, though they be not circumcised; that righteousness might be imputed unto them also:

Note 4

The rite of circumcision was a confirmation of the righteousness that Abraham had already attained by faith. It was meant to be a constant reminder to him of the covenant between God and himself. It was never intended to be something that Abraham would boast about or use to show others his holiness. This was private! No doubt one of the reasons the Lord chose this act as a sign of the covenant instead of some other act was to prevent the very thing that the Jews were doing. How was one to tell if someone else was circumcised? That's not the kind of thing that is public knowledge. It's between God and that individual. God gave the sign of circumcision because it is a very private act; therefore, He never intended circumcision to be used to judge the righteousness of anyone.

Romans 4:12

And the father of circumcision to them who are not of the circumcision only, but who also walk in the steps of that faith of our father Abraham, which he had being yet uncircumcised.

Note 5

Note that Abraham had faith before he had the action of circumcision. Many people have mistakenly thought that actions produce faith, but that's not so (see note 21 at Matthew 23:26 and note 2 at Luke 11:42). Faith produces actions (see note 55 at Matthew 7:21 and note 26 at Matthew 25:40). Acting right doesn't make people right; they have to be born again (see note 2 at John 3:3).

Romans 4:13

For the promise, that he should be the heir of the world, was not to Abraham, or to his seed, through the law, but through the righteousness of faith.

Note 1

There is no Old Testament scripture that states in these words that Abraham would be heir of the world. The closest scriptures would be when the Lord told Abram that all the families of the earth would be blessed through him (Genesis 12:3) and that he had made Abraham the father of many nations (Genesis 17:4-5). The Jews had interpreted God's promises to Abraham as being to his physical descendants only. However, the Apostle Paul's wording of the Old Testament promises to Abraham removed any doubt about the Jews being the only ones to be blessed through God's covenant with Abraham. Abraham's true seed is anyone of any nation or language who places faith in Christ as his or her Savior.

Romans 4:14

For if they which are of the law be heirs, faith is made void, and the promise made of none effect:

Note 2

We are either justified by faith in our works without faith in Christ or we are justified by faith in Christ without faith in our works, but not a combination of the two (Romans 11:6). Trusting in our own goodness as the reason that God would grant us salvation neutralizes faith and renders God's promise to Abraham useless. There are Christians who have put their faith in Christ for their eternal salvation, but then they fall back into the deception that God is going to bless them and use them based on their performance. This is what happened to the Galatians. Paul told them that Christ had become of no benefit to them if they were trusting in what they did in order to be justified with God (Galatians 5:4). Likewise today, many Christians do not experience the full effect of their salvation because they are making faith void by trusting in their own goodness.

Romans 4:15

Because the law worketh wrath: for where no law is, there is no transgression.

LIVING COMMENTARY

Christians are no longer under the Old Testament Law (see my notes at Romans 3:19, 4:16, 6:14, 7:4-6, Romans 8:2; 2 Corinthians 3:7; Galatians 2:19, 3:24-25, 4:21, 5:18; Ephesians 2:14-15; Colossians 2:14; 1 Timothy 1:9; Hebrews 7:18, 8:13, and 10:8-9). Therefore, there is no longer any transgression for those who have accepted Jesus because, as 1 John 3:4 says, "sin is the transgression of the law." Does this mean a Christian can't sin? Absolutely not! There are hundreds of New Testament scriptures that mention believers sinning and admonitions against sinning. First John 1:8 and 10 say that if anyone says they have no sin, they deceive themselves and the truth isn't in them. All of us have been exposed to and lived under the Law. So, even though the Law has now been satisfied through the offering of Jesus and therefore removed, we still know right from wrong because of that Law. James 4:17 says, "Therefore to him that knoweth to do good, and doeth it not, to him it is sin." So, violating the conscience is sin. Whatsoever is not of faith is sin (Romans 14:23). But these sins are not being imputed unto us by God anymore (see my notes at Romans 5:13 and 2 Corinthians 5:19). Our sins are no longer a transgression against God, because the Law has been removed. But sin is not only a transgression against God; it is also an open door to the devil (see my note at Romans 6:16). So, even though God is not imputing our sins unto us, Satan is. Any Christian who just throws the door open to sin is throwing the door open to the devil and will suffer consequences for those sins (Galatians 6:7). Add to this the fact that grace liberates us from sin, not to sin (see my note at Titus 2:12), and you will see that any person who is boldly living in sin and using the grace of God as an excuse is not truly born again (see my note at 1 John 3:3). Grace breaks the dominion of sin; it doesn't encourage or empower sin (see my note at Romans 6:14).

Note 3

The Law of God released the wrath of God (see note 4 at John 3:36). Without the Law, there was no wrath because without the Law, there was no transgression. First John 3:4 says, "Whosoever committeth sin transgresseth also the law: for sin is the transgression of the law." Therefore, before the Law of God was given, people's sins were not being held against them (see note 2 at Romans 5:13). This was why Abraham was not killed for marrying his half sister (see note 5 at Romans 4:3) and Jacob for marrying his wife's sister (Leviticus 18:18). God had not given the Law concerning these things yet, and therefore there was no willful transgression on the part of these men. So when the Law of God was introduced, sin revived and we died (see notes 3 and 4 at Romans 7:9). The Law produced death by releasing God's wrath against our sins (see note 4 at Romans 3:19). Those who seek to keep the Law of God for the purpose of being justified in God's sight will also release the wrath of God in their lives. Praise God for Jesus who brought us out from under the Law and put us under grace (Romans 6:14).

Romans 4:16

Therefore it is of faith, that it might be by grace; to the end the promise might be sure to all the seed; not to that only which is of the law, but to that also which is of the faith of Abraham; who is the father of us all,

Note 4

Paul made it very clear here that the seed of Abraham included more than his physical descendants. Jesus taught on this (see note 10 at John 8:33, note 14 at John 8:37, and note 16 at John 8:41), and Paul mentioned this a number of times (Romans 2:28-29, 4:11-12, 16, 9; and Galatians 3).

Note 5

Since God made salvation available on the basis of faith in what He did, then everyone can be saved. If He had made our holiness the basis of salvation, then no one could have been saved, "for all have sinned, and come short of the glory of God" (Romans 3:23, see note 6 at that verse).

Romans 4:17

(As it is written, I have made thee a father of many nations,) before him whom he believed, even God, who quickeneth the dead, and calleth those things which be not as though they were.

Note 6

The phrase, "and calleth those things which be not as though they were," is referring to the instance Paul had just cited when God changed Abram's name to Abraham (Genesis 17:5). According to Strong's Concordance, the name Abram means "high father," and the name Abraham means "father of a multitude." The Lord changed Abram's name to Abraham one year before the birth of Isaac, thus confessing that Abraham was the father of a multitude before it happened in the physical. This illustrates God's faith. God says things are so before there is physical proof that they are so. The same thing was done at creation (Genesis 1). God spoke everything into existence, and then it was so. He spoke light into existence and then four days later created a source for that light to come from (Genesis 1:3 and 14-19). God has given us the power to create with faith-filled words (Proverbs 18:20-21, see note 4 at Mark 11:14 and note 4 at Mark 11:23). If we are going to operate in God's kind of faith, we have to learn to call those things that are not as though they were.

Romans 4:18

Who against hope believed in hope, that he might become the father of many nations; according to that which was spoken, So shall thy seed be.

Note 7

There was no hope in the natural for Abraham or his wife, Sarah. They were both as good as dead when it came to having children at their age. Therefore, they rejected the natural and believed God with a supernatural hope. There is a natural hope that everyone has, and there is a supernatural hope that is imparted by God (1 Corinthians 13:13). To receive miracles, we have to reject the limitations of natural hope and press on to obtain God's supernatural hope through faith.

Note 8

Abraham's faith was based on God's Word. Every word of God is powerful and contains the faith of God to bring that word to pass (see note 4 at Matthew 14:29). If we will only consider God's Word, then we will only believe (Romans 8:6, see note 9 at Romans 4:19).

Romans 4:19

And being not weak in faith, he considered not his own body now dead, when he was about an hundred years old, neither yet the deadness of Sara's womb:

Note 9

This verse is telling us how Abraham kept from being weak in faith. The key is what he focused his attention on. Some translations and many commentators turn this verse around to say the opposite of what the King James Version says. For instance, the New International Version says, "Without weakening in his faith, he faced the fact that his body was as good as dead." However, that type of reasoning is missing one of the great scriptural keys to strong faith. The word "consider" is defined as "1. To think carefully about. 2. To regard as. 3. To take into account"

(American Heritage Dictionary). The Greek word that was used here for "considered" is "KATANOEO," and it simply means "to observe fully" (Strong's Concordance). Therefore, we can see that Abraham did not think carefully about his age and Sarah's and the impact that would have on the promise God had given him. He did not take those things into account or make any allowance for them. That was not what he paid attention to. That is amazing, and that is exactly the reason many of us would not be able to receive the same miracle. We consider every negative thing that looks contrary to God's promises, and then we try to use our faith to overcome the fear and unbelief that come through those thoughts (see note 3 at Matthew 17:20). That's not the way Abraham was strong in faith. Abram was seventy-five years old when the Lord first promised him that he would have a child and that all the nations of the earth would be blessed through him (Genesis 12:1-4). He was ninety-nine years old in this instance that Paul cited (Genesis 17:1), and Sarah was ninety years old (Genesis 17:17). Yet he didn't even take into account the impossibility of what God had promised him. It is true that Abraham was strong in faith (Romans 4:20), but the thing that made him strong in faith was the fact that he kept his mind stayed on God's promise. Equally important was that he kept his mind off anything that would have been contrary to God's promise. Many people desire the same strong faith that Abraham had, but very few desire to control their thinking the way Abraham did. Faith is a direct result of what you think on. If you think on God's Word, faith comes (Romans 8:6 and 10:17). If you think on other things, unbelief and fear come (Romans 8:6, see note 39 at Matthew 6:22 and notes 40 and 41 at Matthew 6:23). If you want the faith of Abraham working in you, then think the way he thought and never consider anything except God's Word, and you will be strong in faith.

Romans 4:20

He staggered not at the promise of God through unbelief; but was strong in faith, giving glory to God;

LIVING COMMENTARY

Our English word "staggered" in this verse was translated from the Greek word "DIAKRINO," which means "to separate thoroughly i.e. (literal and reflexive) to withdraw from, or (by implication) oppose; figurative to discriminate (by implication decide), or (reflexive) hesitate" (Strong's Concordance). So, Abraham didn't think about what was contrary to what the Lord had told him (Romans 4:19). He didn't hesitate. A large part of giving glory to God is humility, or not depending upon self-effort (see my note at John 7:18). About a decade-and-a-half prior to this, both Abram and Sarai had been proud and gave glory to themselves, thinking they could help God bring the promise to pass through Hagar (Genesis 16:1-4). This produced Ishmael, which only caused problems. Giving glory to God includes trusting God and not ourselves.

Note 10

From the context of this statement, we can see that the unbelief that Abraham refused to consider was the unbelief that would have come through thinking on the natural facts (see note 9 at Romans 4:19). Many of us don't perceive facts as generating unbelief. We have been led to believe that we have to consider all the facts to make a proper decision, but that's not so with God's Word. When we have clear direction from

God's Word, we shouldn't consider anything else. Considering "facts" contrary to God's promises will make us stagger in our faith.

Note 11

Jesus had equated praise with strength (see note 3 at Matthew 21:16). Here we see that this was one thing that made Abraham strong in faith. Praise keeps your mind stayed on God and what He is doing. You cannot praise God and keep your mind on the problem. You will fall into complaining every time. This is why praise makes you strong in faith (see note 9 at Romans 4:19).

Note 12

A person who believes the promises of God brings glory to God. Conversely, a person who disbelieves the promises of God dishonors God.

Romans 4:21

And being fully persuaded that, what he had promised, he was able also to perform.

Note 13

Notice that Abraham wasn't just persuaded; he was fully persuaded. Many people have been persuaded that the promises of God are true, but they stop short of meditating on God's Word until they become fully persuaded. Strong faith belongs to those who continue in God's Word until all doubt is removed.

Note 14

This is so obvious that it should go without saying, but the truth is, we really do doubt that God can perform His promises to us. How could this be? The answer lies in the way God made our hearts. Whatever we focus our attention on is what our hearts will believe, and whatever we neglect is what our hearts will disbelieve (see note 10 at Mark 6:52). If we allow ourselves to meditate on our problems and all the reasons it looks impossible for God to move in our situations, then we will believe that our problems are bigger than God. However, when we keep our minds stayed on the promises of God, nothing is too difficult for Him (Jeremiah 32:17 and 27).

Romans 4:22

And therefore it was imputed to him for righteousness.

LIVING COMMENTARY

The word "impute" is an accounting term. It is speaking of recording our debts or crediting to our accounts. This is made very clear in 2 Timothy 4:16. One of the best examples of this is the way we use a credit card. When we purchase something with a credit card, we don't actually pay for the item at that time. But we give the clerk a credit card that has our information on it so he can bill us later. Then when the bill comes, we pay the charges. If the clerk didn't record the information, the sale would not be imputed to us. If he did, the sale is imputed unto us. God reconciled the world unto Himself by not imputing our sins unto us (2 Corinthians 5:19). Actually

He imputed our sins unto Jesus. That's like instead of having to show our credit cards and have our sins placed on our accounts, God gave His credit card so all the sins of the whole world would be placed on Jesus' account. If I gave my card to pay for your transaction, it would be unjust for the vendor to charge you and me both. In fact, your transaction shouldn't even show on your account if I gave my credit card for that purchase. Likewise, since God paid for our sins by imputing them to Jesus, we don't have any charges shown on our accounts. It's just as if we'd never sinned. That's justified.

Romans 4:23

Now it was not written for his sake alone, that it was imputed to him;

Note 15

Here in Romans 4:23-24, Paul applied to us all these truths he had discussed about Abraham. God is no respecter of persons (Romans 2:11). If He justified Abraham by faith, He will do the same for us.

Romans 4:24

But for us also, to whom it shall be imputed, if we believe on him that raised up Jesus our Lord from the dead;

Living Commentary

Jesus paid the price we needed to pay for salvation. We don't earn salvation. It's a gift from God (Romans 6:23) that we receive by faith (Ephesians 2:8 and Romans 5:2). Romans 10:9-13 reveals what we have to do to receive God's gift of salvation.

Romans 4:25

Who was delivered for our offences, and was raised again for our justification.

Living Commentary

Our sins were imputed to Jesus, and His righteousness was imputed to us. What a trade! Those who think they still have to pay for their sins dishonor Jesus, and those who don't believe they were made righteous dishonor Jesus. See my notes at 2 Corinthians 5:19-21.

ROMANS

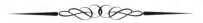

CHAPTER FIVE

Romans 5:1

Therefore being justified by faith, we have peace with God through our Lord Jesus Christ:

Note 1

The word "therefore" means "for that reason; consequently" (American Heritage Dictionary). Paul had just proven through the life of Abraham that justification came by faith. He then made the statement that these truths about Abraham were not written in Scripture for his sake alone but so that we could also be justified by faith (Romans 4:23-24). So, having established justification by faith, here he moved on to some of the benefits of being justified by faith instead of works.

Note 2

The first benefit of being justified by faith, instead of works, that Paul mentioned is peace. Peace can only come when we relate to God on the basis of faith in what He did for us instead of what we do for Him. Those of us who are thinking that we must perform up to some standard to be accepted by God will have no peace. That puts the burden of salvation on our shoulders, and we can't bear that load. We were incapable of living holy enough to please God before we were saved, and we are incapable of living holy enough to please God now that we are saved (Hebrews 11:6). We were saved by faith, and we have to continue to walk with God by faith (Colossians 2:6). Not understanding this has caused many Christians who love God not to enjoy the peace that was provided for them through faith in Jesus. This is the Gospel of peace (Luke 2:14, Romans 10:15, and Ephesians 6:15).

Romans 5:2

By whom also we have access by faith into this grace wherein we stand, and rejoice in hope of the glory of God.

Note 3

The Greek word that was translated "access" here is "PROSAGOGE," and it literally means "admission" (Strong's Concordance). It was only used three times in the New Testament, and it was translated "access" each time (this verse; Ephesians 2:18, and 3:12). Faith is our admission, or ticket, into the grace of God. No one is allowed in without a ticket. Our own good works won't grant us admission. God's grace can only be accessed by faith.

Note 4

The Greek word that was translated "rejoice" here is the same word that was translated "glory" in Romans 5:3 and "joy" in Romans 5:11. That Greek word is "KAUCHAOMAI," and it means "to vaunt (in a good or a bad sense)" (Strong's Concordance). It is derived from an obsolete root word, "AUCHEO," meaning "to boast" (Strong's Concordance). Paul was rejoicing because of the grace that had been given him and the hope of being glorified with Jesus. Anybody could rejoice because of those good things, but Paul went on to say that he had the same rejoicing even in the midst of tribulation. Not many people rejoice during the hard times.

But Paul could make this boast because he was totally convinced of the faithfulness and unconditional grace of God. Those who can't rejoice during tribulation are not convinced.

Note 5

Rejoicing and hope are very closely related. We cannot rejoice in trying times if we have no hope. Therefore, hope is very important in the Christian life (see note 12 at Romans 5:4).

Note 6

The hope that Paul was rejoicing in here was probably what he called the "blessed hope" in Titus 2:13. In that instance, Paul was clearly referring to the Second Coming of Jesus. Therefore, what Paul was probably speaking of here was the return of Jesus and becoming like Him (1 John 3:1-2).

Romans 5:3

And not only so, but we glory in tribulations also: knowing that tribulation worketh patience;

Note 7

Paul had just expressed the joy that he had concerning the Second Coming of Jesus and the glory that would be revealed in us (Romans 8:18, see note 6 at Romans 5:2). Anybody can rejoice about heaven, but here Paul began to say that he had that same rejoicing in the midst of tribulation. This is something that very few people can say, and Paul was presenting this as a direct result of justification by faith. When we believe that God loves us because of our faith in Him, and not because of our performance for Him, then we rejoice—not only in the good times and pleasant things, like thoughts of heaven, but also in the hard times. Our faith remains steadfast. However, those who trust in their own efforts will be devastated in times of trouble because they will know they are getting what they deserve, and they will feel that they have to clean up their act before they can expect any help. Their attention will be on self instead of Jesus, the Author and Finisher of their faith (Hebrews 12:2). Paul continued this same thought on through Romans 5:10. In Romans 5:6-8, he illustrated how great the love of God was for us in that He died for us when we were ungodly. Then he drew a conclusion by way of comparison: if God loved us when we were His enemies, then how much more does He love us now that we are His children? That's the reason Paul could rejoice even in tribulation. If God could work in his life to bring him to justification while he was a sinner, then how much more, now that he was reconciled to God, will God work whatever comes against him for his good!

Note 8

People have taken these scriptures to say that God is the one who brings tribulations to accomplish these positive results in our lives. That is not what these scriptures say. Tribulations exist, not because God creates them, but because there is a battle between the kingdom of God and the kingdom of the devil. And when we operate in faith, God can grant us such victory that we are actually better off because of the battle (see note 9 at this verse). It's just like when an army goes to war. If they win, there are spoils to be gained. But if those soldiers embraced their enemy because of the spoil they were expecting to receive, they would be killed instead of blessed. First, they have to fight and win the war.

Then, and only then, will the spoils be available. The enemy doesn't come to be a blessing, but a blessing can be obtained from the enemy if their opponents are victorious. Likewise, tribulations and adversities are not blessings from God (see note 2 at John 9:2); they are attacks from the enemy intended to steal away the Word of God from our lives (see note 5 at Mark 4:16).

No one should say that the temptation came from God, for God is not the one who tempts anyone (James 1:13). However, there are spoils to be gained when we fight and win over our problems. If problems were what perfected us, then most Christians would have been perfected long ago and those who experience the greatest problems would be the greatest Christians, but that's not the way it is. God's Word is given to make us perfect and thoroughly furnished unto every good work (2 Timothy 3:17). God's Word does not need to be supplemented with problems to accomplish its work. This is a pivotal point. Those who believe God has ordained the problems in their lives to work some redemptive virtue will submit to those problems and therefore to Satan, the author of those problems (see note 3 at Luke 13:16). They have to or else, in their way of thinking, they would be rebelling against God. Yet James 4:7 tells us to submit ourselves to God and resist the devil. If Satan can reverse our thinking on this issue and get us to submit to the problems he brings into our lives, he's got us (Romans 6:16). Paul was simply rejoicing that even in tribulation, he had the opportunity to use, and therefore strengthen, his patience that had already been given him as a fruit of the Spirit (Galatians 5:22-23) and through the Word of God (Romans 15:4). And as he believed that, as he stood in patience, he would gain experience that would cause him to hope even more the next time the devil attacked. Likewise, we can rejoice in tribulation, knowing that regardless of what the devil does, we will win and reap the spoils of victory.

Note 9

The word "worketh" was translated from the Greek word "KATERGA-ZOMAI," and that Greek word means "to work fully, i.e. accomplish; by implication, to finish, fashion" (Strong's Concordance). Paul was not saying that tribulations produced patience. Patience comes from the Scriptures (Romans 15:4). But tribulations cause us to use what God has already given us through His Word, and we therefore become stronger as a result (see note 8 at this verse).

Note 10

According to the American Heritage Dictionary, "patience" means "the capacity, quality, or fact of being patient." One definition of "patient" is "persevering; constant" (AHD). The Greek word used for "patience" here is "HUPOMONE," and it means "cheerful (or hopeful) endurance, constancy" (Strong's Concordance). Patience is not a passive word, as many people use it, but it is an active word. Patience is actually faith—faith that is sustained over a long period of time. Patience comes from the Scriptures (Romans 15:4), just as faith does (Romans 10:17). Patience is a fruit of the Spirit, just like faith (Galatians 5:22-23). It was by faith that Moses endured (the definition of patience, Hebrews 11:27). It was through faith and patience that Abraham received the promises (Hebrews 6:12-15), and not just faith, but a faith that was constant over a twenty-five-year period of time. Therefore, patience is not just passively waiting on God to do something, but it is actively believing for the manifestation of God's promise against all odds, regardless of how long it takes.

That kind of faith will make you perfect and complete, not wanting for any good thing (James 1:4). Patience is a byproduct of hope. Romans 8:25 says, "But if we hope for that we see not, then do we with patience wait for it." When people have hope firmly established in them, then no obstacle or length of time can keep them from enduring. That's why the Scriptures produce patience, because they give people hope (Romans 15:4).

Therefore, patience, hope, and faith are all intertwined. People can't have one without the others. Those who say they are patiently waiting on God yet have lost their hope are deceived. Likewise, those who don't believe God are not operating in patience. First comes hope from a promise of God's Word. Then faith begins to give substance and evidence to those things that were hoped for (Hebrews 11:1). And if time is involved before the manifestation comes, then patience does its work (James 1:4).

Romans 5:4

And patience, experience; and experience, hope:

LIVING COMMENTARY

See my note at Romans 8:24.

Note 11

The Greek word used for "experience" here is "DOKIME," and it means "approved character; the quality of being approved as a result of test and trials" ("Linguistic Key to the Greek New Testament" by Fritz Rienecker). Sanday and Headlam also defined this word in this verse as "the temper of the veteran as opposed to that of the raw recruit." Therefore, this verse is speaking of the character that is produced as a result of having fought battles and won.

Note 12

Hope by itself will never give people victory. Many people have hoped for things and yet have never realized those hopes because they never moved into faith. Faith is the victory that causes people to overcome the world (1 John 5:4), yet faith won't work without hope. Just as a thermostat activates the power unit on an air conditioner, so hope is what activates our faith. Faith only produces what we hope for (Hebrews 11:1).

Therefore, hope is the first step toward faith. The word "hope" means "a desire accompanied by confident expectation" (American Heritage Dictionary), so desiring the things of God with some expectation of obtaining them is the first step in walking in faith. Once this hope is present, then faith begins to bring the desired thing into manifestation. If a delay is encountered, patience completes the work (see note 10 at Romans 5:3). In context, Paul was saying that our experience "worketh" (see note 9 at Romans 5:3) hope. However, he also said in this same epistle (Romans 15:4) that hope comes through the Scriptures. Therefore, it is to be understood that the character that is developed through tribulations just adds to the hope that we have already received through God's Word.

Romans 5:5

And hope maketh not ashamed; because the love of God is shed abroad in our hearts by the Holy Ghost which is given unto us.

LIVING COMMENTARY

Galatians 5:6 says faith works by love, but this verse reveals that hope works by love also. God's great love for us is the motivation for faith and hope. It causes us to be filled with all the fullness of God (Ephesians 3:19).

Romans 5:6

For when we were yet without strength, in due time Christ died for the ungodly.

Note 13

Notice the terms that Paul used to describe us before the transformation of the new birth. We were weak (this verse), ungodly (this verse), sinners (Romans 5:8), and enemies (Romans 5:10). The Lord didn't save us because we deserved it; it was an act of grace. As great as this truth is, Paul didn't stop here. He continued on to make a comparison that if God loved us enough to die for us when we were weak, ungodly, sinners, and enemies, then much more now that we are justified (Romans 5:9) and reconciled (Romans 5:10), He is willing to save us in spite of our actions.

Romans 5:7

For scarcely for a righteous man will one die: yet peradventure for a good man some would even dare to die.

Note 14

Paul was attempting to explain the great love of God shown to us through grace. To illustrate it, he drew on the greatest expression of love known to man: laying down your life for another (John 15:13). However, Paul took it a step further. It is possible to imagine people giving up their lives for others. That has happened many times. But it is inconceivable that they would sacrifice their lives for their enemies. Yet that was exactly what God did (Romans 5:10). Since this is so, how could we ever doubt God's goodness to us now? On our worst days as Christians, we love God infinitely more than our best days as unbelievers.

Romans 5:8

But God commendeth his love toward us, in that, while we were yet sinners, Christ died for us.

LIVING COMMENTARY

The Message puts Romans 5:7-8 into modern language: "We can understand someone dying for a person worth dying for, and we can understand how someone good and noble could inspire us to selfless sacrifice. But God put his love on the line for us by offering his Son in sacrificial death while we were of no use whatever to him." What great love God has for us.

Note 15

This verse is commonly quoted to illustrate the unconditional love that God has toward sinners. While that is certainly true and this verse does clearly teach that, this is not the point that Paul was making. In context, Paul was talking to Christians about the grace of God. He was making a comparison, and Romans 5:9-10 are the point of his comparison. He was using this truth here about God commending His love toward us while we were still sinners as a step to another truth. Not viewing this verse in context has caused many people to accept salvation by grace but then come back under the deception that they have to live good enough for God to use them as Christians. While realizing one truth, they completely missed the whole point of what Paul was saying. These verses, taken in context, conclusively prove that we begin and continue our walk with God through faith in His grace (Colossians 2:6).

Romans 5:9

Much more then, being now justified by his blood, we shall be saved from wrath through him.

Note 16

The phrase "much more" that is used in Romans 5:9-10 is amazing. It would have been wonderful to think that after salvation, God continued to love us with the same love that was manifested toward us through the death of His Son. But Paul was saying that once we are justified by grace through faith, God loves us much more. Being loved the same would be great, more would have been awesome, but much more is beyond our ability to comprehend. Many Christians accept the love of God for the sinners. They extend love toward the drunks or adulterers as long as they are lost, but if the drunks or adulterers receive the forgiveness of God and ever commit one of those sins again, they show no mercy. They actually believe that God loves us much less now that we are saved. We got by with things before we were saved, but now we have to be holy or else. These verses clearly teach that is not the truth. God loves us much more now than He did before our salvation. And before our salvation, He loved us so much that He died for us. He loves us even more now. Does this mean that living a holy life is not necessary? It means that our own holiness is not a requirement. We are acceptable to God by grace through faith. But those of us who are truly born again have had a change of heart. We want to live holy (1 John 3:3). However, we all fail to be as holy as we want to be. When we fail, this knowledge that God loves us more now than when He sent His Son to die for us will keep us from being condemned and draw us back to serving God.

Romans 5:10

For if, when we were enemies, we were reconciled to God by the death of his Son, much more, being reconciled, we shall be saved by his life.

LIVING COMMENTARY

Romans 5:8 is often taken out of context and used to stress that God loves sinners. But Romans 5:9 is the point Paul was getting to. If God loved us as sinners so much that He was willing to die for us, then much more does He love us as saints. These two thoughts are combined in this verse. Jesus' death paid our debt and reconciled us to God. His resurrection gave us His supernatural power to reign in life (Galatians 1:4).

Romans 5:11

And not only so, but we also joy in God through our Lord Jesus Christ, by whom we have now received the atonement.

LIVING COMMENTARY

The Greek word that was translated "atonement" at the end of this verse is "KATALLAGE," and it means "exchange (figuratively, adjustment), i.e. restoration to (the divine) favor" (Strong's Concordance). Christianity is the great exchange. We exchanged our sin for His righteousness (Romans 5:19 and 2 Corinthians 5:21). We exchanged our sickness for His health (1 Peter 2:24). We exchanged our sorrow for His joy (Isaiah 61:3). It's already done. We have received it already. Thank You, Jesus.

Romans 5:12

Wherefore, as by one man sin entered into the world, and death by sin; and so death passed upon all men, for that all have sinned:

LIVING COMMENTARY

The fact that people inherited their sin nature is a totally new concept to many Christians. Most people believe it's what they do that makes them sinners. But this verse clearly teaches that sin entered the earth through one man, Adam (also Romans 5:15-18), and death is a result of that sin (Romans 5:15). It is not our individual actions of sin that separate us from God. It's that sin nature (see my note at Romans 5:21). Our sins don't make us sinners. We were born sinners, and we sin because that is our nature. As Paul said in Ephesians 2:3, "And were by nature the children of wrath." This is why we "must be born again" (John 3:7). We received our sinful nature through our natural birth, and we only receive a new nature through a spiritual birth (see my note at 2 Corinthians 5:17). People have tried to train dogs to abide by human standards. They housetrain them and teach them to beg and pray and do all kinds of human things. But the dogs' nature is still that of a dog. That's why they will lick themselves and relieve themselves on the carpet and do many things that their owners don't want them to do. That's their nature. If left to themselves, they act like dogs, because they are dogs. You can get shampooed, learn to do tricks, and look good on the outside, but if you have not been born again, you are just a housebroken sinner. Your nature hasn't changed. You will still go to hell, because that's where sinners go. But the person who accepts what Jesus did for them and puts their faith in Him gets a new nature and goes to heaven after death. That's where the ones with the new, righteous nature go. It all depends on which nature you have.

Note 1

Paul had already made a strong case for salvation by grace through faith. He used a comparison that illustrated just how great God's grace is (see note 14 at Romans 5:7). Here he used another comparison to make this same point. He began making this point in this verse but inserted a parenthetical phrase in Romans 5:13-17. Therefore, to get the complete thought Paul was expressing, it helps to skip from Romans

5:12-18. He was saying that in the same way that we inherited the sin nature independently of our actions, we also inherit God's righteous nature, not based on our actions, but through the new birth. The reasoning is that if we became sinners through what one man did, then we can also become righteous through one man, the Lord Jesus Christ.

Romans 5:13

(For until the law sin was in the world: but sin is not imputed when there is no law.

LIVING COMMENTARY

A good illustration of imputation is the way credit cards are used. When you buy something with a credit card, you haven't paid for it. You just gave the vendor your credit information, and they bill your credit card company (impute it unto you). Then the credit card company bills you, and you pay them. So, until you've paid the credit card bill, you've only had the charge imputed unto you; it's put on your account. You are now responsible to pay for what you got. Likewise, the Law imputed sin unto us. We became guilty and had a debt that had to be paid (Romans 6:23). But as this verse says, prior to the Law, sin wasn't imputed unto us. It wasn't held against us, not because we hadn't sinned but because God didn't impute it unto us. As the next verse (Romans 5:14) goes on to explain, this didn't mean we got by scot-free. No! Sin had a twofold effect.

God wasn't imputing our sins to us, but Satan was (see my note at Romans 6:16). Sin was destroying the human race even when God was merciful to us in spite of our sin. See my note at Romans 5:14. Compare this verse to Romans 7:9. Sin isn't imputed until there is Law. So, until a child knows they are breaking God's Law, the sin nature they are born with isn't imputed unto them. If a child dies before they reach this place where they are knowingly breaking God's Law (age of accountability), they would go to heaven even though they were born with a sin nature. It would not be imputed unto them (see my note at Romans 7:9).

Note 2

Romans 5:13-17 is a parenthetical phrase. In Romans 5:12, Paul began likening imputed righteousness to imputed sin. He interrupted that thought to briefly explain how God dealt with man's sin nature from the time of Adam until the time of the Law of Moses. Therefore, the point that Paul was making can be received by skipping directly from Romans 5:12-18. However, some very important information is revealed in this parenthetical phrase. Paul said that until the time the Law was given, sin was not imputed unto people. As explained in note 6 at Romans 4:3, the most-used Greek word for "impute" is "LOGIZOMAI," an accounting term meaning that God was not entering people's sins in the account book. In this instance, a different Greek word was used ("ELLOGEO" - used only one other time in New Testament, Philemon 18), but it has virtually the same meaning. This is a radical statement. Most people have interpreted God's dealings with man after Adam's sin to be immediate rejection and banishment from His presence. In other words, it was an immediate imputing of man's sins. However, Paul was stating just the opposite. God was not holding people's sins against them until the time that the Law of Moses was given. With this in mind, it should change the way we think about God's dealings with man between the Fall and the giving of the Law. Adam and Eve were not driven from the Garden of Eden because God could not stand them in His presence anymore. God's dealings with Adam and Eve and their children in Genesis 4 prove His presence was still with them. The reason He drove them from Eden is clearly stated in Genesis 3:22-23; it was to keep them from eating of the Tree of Life and living forever. Instead of this being a punitive act, it was actually an act of mercy. It would have been terrible for people to live forever in sinful bodies, subject to all the emotions and diseases that sin brings. God had a better plan through Jesus. In accordance with what Paul was revealing here, God was merciful to the first murderer (Genesis 4:9-15), even to the point of placing a mark on his forehead and promising vengeance if anyone tried to kill him. In contrast, once the Law was given, the first man to break the ordinance of the Sabbath was stoned to death for picking up sticks (Numbers 15:32-36). That doesn't seem equitable. But the answer is that before the Law, God was not imputing people's sins unto them as He was after the giving of the Law (see note 3 at Romans 5:14). It would appear that the Flood and the destruction of Sodom and Gomorrah were two notable exceptions to this. Actually, these were not exceptions. While these two acts of judgment were punitive on the individuals who received the judgment, they were actually acts of mercy on the human race as a whole. In the same way that a limb or organ will sometimes be sacrificed to save a life, so God had to destroy these sinners to continue His mercy on the human race. The people in Noah's day and the inhabitants of Sodom and Gomorrah were so vile that they were like a cancer that had to be killed. So, for the first 2,000 years after man's Fall (approximate time between the Fall and the giving of the Law), God was not holding people's sins against them. That was why Abram was not killed for marrying his half sister nor Jacob for marrying his wife's sister (see note

3 at Romans 4:15). Therefore, we can see that God's immediate reaction to man's sin was mercy and not judgment. It was over 2,000 years before God began to impute people's sins unto them, and according to Galatians 3:19 and Galatians 3:23-24, that was only a temporary way of dealing with sin until Jesus could come. Through Jesus, God is once again reconciling the world unto Himself, not imputing people's sins unto them (2 Corinthians 5:19).

Romans 5:14

Nevertheless death reigned from Adam to Moses, even over them that had not sinned after the similitude of Adam's transgression, who is the figure of him that was to come.

Note 3

If God was not bringing judgment upon people's sins until the time of the Law of Moses (see note 2 at Romans 5:13), then why were people still dying? Isn't death the wages of sin (Romans 6:23)? Why were people still dying if their sins weren't being counted against them? Sin has a twofold effect. It is not only a transgression against God, worthy of His judgment, but it is also the inroad of Satan into our lives. Romans 6:16 says, "Know ye not, that to whom ye yield yourselves servants to obey, his servants ye are to whom ye obey; whether of sin unto death, or of obedience unto righteousness?" If we yield to sin, we also submit ourselves to Satan, the author of that sin. This was why people were still dying even though God was not bringing His judgment on their sins. Satan was the one who had the power of death (Hebrews 2:14), and it was Satan, through sin, who was causing people to die. As sin multiplied on the earth, the life span of man decreased, not because of God's judgment, but because of the effects of sin on the human race. Therefore, we can see that even when God doesn't judge sin, sin is still deadly. This is why the New Testament believer should resist sin. God doesn't bring judgment on His children for their sins (see note 11 at Romans 4:8), but Satan will. Christians don't live holy in order to avoid God's judgment but so that their enemy won't have any access to them.

Note 4

The people from Adam to Moses had not sinned in the same way that Adam had because they didn't have a direct commandment to violate like Adam did. They were living under their own consciences, and that was enough to make them guilty (see note 2 at Romans 1:18). However, it was not until the time that God revealed the commandments through Moses that people once again began to violate direct commands of God (Romans 4:15).

Note 5

The Greek word translated "figure" here is "TUPOS," and it means "a type, figure, pattern" (Vine's Expository Dictionary). Paul was saying that Adam was a type of Jesus in the sense that in the same way sin entered the world through one man, righteousness entered the world through one man, Jesus.

Romans 5:15

But not as the offence, so also is the free gift. For if through the offence of one many be dead, much more the grace of God, and the gift by grace, which is by one man, Jesus Christ, hath abounded unto many.

LIVING COMMENTARY

In Romans 5:14, Paul said Adam was a like figure to Jesus. Here, in this verse, he showed the similarity but in an opposite comparison, or antithesis. See my note at Romans 5:12 about us being sinners through what Adam did, not just what we do.

Note 1

Paul proceeded to make a series of comparisons about imputed righteousness through Christ being like imputed sin (see note 9 at Romans 5:21) through Adam. Paul made this comparison five times so that there should be no doubt that in the same way that all became sinners through Adam (see note 6 at Romans 5:19), all who put faith in Christ are made righteousness through Him. The religious world has basically accepted this truth of inherited sin from Adam, but this truth of inherited righteousness through the new birth is still a mystery to many. Yet Paul was saying that if one is true, then so is the other. These truths are like two sides of one coin. If you accept one truth, you have to accept the other.

Note 2

These are five comparisons (Romans 5:15-19), but they are opposite comparisons. Adam's sin brought things from good to bad, but Jesus brought things from bad to good. The results are opposite extremes, but the principle involved in both is the same. In the same way that Adam was able to pass sin (see note 9 at Romans 5:21) and its consequences on to his descendants, so Jesus is able to pass righteousness and all its benefits on to those who put faith in Him.

Note 3

The gift by grace spoken of here and in Romans 5:16 and 18 is clearly stated in Romans 5:17. It is the gift of righteousness.

Romans 5:16

And not as it was by one that sinned, so is the gift: for the judgment was by one to condemnation, but the free gift is of many offences unto justification.

LIVING COMMENTARY

In the same way that Adam's one sin brought judgment and condemnation on all mankind, so Jesus' free gift justified from all sin those who receive it.

Note 4

Adam's one sin produced a sin nature in all people (see note 9 at Romans 5:21) that, in turn, caused each person to commit individual acts of sin (see note 6 at Romans 5:19). However, Jesus not only dealt with the original sin that contaminated the human race, but He also dealt with each individual act of sin.

Romans 5:17

For if by one man's offence death reigned by one; much more they which receive abundance of grace and of the gift of righteousness shall reign in life by one, Jesus Christ.)

LIVING COMMENTARY

The "death" spoken of in this verse is not limited to physical death. It includes that, but the wages of sin is death (see my note at Romans 6:23). Anything that comes as a result of sin is death. Shame is death.

Sickness, poverty, divorce, war, and all things that came as a result of the Fall are death. There are many in the modern-day church who will say their sins are forgiven, but they don't believe they are righteous. Yet this verse and its context are saying this gift wasn't just salvation—forgiveness of sins (Ephesians 1:7)—but right standing, or righteousness, with God as a gift. This is foreign to many Christians, but it is the foundation of grace reigning in our lives (Romans 5:21). Notice that we have to receive the abundance of God's grace AND the gift of righteousness to reign in life. Receiving grace is absolutely essential, but it won't produce us reigning until we couple it with our right standing in Christ and all the privileges that come with that.

Note 5

This comparison is repeated again in Romans 5:21 (see note 9 at that verse).

Romans 5:18

Therefore as by the offence of one judgment came upon all men to condemnation; even so by the righteousness of one the free gift came upon all men unto justification of life.

Living Commentary

In the same way that all people became sinners through Adam, so the free gift of righteousness that produces justification has come unto all people through Jesus (Titus 2:11). Some might reason that everyone received the sin nature through Adam and, therefore, everyone just automatically receives a righteous nature through Christ. That is true for everyone who receives the "new birth" (see my note at John 3:3). That's why the new birth is essential. All of us had to have the natural birth to receive the sinful nature, and only those who are born from above by putting their total faith in what Christ has done for them are recipients of the free gift of righteousness. Some have taken this verse out of its context to say that everyone, whether or not they receive salvation through faith in what Jesus did for them, is or will be saved. But in this very chapter, Paul said we have access by faith into this grace (Romans 5:2). It's true that God's grace that brings salvation has come to all (Titus 2:11), but it has to be received by faith (see my note at Ephesians 2:8).

Romans 5:19

For as by one man's disobedience many were made sinners, so by the obedience of one shall many be made righteous.

Note 6

Some people think it is our individual acts of sin that make us sinners, but that is not what Paul was saying in these verses. These scriptures clearly state that Adam's one sin made all people sinners (see note 17 at John 8:44). It is man's sin nature that produces sins, not their sins that produce a sin nature. Therefore, those who are trying to obtain righteousness through their actions are totally missing the point. Even if they could stop all their individual sins, they could not change the sin nature that they were born with. That's the reason people must be born again (see note 2 at John 3:3).

Note 7

These scriptures should provide the ultimate argument for righteousness by faith to everyone who believes the Scriptures to be inspired by God. Paul repeatedly said that believers are made righteous through faith in Christ, independently of their actions, in the same way that all were made sinners, not through their individual sins, but through Adam's one sin.

Romans 5:20

Moreover the law entered, that the offence might abound. But where sin abounded, grace did much more abound:

LIVING COMMENTARY

The Law was added. It wasn't a part of God's original plan (Galatians 3:19). And the purpose of the Law wasn't to provide us something to keep, thereby earning God's favor. It was given to make our offense even greater—not so God would hate us more, but so we would recognize how terrible our sin was; we would quit trying to be right with God through our own goodness.

Note 8

Paul was writing to Jewish Christians who had mistakenly thought that faith in Christ alone was not enough to produce justification. They thought one also had to fulfill a minimum standard of holiness by complying with certain commands of the Old Testament Law. That's what occasioned Paul's whole teaching on justification by faith. Paul had so conclusively proven justification by faith in Christ alone that he knew the legalistic Jews were wondering, "So, what was the purpose of the Law?" He stated that purpose in this verse. The Law was given to make sin increase, or super-abound ("abound" - "PLEONAZO" - "to do, make or be more, i.e. increase...to superabound" [Strong's Concordance]). As explained in note 4 at Romans 3:19, the purpose of the Law was not to strengthen us in our battle against sin but to strengthen sin in its battle against us. Sin had already beaten us; we didn't know it. The Law brought that realization to us so that we would quit trusting in ourselves and call out to God for salvation. So the Law made sin and all its devastating effects abound, but God's grace abounded even more. The Law gave sin so much dominion against us that the grace of God is the only way out.

Romans 5:21

That as sin hath reigned unto death, even so might grace reign through righteousness unto eternal life by Jesus Christ our Lord.

LIVING COMMENTARY

Sin reigned unto death through or by the Law. Once the Law is removed, sin can't reign. Even so, grace reigns unto eternal life through righteousness. If we don't receive the righteousness of Jesus as a gift (Romans 3:25), then we won't experience the eternal life He came to bring.

Note 9

The sin that is being spoken of here is not the individual acts of sin that we commit but rather the propensity for sin itself. The American Heritage Dictionary defines "propensity" as "an innate inclination; tendency." It is this inherited inclination to sin that Paul was speaking of. The word "sin" is used forty-five times in the book of Romans (Romans 3:9, 20; 4:8; 5:12-13, 20-21; 6:1-2, 6-7, 10-18, 20, 22-23; 7:7-9, 11, 13-14 17, 20, 23, 25; 8:2-3, 10; and 14:23). The plural, "sins," is used four times , Romans 3:25 4:7, 7:5, and 11:27). Of this total of forty-nine times that "sin" or "sins" is used in Romans, these two English words come from three Greek words. One of these Greek words, "HAMARTEMA," is only used once, in Romans 3:25, and only three other times in all the New Testament (Mark 3:28, 4:12; and 1 Corinthians 6:18). Of the remaining forty-eight times, the Greek word "HAMARTIA" was used forty-seven times and "HAMARTANO" just once (Romans 6:15). This is very significant because the Greek word HAMARTIA is a noun, while HAMARTANO is a verb. A noun denotes a person, place, or thing, while a verb describes the action of a noun. Therefore, in all but one instance in the book of Romans, the words "sin" and "sins" describe man's tendency toward sin and not the individual acts of sins themselves. If you think of the word "sin" in these chapters as denoting the act of sin, you will miss what Paul was saying. As believers, our fight is not against individual acts of sin but against the inner tendency to sin. If the propensity to sin can be broken, then the actions of sin will cease. Our individual acts of sin are only an expression or indication of how well we are doing in our war against this condition of the heart that causes us to sin. Romans 5:12 says that this propensity to sin (or what many call the "sin nature") entered the world through Adam. It is this sin nature that caused us to sin, not our individual acts of sin that gave us a sin nature (see note 17 at John 8:44, note 6 at Romans 5:19, and note 3 at Romans 7:9). At salvation, the "old man" (Romans 6:6), or sin nature, died, but the tendency to sin remained through the thoughts and emotions that the "old man" left behind. Christians no longer have a sin nature that compels them to sin; they are simply dealing with the renewing of their minds.

Note 10

Sin (see note 9 at this verse) ruled like a king (the Greek word for "reigned" in Romans 5:17 was also translated "king") through condemnation (Romans 5:16) to bring death upon everyone. Condemnation is like the general of sin that enforced its power. Likewise, now God's grace rules like a king through righteousness to bring all who are in Christ into eternal life. Righteousness is the general of grace who defends us against all the wiles of the devil. Sin would ultimately bring death to all people whether they were condemned or not (Romans 6:23). But to those who are guilt-ridden and condemned over their sins, sin has a particularly devastating effect. Likewise, those who put faith in Christ will ultimately experience God's eternal life. But those who understand righteousness as a gift to be received and not a wage to be earned are the ones who reign like kings, over sin and all its effects, in this life. Remove guilt or condemnation, and sin loses its strength to rule (1 Corinthians

15:56). Remove the knowledge of righteousness by faith, and grace loses its power to release eternal life in our daily lives.

ROMANS

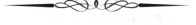

CHAPTER SIX

Romans 6:1

What shall we say then? Shall we continue in sin, that grace may abound?

LIVING COMMENTARY

Of course, Paul is not arguing for us to continue in sin because God loves us by grace instead of performance. But he did bring up this question because it would be a logical question from his teaching. In fact, he answered this question three times in his book (Romans 3:8; here; and 6:15). Therefore, we can say, if we aren't ever asked, "Are you saying we can keep on sinning because God loves us?" then we aren't preaching the same Gospel Paul preached.

Note 1

Paul had stated God's grace (see note 5 at Acts 20:24 and note 5 at Romans 1:5) in such a way that it was inevitable that someone would ask, "Can we just keep on sinning, since we are saved by grace?" Of course, that is not what Paul was saying at all. He had already answered this argument before (Romans 3:8), and he did it again in Romans 6:15, making a total of three times in this epistle he had to overcome misunderstandings about his grace teaching encouraging sin. Paul spoke this revelation of God's grace under the inspiration of the Holy Ghost with perfect balance, yet he was still misunderstood. Therefore, those who are teaching grace but do not encounter the same arguments causing them to explain that they are not advocating a life of sin have not preached grace the way that Paul did. If, in their efforts to prevent misuse, they present grace in such a way that no one ever accuses them of giving people a license to sin, then they haven't presented grace correctly.

Romans 6:2

God forbid. How shall we, that are dead to sin, live any longer therein?

LIVING COMMENTARY

Ephesians 2:1 and Colossians 2:13 say we were dead IN trespasses and sins. But through Christ, we have become dead TO sin, as this verse says. What a swap! How can it be that we are dead to sin when observation proves we are very capable of sin? This is speaking of our spirits. Our born-again spirits are totally new and dead to sin. Our physical bodies and souls are still capable of sin, but in our new spirits, we are identical to Jesus (1 John 4:17 and 1 Corinthians 6:17). Our new spirits (new man) were created in righteousness and true holiness (Ephesians 4:24) and then sealed with the Holy Spirit (Ephesians 1:13). Therefore, a born-again person cannot sin in their spirit (see my note at 1 John 3:9).

Note 2

Paul had so convincingly proven salvation by grace that no theological argument against it was left. Yet the most common complaint against grace is not theological; it concerns the practical application. Most people who can't handle grace think, "If I'm saved by grace, then why resist sin?" Paul answered this question in two ways in this chapter. First, we as Christians don't live lives of sin because we are dead to sin (see note 3 at this verse). This was the point Paul was making in Romans 6:1-14. Second, although God is not imputing our sins unto us, Satan is. Beginning with Romans 6:15, Paul clearly stated that sin is an inroad of the enemy into our lives (see note 3 at Romans 5:14). Therefore, Paul stated that sin is still deadly and something to be resisted, but he changed the motivation for living holy. No longer do we resist sin to try to be accepted by God, but we live holy lives because our nature has been changed and because actions of sin give place to the devil.

Note 3

What does it mean that we are dead to sin? From the context and also from personal experience, we can easily see what it doesn't mean. It clearly doesn't mean that we as Christians are incapable of committing sins. Once again, the Greek word translated "sin" here is "HAMARTIA," a noun describing the propensity for sin, or what many call the sin nature (see note 9 at Romans 5:21). The New International Version translation calls this the old self. Our "old selves" were the driving force behind our acts of sin. Paul was saying that since our old selves that loved to sin are dead, it is not the nature of us Christians to commit acts of sin as it was before we were born again (see note 2 at John 3:3). That's the number-one reason that we don't sin. We don't want to sin. However, by Paul saying that the part of us that compelled us to sin is dead, new questions are raised. If we no longer have a sin nature that compels us to sin, then why do we do it?

Some Christians believe they are still driven to sin and quote Paul's statements in Romans 7 to justify this. Paul went on to answer this question in Romans 6:6 (see note 7 at that verse).

Romans 6:3

Know ye not, that so many of us as were baptized into Jesus Christ were baptized into his death?

Note 4

Our spirits are the part of us that became born again (see note 2 at John 3:3), and this is the part of us that Paul was referring to as being baptized into Jesus and His death (see note 3 at Matthew 26:41). Our physical bodies are not dead, and our souls are not dead. But our "old man" died with Christ (see note 8 at Romans 6:6).

Note 5

The baptism that is being spoken of here in Romans 6:3-4 is not water baptism. Hebrews 6:2 speaks of the doctrine of baptisms (plural), clearly stating that there is more than one kind of baptism. It is easy to see that there is a difference between the baptism of the Holy Spirit and the baptism into the body of Christ. When John the Baptist spoke of the baptism of the Holy Spirit in Matthew 3:11, he said that Jesus is the baptizer and the Holy Spirit is the one that we are being baptized with. But in 1 Corinthians 12:13, Paul said that the Holy Spirit is the baptizer and the body of Christ is what we are being baptized into. So, there are two different baptizers and two different elements that we are being baptized into, leaving no doubt that these are two different baptisms. The mistake of always associating the word "baptism" with water baptism has led many people to incorrectly interpret Romans 6:3-4 as speaking of water baptism. Some have even attempted to use these verses to prove that water baptism is the act that causes salvation. However, that is not what Paul was saying and, in fact, is the exact opposite of every point that he had made in the book of Romans for salvation by grace through faith. This is not speaking of the sign of water baptism (see note 9 at Mark 16:16 and note 2 at Acts 2:38). Paul was speaking of the act where all of us who put saving faith in Jesus as our Lord are automatically and instantaneously baptized into Jesus and all that He purchased for us (1 Corinthians 12:13 and Colossians 2:12). He was simply stating that as believers, we have become dead to sin (Romans 6:6) through the death of Jesus. Jesus didn't die for His sins; He had none. He died for our sins (1 Peter 2:24). Therefore, His death was for us, and all the benefits to be obtained through His death and resurrection are our benefits.

Romans 6:4

Therefore we are buried with him by baptism into death: that like as Christ was raised up from the dead by the glory of the Father, even so we also should walk in newness of life.

Note 6

This verse states our death with Christ (see note 7 at Romans 6:6) as an accomplished fact and our resurrection with Christ as what should be the result of that death. That might lead some to speculate that our death with Christ to sin has already been accomplished, while our resurrection with Him (in context, spiritual resurrection) has yet to be accomplished. Yet comparison with other scripture will reveal that is not so Ephesians 2:5-6 states our spiritual resurrection with Christ as an accomplished fact that happens at salvation.

Colossians 2:12-13 makes the same claim. In Colossians 3:1, Paul used the reasoning that if we are risen with Christ, then we should seek those things that are above. Just as surely as all Christians are to seek heavenly things, likewise, all Christians have been raised with Christ. Our spirits (see note 3 at Matthew 26:41) died to sin and are already resurrected with Christ unto newness of life. These things are already realities in our new spirits. Yet to see these facts become realities in our physical lives, we have to first know what happened to us in our spirits at salvation and then believe this good news. To the degree that we think, believe, and act like who we are in our spirits, to that degree we will experience the life of Christ in our flesh.

Romans 6:5

For if we have been planted together in the likeness of his death, we shall be also in the likeness of his resurrection:

LIVING COMMENTARY

This verse is not a complete sentence, and therefore, it would be incorrect to base a doctrine on a partial sentence. The next verse clearly states that we have to know some things in order for this resurrection life to manifest in our lives. See my note at Romans 6:6.

Romans 6:6

Knowing this, that our old man is crucified with him, that the body of sin might be destroyed, that henceforth we should not serve sin.

Note 7

As explained in note 6 at Romans 6:4, our spirits have already died with Christ unto sin and are already resurrected unto newness of life. Yet this newness of life, which is a reality in our spirits, does not automatically manifest itself in our flesh. This verse makes it very clear that we have to know some things before this resurrection life flows from our spirits into our flesh. Facts, whether spiritual or natural, don't govern your life. It's your knowledge or perception of truths that controls your physical emotions and experiences (Proverbs 23:7). If someone lied to you about a family member having just died, you would experience sorrow or other negative emotions even though there was no factual basis to feel that way. In the same way, if you were told that a family member had died and it was true but you didn't believe the report, you would be spared those emotions. Likewise, we have had the power of sin broken in our lives by our death to sin (see note 8 at this verse), and we have the resurrection power of Christ's life in our spirits. But these facts won't change our experiences until we know them and begin to act accordingly. All Christians are already blessed with all spiritual blessings (Ephesians 1:3). However, few Christians know that, and even fewer understand it to a degree that it impacts their lives. "My people are destroyed for lack of knowledge" (Hosea 4:6).

Note 8

Walking in resurrection power in our physical lives is dependent on knowing that our "old man" (New International Version - old self) is crucified. If we don't believe that, then there won't be newness of life (Romans 6:4) or victory for us (see note 7 at this verse). As explained in note 6 at Romans 6:4, our old selves are already crucified. Yet some people have effectively voided the power of that truth (Mark 7:13) by teaching that we still have an old self, or sin nature, that is constantly being resurrected from the dead. There is no scripture that mentions a daily or even periodical resurrection of our "old man." Only Jesus has that power. Satan has no power to accomplish resurrection of any kind. This common belief that people still have an "old man," or sin nature, does not come from Scripture but through observation. People observe a drive to sin, and they assume that it is their old sin nature that drives them to it. The Scripture does teach that sin produced death (Genesis 2:17; Romans 5:12, 15, 17, 6:23; and Ephesians 2:1), and therefore everyone was born with a spirit that was dead to (or separated from) God. This is the part of people that the Bible calls sin (see note 9 at Romans 5:21), or the "old man" (this verse). Therefore, the Scriptures do teach that everyone was born with a sin nature, or "old man" (see note 4 at Romans 7:9). But Paul was making a very clear presentation in these verses that for the Christian, the old self is dead. Christians do not have a nature that is driving them to sin (see note 2 at Romans 6:2). If that is so, then why do we seem so bound to sin even after we experience the new birth? The reason is that the old self left behind what this verse calls a "body." Just as a person's spirit and soul leave behind a physical body at death, so the old self left behind habits and strongholds in our thoughts and emotions. The reason we as Christians tend to sin is because of un-renewed minds, not because of a sin nature. God made the mental part of us similar to a computer. We can program our minds so that certain actions and attitudes become automatic. For instance, when we were children, it was a major effort to tie our shoelaces or button our shirts, but as adults, we can now perform those tasks without even thinking about what we are doing. It's like it is just a part of us, but in actuality it was an acquired trait. Likewise, our "old man" ruled our thinking before we were born again. Our "old man" taught us such things as selfishness, hatred, and fear, as well as placed within us the desire for sin. The old self is now gone, but these negative parts of the old self's body remain. Just as a computer will continue to perform according to its programming until reprogrammed, so our minds continue to lead us on the course that our "old man" charted until renewed (Romans 12:2). Therefore, Christians do not have a part of them that is still of the devil and is driving them to sin. Instead, Christians have been liberated from the part of them that was dead in sin (i.e., the old self, Ephesians 2:1), and the rest of the Christian life is a renewing of the mind that results in the resurrection life of Jesus being manifest in their physical bodies (2 Corinthians 4:11). Someone might say, "What's the difference? Whether it's my 'old man' or an un-renewed mind, I still struggle with the desire to sin." The difference is enormous! If we still have a sin nature, then we are doomed to lives of schizophrenia (i.e., a split mind), but if it is just our un-renewed minds that cause the problem, then we can see the situation improve as we renew our minds. If people retained a sin nature even after the new birth, then those who were bound by particular sins before salvation would still be bound by them after salvation. They would just have to refrain from the physical acts, but in their hearts, they would continue to be guilty of committing those sins in thought (see note 12 at Matthew 5:22). Yet there are millions of examples of people who experience the new birth and are so changed that the very sins that used to enslave them before salvation are now so repulsive to them that they have no desire to commit those acts. They can't even relate to their old selves that did those things, because they are new people (2 Corinthians 5:17) with renewed minds. It is truly liberating to learn that we don't **have** to commit sins; we choose to do so. Therefore, we can change through the renewing of our minds (Romans 12:2) because there is no longer a part of us that is a sinner by nature. This is the point that Paul was making in this verse. To experience the resurrection life of Jesus, we have to know that the old self is dead, and then through the renewing of our minds, we destroy the body that the old self left behind, with the end result being that we will not serve sin any longer.

Romans 6:7

For he that is dead is freed from sin.

Note 9

There is a difference between being "freed" and being "free." In the 1860s, President Abraham Lincoln issued the Emancipation Proclamation that "freed" the American slaves. Many slaves, however, continued to serve their masters in slavery because the truth was hidden from them or in some cases, the slaves were afraid that they couldn't make it on their own. Likewise, Christians have been "freed" from sin, but that doesn't automatically mean all Christians experience that freedom. Through ignorance and deception, Satan continues to maintain mastery over those who have not yet realized their death and resurrection with Christ.

Romans 6:8

Now if we be dead with Christ, we believe that we shall also live with him:

LIVING COMMENTARY

The statement in this verse is dependent upon us knowing that death's dominion has been broken (Romans 6:9). If we are ignorant of this truth, then the resurrection life spoken of here won't manifest in our thoughts and actions—until we come to know this truth.

Romans 6:9

Knowing that Christ being raised from the dead dieth no more; death hath no more dominion over him.

Note 10

Our death to sin and resurrection to life with Christ is already a reality in our spirits (see note 7 at Romans 6:6), but it will only become a physical reality as we know and believe these truths (see note 8 at Romans 6:6). In this verse, Paul was stressing that this resurrection life is dependent on knowing that our death with Jesus unto sin is a one-time death that does not have to be repeated (see note 11 at this verse).

Note 11

Much current theology believes that we died unto sin but that we resurrect unto sin every morning and therefore must continually repeat this process. That is not what happened to Jesus, and these verses are comparing our death to sin with Jesus' death to sin (see note 3 at Romans 6:11). It is true that we continually have to appropriate this death to sin, but there is a big difference between dying over and over and over and just renewing our minds with an accomplished fact.

Note 12

In the same way that Jesus died unto sin once (Romans 6:10) and now death has no more dominion over Him, those who recognize their death with Christ unto sin will not have sin rule over them anymore either (Romans 6:14). Christians who are struggling with sin have not recognized that they are dead unto sin (see notes 7-8 at Romans 6:6).

Romans 6:10

For in that he died, he died unto sin once: but in that he liveth, he liveth unto God.

LIVING COMMENTARY

Our death to sin (the old sin nature - see my note at Romans 6:6) is a one-time experience, just as it was for Jesus. We don't die to sin over and over and over.

Romans 6:11

Likewise reckon ye also yourselves to be dead indeed unto sin, but alive unto God through Jesus Christ our Lord.

Note 1

As already discussed in note 3 at Romans 6:2 and note 6 at Romans 6:2, our "old man" is dead. However, because a lust to sin is still present even after the new birth, many teach that the "old man" is constantly being resurrected. That's not so. This verse makes it very clear that we are to reckon ourselves dead to sin in the same manner as Christ is dead to sin. The Greek word that was translated "likewise" in this verse is "HOUTO," and it means "in this way (referring to what precedes or follows)" (Strong's Concordance). The American Heritage Dictionary defines "likewise" as "in the same way; similarly." Therefore, we are dead to sin in the same way that Christ is dead to sin. Of course, Jesus only died to sin once, so therefore we only die to sin once (Romans 6:9-10). After that, we simply reckon (see note 2 at this verse) ourselves to be dead to sin and alive unto God.

Note 2

In note 6 at Romans 4:3, the Greek word "LOGIZOMAI," which was translated "reckon" here, is explained in detail. The word conveys no causative meaning but rather only an inventory or assessment of a condition that already exists. Therefore, the state of being dead to sin already exists for us as Christians, but we have to seize this benefit by reckoning it to be so. The use of the word "indeed" in this verse further establishes that this is already an accomplished work of Christ that we are simply appropriating.

Note 3

Many people focus on the death to sin that is mentioned in this verse and omit, or at least put secondarily, the part about being alive unto God. It is assumed that if people will just die to sin, then life with Christ comes automatically. That's no more so than physical death automatically producing physical resurrection. God doesn't need dead people; He needs people who have risen from the dead spiritually. People who are preoccupied with dying to themselves will not experience their new lives with Christ. This verse emphatically states that they are to believe unquestionably, without a doubt, that they are, in reality, already dead to sin (see note 2 at this verse) in the same way that Christ is already dead to sin (see note 1 at this verse). As explained in note 9 at Romans 5:21, being dead to sin is not a struggle against or victory over sin that we are accomplishing; it is deliverance from our "old man" (sin nature) that enslaved us to sin. Our "old man" no longer exists and, therefore, no longer can dominate us if we know the truth (see note 7 at Romans 6:6). It is wrong to teach that dying to sin is something that we still have to accomplish by acknowledging all our sinfulness and forsaking it. This actually causes us to focus on self (sinful self) more than ever before and, therefore, actually strengthens the hold of what's left of the "old man" (see note 8 at Romans 6:6) in our lives. The way to get rid of the residual effect of the "old man" in our lives is not to focus on our sins but to focus on our resurrected union with Christ. Therefore, according to the instruction of this verse, we are to unquestionably count on the fact that our "old man" is gone and just as certainly reckon that our new man is alive with Christ, desiring only those things that please the Father. Doing this will transform us outwardly in our flesh into people who reflect who we already are inwardly in our spirits.

Romans 6:12

Let not sin therefore reign in your mortal body, that ye should obey it in the lusts thereof.

LIVING COMMENTARY

Paul gives us a command not to let sin reign in our mortal bodies. He would be unjust to command us to do something beyond our ability. Therefore, it's a lie to say that we can't help but sin or "I can't control myself." That's a lie of the devil and only applies if we believe Satan's lie. The only way sin can reign is through the Law (Romans 5:21). A person who is freed from the Law because of the grace of God can always successfully resist sin.

Note 4

If this sentence were to be diagrammed the way we were taught in school for the purpose of identifying the subject and verb, then the understood subject of this sentence would be "you." Paul was saying, "[You] let not sin therefore reign in your mortal body" (brackets mine). You have the power to stop the reign of sin in your life, or the Lord would not have given you this command. A mistaken belief that we can't help but sin is one of the biggest reasons that we do sin. The power of sin (see note 9 at Romans 5:21) has been broken in our lives, and the only reason we Christians sin is because we haven't renewed our minds with the reality of our new lives with Christ (see notes 7 and 8 at Romans 6:6).

Note 5

The word "therefore" makes our ability to end sin's reign in our lives that this verse speaks of, dependent on the truth that was just expressed in Romans 6:11 (see note 3 at that verse). We have to know beyond any doubt that our "old man" is dead and gone; then, and only then, will we be able to renew our minds and end the dictatorship of sin in our lives.

Romans 6:13

Neither yield ye your members as instruments of unrighteousness unto sin: but yield yourselves unto God, as those that are alive from the dead, and your members as instruments of righteousness unto God.

LIVING COMMENTARY

Notice we have to yield our members unto sin. Sin can't force us to do anything. We are dead to sin. It is only those who don't know what has happened and what they now have in Christ who are susceptible to Satan's lies about this. Knowing that our "old man" is crucified with Christ will break the dominion of sin in our lives (see my notes at Romans 6:6-7).

Romans 6:14

For sin shall not have dominion over you: for ye are not under the law, but under grace.

LIVING COMMENTARY

Sin can't dominate us when we are under grace. Grace liberates us from sin, while the Law strengthens sin (see my note at 1 Corinthians 15:56). If we are being dominated by sin, it's because we are under the Law. And this verse makes it very clear that a true believer is not under the Law. Grace sets us free from sin, not free to sin. See my note at Titus 2:12.

Note 6

The "old man" (sin, see note 9 at Romans 5:21) is dead and gone. Yet there is a "residual old man", or the un-renewed mind and emotions that the "old man" left behind (see note 8 at Romans 6:6). It is these lingering effects of the "old man," or sin, to which Paul was referring. Paul made a very clear statement that the reason this sin shall not have dominion over us is because we are not under Law (see note 3 at Romans 3:19) but under grace (see note 5 at Romans 1:5). However, most Christians today are still operating under the Law, so it's no surprise that sin still has dominion over them. Understanding our freedom from the Old Testament Law is a prerequisite to breaking the dominion of sin in our lives. The reason this is so is because the Law strengthened sin by producing guilt that condemned us and killed us (see note 4 at Romans 3:19). The Law also brought the wrath of God against our sins (see note 3 at Romans 4:15). However, once we accept the atonement of Christ for our sins, we no longer need to fear the wrath of God; that was placed on Jesus. We also don't need the Law to condemn us and kill us. We have already come to Christ for salvation, which is what the Law was designed to do (Galatians 3:24-25). Knowing this (see note 7 at Romans 6:6) frees us **from** sin; it doesn't free us **to** sin. As Christians, all of us continue to sin to some degree, not because we have to, but because we are still in the process of renewing our minds (see note 4 at Romans 6:12). However, when we aren't condemned and feeling separated from God because of our sins, we are free to run to God for help instead of away from God in fear. Therefore, understanding God's grace and our freedom from the Law is the key to breaking the dominance of sin in our lives.

Romans 6:15

What then? shall we sin, because we are not under the law, but under grace? God forbid.

LIVING COMMENTARY

This is the third time in this book that Paul brought up this question (Romans 3:8; 6:1, and this verse). If no one ever asks us if we are saying that people can just continue living in sin, then we haven't preached the Gospel the way Paul preached it (see my note at Romans 6:1).

Note 7

Paul had started this sixth chapter with a similar question as to whether or not his teaching was encouraging people to sin (see note 1 at Romans 6:1). In Romans 6:1-13, he explained that as Christians, we don't sin, because we are dead to sin (see note 3 at Romans 6:2 and note 6 at

Romans 6:4). Then in Romans 6:14, he brought up our deliverance from the Law again, which prompted this similar question. He then went on through the rest of this chapter to explain that the second reason we don't sin is because it gives Satan an inroad into our lives (see note 8 at Romans 6:16).

Romans 6:16

Know ye not, that to whom ye yield yourselves servants to obey, his servants ye are to whom ye obey; whether of sin unto death, or of obedience unto righteousness?

LIVING COMMENTARY

This is one of two reasons presented in this chapter (first—Romans 6:2) as to why Christians don't sin. It is because it gives the author of sin (Satan) control over us. If we sin, God still loves us, but Satan will eat our lunch and pop the bag.

Note 8

This is the second argument that Paul presented in this chapter as to why Christians don't live in sin (see note 2 at Romans 6:2). The legalistic Jews were pursuing sinless lives so that they could earn God's favor. Paul had conclusively proven that no one could keep the precepts of the Law and that the Law was never given for the purpose of justification (see note 4 at Romans 3:19 and note 14 at Romans 3:31). Therefore, he was explaining that Christians still seek to live holy but for different reasons. This second reason Paul gave for holiness in our lives as believers is that when we obey sin, we yield ourselves to Satan, the author of that sin. Notice the use of the personal pronoun "whom" in this verse. Yielding to sin is yielding to a person—Satan.

God doesn't impute the sin to us (see note 2 at Romans 5:13), but the devil does (see note 3 at Romans 5:14). Our actions release in us either the power of Satan or the power of God. Therefore, although God is not imputing our sins unto us, we cannot afford the luxury of sin because it allows Satan to have access to us.

When we do sin and allow the devil opportunity to produce his death in our lives, then the way to stop that is to confess the sin, and God is faithful and just to take the forgiveness that is already present in our born-again spirits and release it in our flesh, thereby removing Satan and his strongholds (see note 11 at Romans 4:8).

Note 9

The Greek word that was translated "servants" twice in this verse is "DOULOS," and it denotes "a slave" (Strong's Concordance) (see note 1 at Romans 1:1). Therefore, Paul was not speaking of an infrequent error on our part but rather a servile condition where one "gives himself up wholly to another's will" (Thayer's Lexicon). So Paul was stating that those who abandon themselves to sin are in actuality becoming slaves of the devil (see note 8 at this verse), while those who obey righteousness are actually yielding themselves to the Lord. This is the second reason in this chapter as to why a Christian should live holy.

Romans 6:17

But God be thanked, that ye were the servants of sin, but ye have obeyed from the heart that form of doctrine which was delivered you.

LIVING COMMENTARY

As mentioned in my note at Romans 6:16, the Greek word that was translated "servants" here is "DOULOS" and signifies a slave. We were all slaves to sin (see my note at Romans 5:21) before we were born again (see my note at Romans 5:12). This verse clearly shows how we break the slavery of sin: We obey, from the heart, the proper doctrine. The doctrine promoted throughout this entire letter is the Gospel of grace (see my note at Romans 1:16).

Romans 6:18

Being then made free from sin, ye became the servants of righteousness.

Note 10

Jesus said, "No man can serve two masters: for either he will hate the one, and love the other; or else he will hold to the one, and despise the other. Ye cannot serve God and mammon" (Matthew 6:24). We cannot become the servants of righteousness until we are made free from serving sin. As discussed in note 9 at Romans 6:16 "servants" here denotes slavery. Christians still sin (1 John 1:7 and 9), but they aren't the slaves of sin (see note 9 at Romans 5:21) anymore. Those who believe that the "old man" still lives and exerts mastery in their lives (see notes 1-3 at Romans 6:11) will not experience the joy of being servants to righteousness.

Romans 6:19

> *I speak after the manner of men because of the infirmity of your flesh: for as ye have yielded your members servants to uncleanness and to iniquity unto iniquity; even so now yield your members servants to righteousness unto holiness.*

LIVING COMMENTARY

Paul said in 1 Corinthians 2:13 that he compared spiritual things with spiritual things. That's the way it should be and the way he preferred to communicate. But because the people were carnal and he wanted them to get these points, he came down to their level and spoke in terms they could understand. Just as they had yielded themselves to sin in all its lusts, likewise they should yield themselves as slaves to righteousness and holiness.

Romans 6:20

> *For when ye were the servants of sin, ye were free from righteousness.*

Note 1

Paul had just made a statement in Romans 6:19 that we should serve the Lord with the same fervor that we served the devil with before we were born again. He continued that comparison through Romans 6:22 and made an amazing point. He was saying that in the same way that our good acts could not change our sinful nature before we were born again, likewise, our sinful acts cannot change our righteous nature now that we have become new creatures in Christ Jesus. In this verse, the phrase, "servants of sin," is describing people before they are born again. The phrase, "free from righteousness," is not saying that lost people cannot do anything that is right, but rather all of their good acts aren't enough to change their nature. They must be born again (see note 2 at John 3:3). Most Christians have accepted this truth unquestionably. They were saved by believing that. Yet this exact terminology is used again in Romans 6:22 in a way that very few Christians accept. The same logic that was used in this verse is reversed in Romans 6:22. If "servants of sin" in this verse signified people before salvation, then "servants to God" in Romans 6:22 denotes just the opposite—people who have been saved through faith in Christ. If "free from righteousness" in this verse described lost people who were incapable of changing their sinful nature by their own good works, then "free from sin" in Romans 6:22 describes Christians as being unable to change their righteous nature through their sins. This is a powerful truth. In the same way that our sinful nature could not be changed by our own actions, now our new, born-again spirits cannot be changed by our actions either. If we are going to accept one of these truths, we have to accept the other. We cannot honestly accept this verse and reject Romans 6:22 when the exact same terminology is used in the same context. Actions cannot produce the new birth, and actions cannot destroy the new birth. We had to believe to receive salvation, and we have to willfully reject that faith in Christ to become reprobate (see note 6 at Romans 1:28 and note 9 at Romans 1:32).

Romans 6:21

What fruit had ye then in those things whereof ye are now ashamed? for the end of those things is death.

LIVING COMMENTARY

The question is, how fruitful were we in sin when we were slaves to sin? The answer is, very! Anything we profess as our master will dominate us. Many of us Christians, through ignorance of the truths presented in this chapter, profess sin (our old sin nature) as our master, and we suffer because of it. But if we can understand and believe the truths in this chapter about our "old man" being dead (see my notes at Romans 6:3-12), then sin will cease to produce fruit in us and we will yield the fruit of holiness and everlasting life (see my note at John 17:3) instead.

Romans 6:22

But now being made free from sin, and become servants to God, ye have your fruit unto holiness, and the end everlasting life.

LIVING COMMENTARY

This is the exact same truth presented in Romans 6:20 but applied in the opposite direction. We were slaves to sin before our salvation, and therefore, all our good works were useless to change our condition. In the same way, now that we are slaves to God, all our ungodliness can't change our new birth. See my note at Romans 6:20.

Note 2

Notice that holiness is a fruit, and not a root, of salvation. That is to say that holiness is a byproduct of relationship with God; it does not produce relationship with God (see note 21 at Matthew 23:26).

Romans 6:23

For the wages of sin is death; but the gift of God is eternal life through Jesus Christ our Lord.

LIVING COMMENTARY

When we were slaves to sin, we got paid. The payment was death. But now that we are slaves to righteousness, we don't get things from God on the basis of our effort. Instead, it's on the basis of faith. It's a gift. And that gift is eternal life.

Note 3

The American Heritage Dictionary defines "wages" as "a suitable return or reward." Sin has a wage that it pays, and no one can avoid "payday" without faith in Jesus. As explained in note 9 at Romans 5:21, the sin spoken of here is not an individual act of sin but rather the sin nature, or "old man," itself. Those who do not receive the new birth (see note 2 at John 3:3) will be held liable for all the wrongs committed as a result of their sinful nature (see note 4 at Mark 3:29). However, those who receive the new birth through faith in Jesus don't have a sin nature (see note 8 at Romans 6:6) and will therefore not receive this payment of death. The physical death of our bodies is not really what is being spoken of here. Physical death, as well as all results of the sin nature (i.e., sickness, depression, fear, etc.), is only a byproduct of the spiritual death that was already present on the inside of us. The Lord told Adam that in the day he ate of the forbidden tree, he would surely die (Genesis 2:17). Adam didn't die physically that day, but he did die spiritually. Physical death came at age 930 for Adam (Genesis 5:5) as a byproduct of spiritual death. The wages (plural) of death that those who are not born again will receive can be broken into two categories. The Bible speaks of a second death (Revelation 2:11; 20:6, 14; and 21:8)—banishment to the lake of fire (see note 4 at Mark 3:29) on the Day of Judgment. The first death is this separation from God (or spiritual death) that was inherited through Adam (see note 4 at Romans 5:16 and note 6 at Romans 5:19). So this verse is specifically speaking of the spiritual death that was inherited through Adam and then the second death, which is eternal banishment from God and torment in the lake of fire. However, any negative results of sin, which were not part of God's original plan for man, can also be included in the term "death," since they are a direct result of this spiritual death.

Note 4

Eternal life (see note 94 at John 17:3) is a gift. The American Heritage Dictionary defines "gift" as "something bestowed voluntarily and without compensation." We have nothing to do with earning this gift. Eternal life would cease to be a gift if we earned it (Romans 11:6). We simply receive it by faith.

ROMANS

CHAPTER SEVEN

Romans 7:1

Know ye not, brethren, (for I speak to them that know the law,) how that the law hath dominion over a man as long as he liveth?

Note 1

Remember that Paul wrote this epistle to all the saints in Rome (Romans 1:7). Therefore, even though this term "brethren" can be used to designate fellow countrymen, as in Romans 9:3, here it is specifying fellow believers, especially the Jewish believers who were knowledgeable of the Law.

Note 2

Paul was saying that the only way to get out from under the Old Testament Law is through death. He had just taught that the "old man" is once and for all dead (see note 6 at Romans 6:4 and note 8 at Romans 6:6). Here he used the natural illustration of marriage to further make this point. In the same way that the marriage vow was intended by God to be binding until "death do us part" (see note 5 at Matthew 19:7), so our bondage under the tyranny of the sin nature (see note 9 at Romans 5:21) was inescapable except through death.

Therefore, this knowledge of our death to the old self is crucial to escaping the carnal life that the old self put in place in our lives.

Romans 7:2

For the woman which hath an husband is bound by the law to her husband so long as he liveth; but if the husband be dead, she is loosed from the law of her husband.

Note 3

Paul likened our death to sin, which he had explained in Romans 6, to the laws governing a marriage relationship. The husband is our "old man," the wife is the soul and body part of us, or our personality, and the binding civil and moral code that enforces a marriage is like the Old Testament Law. We, the wife, were enslaved to a wicked husband, the old self. In Old Testament times, the Law gave the wife no option of divorce. The man could divorce his wife (Deuteronomy 24:1), but the wife could not divorce her husband. Therefore, the only hope a woman could ever have of being delivered from that situation was that her "old man" would die. Then she was delivered from that moral and civil code that kept her from having relationship with someone else. Likewise, we were in bondage to the old self. We wanted out of the relationship, but we were by nature slaves to sin (Ephesians 2:3). The Old Testament Law only made the situation worse. It strengthened the control of the old self over us. The Law actually empowered sin, or our wicked husband, against us (see note 4 at Romans 3:19). Then Jesus entered the scene. He took the old self with Him to the cross, and when He died, the old self died too. But Jesus rose from the dead, and the old self didn't. Now we are free from the old self and the Law that bound us to it so that we can be married to Him who is risen from the dead.

Romans 7:3

So then if, while her husband liveth, she be married to another man, she shall be called an adulteress: but if her husband be dead, she is free from that law; so that she is no adulteress, though she be married to another man.

Note 4

In this comparison, it is clearly understood that a woman who has two husbands would be living in adultery. Likewise, Paul was saying that a Christian who has two natures would be living in adultery. Those of us who do not understand that the old self is dead will constantly feel the guilt of the Old Testament Law that bound us to our first husband, the "old man."

Romans 7:4

Wherefore, my brethren, ye also are become dead to the law by the body of Christ; that ye should be married to another, even to him who is raised from the dead, that we should bring forth fruit unto God.

Note 5

Through Jesus, not only is the old self dead, but we also are dead to the Law that enforced the tyranny of the old self over us. The Law was only made for the old self (1 Timothy 1:9-10). Once it is dead, we are no longer under the Law (see note 6 at Romans 6:14). Failure to understand this will produce the same end results as if our "old man" was not dead.

Note 6

Christ didn't free us from the relationship to our first husband, the "old man," so we could just run around and do whatever we want; He freed us from that first marriage so we could marry Him. As Christians, our freedom is not the freedom to do "our own thing," but it is freedom from the old nature so that we can now serve Christ in newness of spirit (Romans 7:6).

Note 7

Just as it is normal for a physical marriage to produce children, so our marriage to Christ is intended to bring forth fruit (see note 47 at John 15:2)

Romans 7:5

For when we were in the flesh, the motions of sins, which were by the law, did work in our members to bring forth fruit unto death.

Note 8

Christians are not **in** the flesh even though they walk **after** the flesh at times. There is a difference, and Paul made a major point in Romans 8 concerning the difference between being in the flesh and after the flesh (see note 20 at Romans 8:9).

Note 9

Notice that the motions or influences of sin were by the Law. The Law actually made sin come alive in us (see notes 3 and 4 at Romans 7:9).

Note 10

This is the same phrase that was used in the last part of Romans 7:4. In the same way that relationship with the old self produced death, now realizing our new relationship with Christ produces the fruit of holiness (see note 2 at Romans 6:22).

Romans 7:6

But now we are delivered from the law, that being dead wherein we were held; that we should serve in newness of spirit, and not in the oldness of the letter.

Note 11

In these first six verses of Romans 7, Paul said we are "loosed from the law" (Romans 7:2), "free from that law" (Romans 7:3), "dead to the law" (Romans 7:4), and "delivered from the law" (this verse). Romans 6:14 says that we "are not under the law." How could it be made any clearer that the Law was not made for a born-again person (1 Timothy 1:9)?

Note 12

The American Heritage Dictionary defines "spirit," when used as in this verse, as "the actual though unstated sense or significance of something." Just as Jesus taught against ritualistic observance of laws (see note 21 at Matthew 23:26), so Paul was saying a Christian is someone who fulfills the real sense or significance of the Law, not every detail. God is more pleased with someone who has a pure heart and yet fails Him in actions (example: Luke 7:36-50) than someone who does the right things with an impure heart (1 Samuel 16:7). Second Corinthians 3:6 says, "The letter killeth, but the spirit giveth life." True Christianity is not the observance of a different set of rules than some other religion;

it is a change of the heart (Ezekiel 11:19, 36:26; and 2 Corinthians 5:17). Once people's hearts are changed, they will serve God, not because they have to, but because they want to.

Romans 7:7

What shall we say then? Is the law sin? God forbid. Nay, I had not known sin, but by the law: for I had not known lust, except the law had said, Thou shalt not covet.

Note 1

Remember, in context, the sin being spoken of here is not an individual act of sin but rather the sin nature that compelled us to sin (see note 9 at Romans 5:21). Paul was saying, "Is it the Law that compelled us to sin?" The answer to this is no. Paul had just spoken of being "loosed from," "free from," "dead to," and "delivered from" the Law (see note 11 at Romans 7:6). Here he was clarifying his statements so that someone wouldn't think he was saying that the Law is the thing that drove us to sin. The Law of God simply made clear to us that we already had a depraved nature. When the Law said, "Thou shalt not covet," that commandment didn't make covetousness come; it made the lust that was already present revive (Romans 7:9) and strengthened it (1 Corinthians 15:56) so that we could not be deceived any longer into thinking that we could produce salvation on our own (see note 4 at Romans 3:19). God's commandments are holy, just, and good (Romans 7:12), but man apart from God is sinful. Therefore, it was impossible that a revelation of God's true standards could change our nature; only the new birth can do that. The Law simply stripped our sinful nature of its disguise so that we could properly assess how bad the situation was.

Note 2

As explained in note 2 at Romans 1:18, there is an intuitive knowledge of right and wrong inside every person. How does that harmonize with Paul's statement here? The answer is that the Law brought sin into focus. Every person has an intuitive picture of what sin is, but hardness of the heart caused this image to become blurred. Once the Law comes to an individual, all blindness is removed, and it is very clear what God's standard of right and wrong is.

Romans 7:8

But sin, taking occasion by the commandment, wrought in me all manner of concupiscence. For without the law sin was dead.

LIVING COMMENTARY

The Law gave occasion to sin. Sin is the transgression of the Law (1 John 3:4). Therefore, where there is no Law, there is no transgression (Romans 4:15).

Romans 7:9

For I was alive without the law once: but when the commandment came, sin revived, and I died.

Note 3

Paul stated that there was a time in his life when he (his soulish, emotional, or personality part) was not separated from God. This was before the Law came. But the Law of God was communicated thousands of years before Paul was born, so what does this mean? When Paul spoke of the Law coming, he was speaking of the time in all people's lives when they recognize that they are violating a command of God. Children may know they've been told not to do certain things and that if they do them, they will be punished. However, there comes a time when they realize that it is not just Mom or Dad or society that they are disobeying, but this is disobedience to God. That's when the Law comes and God imputes their sins from that time. Prior to that time, their sin nature is not being imputed to them (see note 2 at Romans 5:13), and they can fellowship with God. Notice that Paul said, "When the commandment came, sin revived." He did not say, "Sin **came**." You cannot revive something that doesn't already exist. The sin nature already exists in every human at birth (see note 1 at Romans 5:15 and note 4 at Romans 5:16), but until the Law comes, that nature is dead (Romans 7:8). That does not mean that it is not functional. Observation tells us that very young children have a functional sin nature. But God is not imputing sin unto people until the time that they knowingly violate God's Law. This is why children can receive from God even before they are born again, and it also explains why infants who die go to heaven. Until the time that Paul calls "when the commandment comes," or what many call "the age of accountability," the sin nature does exist, but God is not imputing that sin. Therefore, they are not bearing God's judgment against sin. But once the commandment comes, then the wrath of God against sin is released (see note 3 at Romans 4:15), and unless they receive Jesus as their Savior, they will bear the eternal punishment of God (see note 4 at Mark 3:29). It is impossible to fix a certain age when this accountability occurs. That varies from person to person. For some, such as in cases of retardation, it is possible that this age of accountability is never reached. We can be sure that our all-knowing God will be righteous in His judgment of each individual.

Note 4

All people are born with a nature that is dead in trespasses and sin (Ephesians 2:1-3), but until they reach an understanding where they are accountable to God, sin is not imputed unto them (see note 3 at this verse).

Until that time, people are alive in the sense that they can communicate with God without the barrier of sin. However, once the Law comes and sin is imputed, there is a separation from (or death to) God that can only be remedied by the new birth (see note 2 at John 3:3) through faith in Jesus.

Romans 7:10

And the commandment, which was ordained to life, I found to be unto death.

LIVING COMMENTARY

If we could have kept the Law, then our compliance with it would have produced life. So, in that sense, it was ordained to life. But the sad fact is that no one ever kept the Law except Jesus. Therefore, instead of life coming through the Law, it produced death, because we all sinned and came short of the Law's demands (Romans 3:23).

Romans 7:11

For sin, taking occasion by the commandment, deceived me, and by it slew me.

LIVING COMMENTARY

The Amplified Bible translated this verse as "For sin, seizing the opportunity and getting a hold on me [by taking its incentive] from the commandment, beguiled and entrapped and cheated me, and using it [as a weapon], killed me." The letter (Law) kills (2 Corinthians 3:6).

Note 5

The ministry of the Law actually gave sin (the sin nature, see note 9 at Romans 5:21) an occasion against people. The corrupt rebellious nature of man will always lust for what it cannot have. Forbid people to do something that they were only mildly interested in before, and they will develop an uncontrollable lust for that very thing. This is how the Law worked. Sin was already at work in man, but when the Law came, condemning their actions, sin came alive (Romans 7:9) in comparison to what it was before. The reason God did this was because mankind had been blinded to what sin was and its consequences. Sin had already beaten and enslaved people, but they didn't realize it. They thought they were good enough, until the Law came.

Once they were forbidden to do and think certain ways, sin began to abound (Romans 5:20), and they became aware that they were, by nature, children of the devil (Ephesians 2:3) and needed a savior. That was the purpose and ministry of the Old Testament Law (see note 4 at Romans 3:19). Failure to understand this truth has led many well-meaning religious people to attempt to get others to stop sinning through the proclamation of God's laws against, and punishments for, sin. That wasn't the purpose of the Law. According to these verses, sin actually revives and gains an occasion against people when the Law is used. The right use of the Law is to give knowledge of sin (Romans 3:20) and convince people that they are doomed without a savior.

The Law is powerless to overcome sin. Only the grace of God can cause people to overcome sin (Romans 6:14).

Romans 7:12

Wherefore the law is holy, and the commandment holy, and just, and good.

LIVING COMMENTARY

The problem was not with the Old Testament Law. It was holy, just, and good. The problem was with us— mankind. We were sold under sin (Romans 7:14) and couldn't keep the Law. Therefore, the only thing the Law could justly do was condemn us.

Romans 7:13

Was then that which is good made death unto me? God forbid. But sin, that it might appear sin, working death in me by that which is good; that sin by the commandment might become exceeding sinful.

LIVING COMMENTARY

The Law wasn't the problem. Our sin nature was the problem, and the Law just brought that sin nature out in the open where we could see it and deal with it. Before we could receive the salvation that Jesus provided, we had to come to the end of our self-righteousness. We had to quit trying to earn salvation by our own goodness. The Law helped with that. Before the Law, people could compare themselves with others and come to wrong conclusions about their relative holiness (2 Corinthians 10:12). But when the Law was given, this deception was removed. The Law clearly stated God's righteous standard, which condemned everyone (Romans 3:19-20). I might be better than some other sinner, but who wants to be the best sinner who ever went to hell? All have sinned and come short of God's glory (Romans 3:23), which is Jesus. The Law showed us our need for a Savior, but the Law wasn't that Savior. Jesus is the only Savior.

Note 6

Even though the Law was called "the ministration of death" (2 Corinthians 3:7), the Law itself was not death. Death was already at work in us through the sin nature (see note 9 at Romans 5:21). The Law simply drew out what was already there so that we could see how sinful we were and realize that we needed a savior. The deceitfulness of sin evaporates in the presence of the Law, and sin becomes exceedingly sinful.

Romans 7:14

For we know that the law is spiritual: but I am carnal, sold under sin.

Note 7

This is why the Law could not produce life for us. It is because the Law is spiritual, but we are carnal. Another way of saying this is, the Law is perfect, but we aren't. If we could have lived up to every detail of the Law, then we could have obtained salvation through it. But all have sinned and come short of God's perfect standard (Romans 3:23), all except for one, and that is Jesus. The Law did provide life for one man, the man Christ Jesus, because He was the only man who was ever perfect. Jesus was without any sin whatsoever, and therefore He deserved eternal life as a payment, not a gift. Those who put their faith in Jesus as their Savior benefit from His keeping of the Law (Romans 8:4).

Romans 7:15

For that which I do I allow not: for what I would, that do I not; but what I hate, that do I.

Note 1

Many debates have occurred over whether here Paul was describing himself before his conversion or whether he was describing the carnality that still existed in him after all those years of walking with the Lord. Was Paul describing a condition that has already been taken care of through the new birth, or was he saying that even mature Christians are doomed to lives of schizophrenia (i.e., a split mind) where part of us wants to serve God and part of us wants to serve the devil? Actually, Paul was not stating either one of those positions. He was expounding the impossibility of serving God in our own power, whether lost or saved. The flesh (see note 3 at Romans 7:18) is unwilling and unable to fulfill the Law of God, and if we as Christians try to fulfill the righteousness of the Law through our own willpower, we will fail just the same as unregenerate people would. Paul was describing the futility of trying to obtain favor with God through our own goodness whether Christian or non-Christian. That has been the theme throughout the book of Romans. Paul only used the term "spirit" once in Romans 7 (Romans 7:6), a chapter that described the hopelessness of people to ever keep the righteousness of the Law in their own strength. In contrast, the word "spirit" (or "Spirit") is used twenty-one times in Romans 8, a chapter that gives the answer to the hopelessness of Romans 7. In these verses of Romans 7, Paul was not describing warfare that wages between the new man and the old man. He was contrasting the complete inability of people to save themselves because of their corrupted flesh (see note 3 at Romans 7:18) versus the life-transforming power of Christ described in Romans 8. The Apostle Paul was not living a life of constant failure where the good that he wanted to do, he was unable to accomplish, but the evil that he didn't want to do, he did. He wasn't living that kind of life because it was no longer him living, but Christ living in him (Galatians 2:20). Christ in Paul was manifesting holiness in Paul's life that was second to none. However, if Paul had abandoned his dependency upon Christ and had started trying to live the Christian life out of his own resources, then the condition described in Romans 7:15-24 would have been his experience. Our flesh has been corrupted through sin, and though we can renew our minds through God's Word (Romans 12:2), we can never elevate our flesh to a place where it can fulfill the Law of God. Hence, the good news of Romans 8 that what the Law couldn't do, because of the weakness of our flesh (Romans 8:3), God did for us, and all we have to do is receive by faith.

Romans 7:16

If then I do that which I would not, I consent unto the law that it is good.

LIVING COMMENTARY

The Law is good if we use it for what it was intended to do (see my notes at 1 Timothy 1:8-10). The Law can only show us our sin and our need for salvation. It is powerless to save us. All it does is condemn (2 Corinthians 3:9). But this is good. We need to come to the end of ourselves before we can get into God. The Law helped us do that.

Romans 7:17

Now then it is no more I that do it, but sin that dwelleth in me.

Note 2

As already stated in note 9 at Romans 5:21, this sin is not speaking of an individual act of sin but of the "old man," or "sin nature," itself. This looks like a direct contradiction to Paul's statements in Romans 6 about the old self being dead (see note 6 at Romans 6:4). To harmonize these apparently opposite accounts, most people have said that the death spoken of in Romans 6 is not a one-time experience but an ongoing process. Experience and Paul's testimony here seem to bear that out. However, Romans 6:9-11 makes a specific point of comparing our death to sin with Christ's death to sin. Romans 6:10 clearly states that Christ died unto sin once (see note 11 at Romans 6:9), and Romans 6:11 says we should likewise reckon ourselves to be dead unto sin (see note 1 at that verse). To further strengthen this point, Paul began Romans 7 with the illustration of marriage (see note 3 at Romans 7:2). In the same way that a woman cannot have two husbands, a Christian cannot have two natures (see note 4 at Romans 7:3). So, in context, there is a very strong case for our "old man" being dead in the absolute sense. But what about Paul's statements here and in Romans 7:20 about sin dwelling in him? The key is in Romans 7:23 where Paul spoke of a law (influence) of sin that dwelt in his members, not sin itself (see note 5 at that verse). Therefore, this passage is referring to the force or influence of the "old man," which does still exist, but not the "old man" itself. The argument for the complete abolishment of the sin nature is further strengthened in Romans 7:24 (see note 2 at that verse) where Paul referred to "the body of this death." This is referring to the same thing that Paul spoke of in Romans 6:6 where he used the terminology "the body of sin" (see note 8 at that verse).

Romans 7:18

For I know that in me (that is, in my flesh,) dwelleth no good thing: for to will is present with me; but how to perform that which is good I find not.

LIVING COMMENTARY

The word "flesh" here is referring to all that is carnal in us. I believe the Greek word "SARX" that was translated "flesh" in the King James Version has been incorrectly interpreted "sinful nature" in the New International Version. This isn't a translation but an interpretation based on the belief that Christians still have old sinful natures. We no longer have sinful natures after being born again. The sinful nature was crucified and is gone (see my note at Romans 6:6). The only nature we have is that of God. The only reason we still have a tendency to sin is because we haven't renewed our minds. The sinful nature taught our minds how to think, and they have to be reprogrammed. Our minds will continue to operate in lust and selfishness until we renew them by the Word of God. Therefore, the King James Version's "flesh" is a much better rendering than the New International Version's "sinful nature."

Note 3

The term "flesh" comes from the Greek word "SARX." SARX was translated "flesh" 147 times, "carnal" 2 times (Romans 8:7 and Hebrews 9:10), "carnally" 1 time (Romans 8:6), and "fleshly" 1 time (Colossians 2:18). There are many ways that the word "flesh" was used in the New Testament, but for simplification, we will group its usage into three main categories. First, it can refer to the physical flesh of man (Luke 24:39) or beasts (1 Corinthians 15:39). When used in that context, the term is descriptive of only the physical makeup of man and is neither good nor bad, as can be seen by the fact that Jesus was made "flesh" (John 1:14).

Second, "flesh" can describe the weakness and frailty of people, or people apart from God. This was the way Paul used the term in Romans 8:3 when he said, "For what the law could not do, in that it was weak through the flesh." Paul was saying that people, without the quickening power of God in their lives, were unable to keep the Law. Paul described his own efforts at holiness without the power of Christ as works of the flesh (Philippians 3:3-9). "The flesh is weak" (Matthew 26:41). Third, "flesh" can refer to all that is sinful in man. In Galatians 5:19-21, Paul described the works of the flesh as "Adultery, fornication, uncleanness, lasciviousness, Idolatry, witchcraft, hatred, variance, emulations, wrath, strife, seditions, heresies, envyings, murders, drunkenness, revellings,

and such like." In this sense, the term "flesh" can be used almost interchangeably with the "sin nature" when describing those who are not
born again or the effects of the residual old self (see note 6 at Romans
6:14) on those who are born again. In this instance, when Paul used this
parenthetical phrase, "that is, in my flesh," he was specifying the natural
part of his person, or the second category of "flesh" described above.
He was stating that in himself, apart from his born-again spirit, there
was no good thing. He had to include this explanation, or his statement
would not have been accurate, for in his spirit there was a good thing
(i.e., Christ).

Romans 7:19

*For the good that I would I do not: but the evil which I would not,
that I do.*

LIVING COMMENTARY

All of us have experienced what Paul was speaking
about here. We want to do one thing but wind up doing
the opposite. Before people are born again, the only
thing they have to fight against this inner conflict is willpower. That can modify actions to a degree, but it can't
do a thing to stamp out the inner desire. Jesus said that
desiring it in our hearts is as bad as doing it (Matthew
5:27-28). But when we are saved, our "old man"—our
old nature—is gone (see my note at Romans 6:6). The
driving force that compels us to sin is gone. The only
thing that is left is an un-renewed mind (Romans 12:2).
Through the power of the Holy Spirit, we can renew our

minds and break the dominion of sin (Romans 4:15 and 7:25).

Romans 7:20

Now if I do that I would not, it is no more I that do it, but sin that dwelleth in me.

LIVING COMMENTARY

See my note at Romans 7:17. This is the same thing. The sin nature is gone (see my note at Romans 6:6), but it left behind a body (i.e., an un-renewed mind) that has to be destroyed (transformed, Romans 12:2).

Romans 7:21

I find then a law, that, when I would do good, evil is present with me.

Note 4

This law (force or influence, see note 5 at Romans 7:23) was present, but Paul was not living under the dominance of it (Romans 6:14). He clearly stated in Romans 8:2 that the law of the Spirit of life in Christ Jesus had made him free from the law of sin and death (see note 1 at Romans 7:15).

Romans 7:22

For I delight in the law of God after the inward man:

> ## LIVING COMMENTARY
>
> Paul's inward man (spirit) was born again (see my note at 2 Corinthians 5:17). And in his spirit, he delighted in the same godly things the Law commanded.

Romans 7:23

But I see another law in my members, warring against the law of my mind, and bringing me into captivity to the law of sin which is in my members.

Note 5

The Greek word translated "law" three times in this verse is "NOMOS," and it means "a force or influence impelling to action" (Vine's Expository Dictionary). So these verses are not speaking of the "old self," or "sin nature," directly but rather of its influence. In Romans 7:22, this same Greek word was used to refer to the Law of God. In that instance it is clear that this is speaking of the influence of God through His precepts and not the divine person Himself. Likewise, in Romans 7:23, the influence of the "old man" is what is being spoken of. As explained in note 8 at Romans 6:6, the old self is dead and gone, but it left behind a body.

Attitudes and emotions that still influence us until we renew our minds, are the body of the old self. We are not dealing directly with the "old sin nature" but with its influence that is still being exerted through our unregenerate flesh. So the Christian life is a renewal of our minds to who we have become in Christ, not a hatred for who we are in our "old self."

Romans 7:24

O wretched man that I am! who shall deliver me from the body of this death?

Note 1

Paul was not describing his spiritual condition when he said, "O wretched man that I am!" He was speaking of his flesh (see note 3 at Romans 7:18). He made this distinction clear in Romans 7:18 when he said, "I know that in me (that is, in my flesh,) dwelleth no good thing." So as explained in note 1 at Romans 7:15, Paul was describing the absolute wretchedness of his flesh.

Note 2

In context, Paul was summarizing his statements from Romans 7:14-23. He didn't say, "Who shall deliver me from this death?" for the Christian has already been delivered from the death that is the wages of sin (see note 3 at Romans 6:23). He made special mention of the **body** of this death. The terminology "the body of this death" corresponds to what Paul called "the body of sin" in Romans 6:6. He was not speaking of the sin nature itself, for a Christian no longer has a sin nature (see note 8 at Romans 6:6), but he was rather speaking of the "old man" or the lingering influence of the sin nature that still exerts itself through the un-renewed mind. So death, or the "old man," is gone, but the body that it left behind (i.e., the thoughts, attitudes, and emotions) still poses a problem to us as Christians. How do we overcome this flesh (see note 3 at Romans 7:18)? The answer is stated in Romans 7:25 and then explained in Romans 8.

Romans 7:25

I thank God through Jesus Christ our Lord. So then with the mind I myself serve the law of God; but with the flesh the law of sin.

Note 3

Paul was not just stating that he was thanking God through Jesus Christ; he was specifically thanking God for the deliverance from this body of death, and that deliverance only comes through our Lord Jesus Christ.

Note 4

Here is the conclusion of Paul's arguments from Romans 7:14-24. He desired to serve the Law of God, but his flesh was incapable of doing so. How then can we overcome this frustration? The answer is given in Romans 8 as Paul explained how to escape the flesh and walk in the Spirit.

ROMANS

CHAPTER EIGHT

Romans 8:1

There is therefore now no condemnation to them which are in Christ Jesus, who walk not after the flesh, but after the Spirit.

LIVING COMMENTARY

I believe the use of the words "in" and "after" in this chapter are significant. "In" denotes a fixed place or position. "After" denotes a lifestyle. So, Christians are "in" Christ and should walk "after" Christ. But it is possible for a person who is "in" Christ to walk "after" the flesh. But a true Christian cannot be "in" the flesh (Romans 8:9). We are now new creatures in Christ (2 Corinthians 5:17) and have a new identity, which is our spiritual man, not the flesh. Likewise, an unbeliever might try to walk "after" Christ, but the truth is they will always be "in" the flesh until they put their faith in Christ alone. Out of sixteen translations that I checked, eleven left out the phrase "who walk not after the flesh, but after the Spirit." The point is that there is NO condemnation from the Lord to those who are in Him, PERIOD. But if believers walk "after" the flesh, there can be condemnation against them from other sources. A Christian who breaks the law will be condemned by the legal authorities. Christians who walk "after" the flesh can be condemned by their own consciences and the devil's accusations, but that condemnation isn't from the Lord.

Note 1

The American Heritage Dictionary defines the word "therefore" as "for that reason; consequently." This word ties Paul's statement here in this verse to the previous verses. Paul was giving us the answer to the hopeless situation he described in Romans 7:14-24. Prior to Romans 8, the Holy Spirit was only mentioned once in this epistle (Romans 5:5 - Holy Ghost). In this chapter alone, the Holy Spirit is referred to nineteen times (compare with note 1 at Romans 7:15). Paul was making the point that the only way to overcome the effects of sin in our lives is through the indwelling presence and power of the Holy Spirit.

Note 2

Nine Greek words are used in the New Testament that were translated "now." Some of these words simply provide a transition between thoughts. However, the Greek word translated "now" in this verse is "NUN," and it is "a primary particle of present time; 'now'" (Strong's Concordance), "the immediate present" (Vine's Expository Dictionary). Thus, Paul's use of this word makes it very clear that living with no condemnation is a present-tense experience of the believer, not something reserved for the future.

Note 3

The Greek word that was translated "no" in this verse is "OUDEIS." This is an emphatic term meaning "not even one…i.e. none" (Strong's Concordance). Wuest translated this as "There is not even one bit of condemnation" (The New Testament: An Expanded Translation by Kenneth S. Wuest).

Note 4

The Greek word translated "condemnation" here is "KATAKRIMA," and it means "an adverse sentence (the verdict)" (Strong's Concordance). Paul was stating that God has no adverse sentence against us once we accept Him. All our punishment has been placed on Jesus, and we don't bear it. Those of us who still walk in condemnation are being condemned by the devil or are condemning ourselves. It's not God who condemns us (Romans 8:34). Second Corinthians 3:9 called the Law a "ministration of condemnation." It was the Law that brought God's adverse sentence against us. Romans 3:19 says the Law was given to make us guilty before God. Guilt is the emotional response to condemnation. This can be illustrated by the way a building is condemned. When the government condemns a building, it is declared unfit for use and must be destroyed. Likewise, when Satan condemns us, he makes us feel unfit for use and ready to be destroyed. Since we as Christians are no longer under the Law (see note 3 at Romans 4:15), we should no longer be condemned or feel unfit for use. We have been accepted by the Father through Jesus (Ephesians 1:6).

Note 5

God placed the judgment that the Law prescribed against us upon His Son. Therefore, those of us who accept Jesus as our Savior will not be condemned, because Jesus was condemned for us (Romans 8:3). This truth, and the fact that this phrase, "who walk not after the flesh, but after the Spirit," is not in some of the old Greek manuscripts, has led many scholars to believe that this phrase does not belong here. They say it was borrowed from Romans 8:4 by some scribe who was copying out the scriptures. Condemnation still exists, as any Christian knows. This verse has rightly portrayed that only those who are living in the power of the Holy Spirit escape that condemnation. Compare this to the law of gravity. Gravity is a law that never quits exerting its power, but it can be overcome. Through the laws of aerodynamics, man can actually fly and send space ships beyond Earth's gravity. But it takes power to do this. If the power is shut off, the law of gravity is still at work and will cause the vehicle to fall. Likewise, the law of sin and death still exists. If Christians shut off the power of the Spirit of life and begin to start walking in the power of their own flesh, Satan will use this law of sin and death to make sure they crash and are condemned. God convicts of sin, but He doesn't condemn (Romans 8:34). Conviction is solely for our profit and is free of malice, while condemnation includes punishment (see note 4 at this verse). Satan is the one who condemns us, but the Holy Spirit has given us the power to escape that condemnation.

Romans 8:2

For the law of the Spirit of life in Christ Jesus hath made me free from the law of sin and death.

Living Commentary

A law is something that is consistent and universal, like the law of gravity. If gravity only worked in one country, or if it only worked sometimes, then it would be a phenomenon, not a law. The life the Spirit brings to the believer is consistent and universal. It never fails to set believers free from the consistent and universal death that sin produces. But this freedom has to be appropriated. Many slaves were freed by the Emancipation Act, but not all of them went free immediately because they had the truth hidden from them.

Likewise, we have been freed, but not all Christians experience that freedom because they are ignorant of what is rightfully theirs.

Note 6

Romans 7:15-24 describes the hopelessness of those attempting to overcome the law (see note 5 at Romans 7:23) of sin and death in their own ability or holiness (see note 1 at Romans 7:15). But Romans 8, and specifically this verse, brings people the good news that what could not be done by human effort has been done through the power of the Holy Spirit. Christians are no longer slaves to the law of sin and death.

According to Romans 6:23, death is the wages of sin (see note 3 at Romans 6:23). Therefore, this phrase, "the law of sin and death," is referring to the influence of sin and the resulting wages of that sin. Another way of saying "the law of sin and death" is "the law that when we sin, we receive death instead of life" or "when we sin, we reap the curse instead of the blessing." Deuteronomy 28:1-14 lists the blessings that come if we keep the whole Law. Deuteronomy 28:15-68 lists all the curses that come as the wages of not keeping the Law.

Because the law of the Spirit of life has set us free from the law of sin and death, we no longer reap Deuteronomy 28:15-68, even though we haven't kept every precept of the Law. Christ redeemed us from these curses of the Law (Galatians 3:13). Praise God that we don't have to receive the wages of sin, which is death. Not only have we been redeemed from the curses of Deuteronomy 28:15-68, but also, through Jesus, we have the righteousness of the Law fulfilled in us (see note 9 at Romans 8:4) so that the blessings of Deuteronomy 28:1-14 are now ours. So, through Christ, we receive what we don't deserve (the blessings of Deuteronomy 28:1-14), and we don't receive what we do deserve (the curses of Deuteronomy 28:15-68).

Romans 8:3

For what the law could not do, in that it was weak through the flesh, God sending his own Son in the likeness of sinful flesh, and for sin, condemned sin in the flesh:

LIVING COMMENTARY

The Law wasn't weak. It was perfect, but we weren't (see my notes at Romans 7:12-13). It was our flesh that was weak, and therefore, the Law could never set anyone free from the bondages of sin. All the Law did was point out our sin (Romans 3:20). God placed all the sin of the world on the flesh of Jesus and condemned Him in our place (see my note at John 12:32). I believe the New International Version's interpretation of the Greek word "SARX" as "sinful nature" in this verse does this passage an injustice. No doubt our sinful nature kept us from fulfilling the Law, but it wasn't only our sinful nature that caused that weakness. As Christians, without a sinful nature, we are still incapable of fulfilling the Law in our flesh. Turning the other cheek is against the way most of us have programmed ourselves. The

Amplified Bible translated this as "flesh," the same as the King James Version, and gives further amplification: "the entire nature of man without the Holy Spirit." That is more accurate than just to say "the sinful nature," because a carnal Christian's soul is flesh that will stop the power of God from manifesting in their life.

Note 7

The Law itself was not weak. In Romans 7:12 Paul said, "The law is holy, and the commandment holy, and just, and good." The Law wasn't weak, but our flesh (see note 3 at Romans 7:18) was. The Law and our flesh were linked together like a chain, and a chain is no stronger than its weakest link. Our flesh was the weak link in the chain. Although the Law was strong, it couldn't accomplish righteousness, because of the weakness of our flesh.

Note 8

This last "flesh" in Romans 8:3 is speaking of the flesh of Jesus. God placed the condemnation that was directed toward us upon the flesh of His Son, Jesus. As stated in note 7 at this verse, the Law was strong enough to produce life **if** we would have been able to keep it, but our human flesh rendered us impotent. This was a dilemma. The Law was ordained to life (Romans 7:10), but none of us could keep it (Isaiah 59:16). So God Himself became flesh (John 1:14 and 1 Timothy 3:16). He did what no sinful flesh had ever done: He kept the Law, thereby winning the life of God as the prize for keeping the Law. This granted Him eternal life, but before He could give it to us, we still had a debt that had to be paid. This is similar to a man receiving the death penalty for some hideous crime, and then some billionaire leaves his whole estate to him. It would do the condemned man no good. But if that same billionaire could somehow take that man's place and die for him, then he could go free and enjoy his new wealth. That's what Jesus did for us. He took our sins and gave us His righteousness. Jesus did much more than just obtain eternal life for us; He also paid all the wages of our sins (Romans 6:23). God literally placed the condemnation, or judgment, that was against us upon His own Son. Jesus' perfect flesh was condemned so our defiled flesh could go free. What a trade! Since Jesus bore our sentence (condemnation), we don't have to bear it. The debt has already been paid. It would be double jeopardy if we also had to bear any condemnation.

Romans 8:4

That the righteousness of the law might be fulfilled in us, who walk not after the flesh, but after the Spirit.

LIVING COMMENTARY

What was the result of God placing our condemnation on Jesus? It was that now we have the righteousness of the Law given to us as a gift. Jesus paid a debt He didn't owe, and I owed a debt I couldn't pay. He received my sin and condemnation, and I received His righteousness (2 Corinthians 5:21). Walking "after" the Spirit doesn't mean we are perfect and holy. It simply means we are seeking to follow after the Lord. In the same way that there are varying degrees of being "after" the flesh, there are likewise varying degrees of being "after" the Spirit (see my note at Romans 8:1).

Note 9

This verse is saying that through the sacrificial death of Jesus, we can now fulfill the righteousness of the Law. There are two ways that we need to understand this. First, the righteousness of the Law is now fulfilled in our new, born-again spirits (see note 11 at Romans 4:8). Jesus fulfilled the Law (Matthew 5:17) and has given us His righteousness (see note 10 at Romans 3:26). Every believer's spirit is righteous and truly holy. Second, through the Holy Spirit, we are now empowered to live, outwardly in our actions, the holy lives that the Law demanded but we were unable to do in our own strength. That's what Paul was referring to when he said, "Who walk not after the flesh, but after the Spirit." It needs to be pointed out that although as Spirit-filled believers, we will live holy lives, we will never keep every detail of the Law. That could not be done before salvation, and it cannot be done after salvation. The same Greek word that was translated "righteousness" in Romans 8:4 was translated "ordinances" in Luke 1:6. Luke was speaking of Zacharias and Elizabeth, that "they were both righteous before God, walking in all the commandments and ordinances of the Lord blameless." Notice that they were both righteous and blameless before the Lord but not sinless (see note 2 at Luke 1:6). So the righteousness of the Law can be fulfilled without keeping every commandment.

The purpose of the Law was to make us despair of saving ourselves and to point us to a Savior (see note 4 at Romans 3:19). When we come to put faith in Jesus as our Savior, then we are fulfilling the purpose of the Law. So this verse is speaking of us as believers being empowered to live holy lives, but fulfilling the righteousness of the Law is not the same as keeping every detail of the Law (see note 12 at Romans 7:6). Therefore, all Christians have fulfilled the righteousness of the Law in their spiritual man through Jesus. But only those Christians who are under the control of the Spirit of God are fulfilling the spirit of the Law in their actions.

Note 10

The word "walk" in this phrase is translated from the Greek word "PERIPATEO," and it means "to tread all around, i.e. walk at large... figuratively, to live, deport oneself, follow" (Strong's Concordance). The American Heritage Dictionary defines it as "to conduct oneself in a particular manner." Therefore, this phrase, "who walk not after the flesh, but after the Spirit," is speaking of those who do not conduct their lives according to the flesh but follow the leading of the Spirit. Romans 8:5 goes on to further explain this and uses the terminology "mind the things of the flesh" to describe those who "walk after the flesh" and "[mind] the things of the Spirit" (brackets mine) to describe those who "walk after the Spirit." So "walking after the flesh" is simply having your mind focused on carnal things, and "walking after the Spirit" is having your mind stayed on spiritual things (John 6:63).

Romans 8:5
> *For they that are after the flesh do mind the things of the flesh; but they that are after the Spirit the things of the Spirit.*

LIVING COMMENTARY

Many people desire to walk after the Spirit and not after the flesh but there is a lot of confusion about how to do that. This verse makes it very simple. Those who mind spiritual things are walking after the Spirit and those who mind carnal things are after the flesh. We can evaluate our carnality or spirituality by examining where our minds are focused. The Greek word that was translated "mind" here is "PHRONEO," and it means "to exercise the mind, i.e. entertain or have a sentiment or opinion;

by implication, to be (mentally) disposed (more or less earnestly in a certain direction); intensively, to interest oneself in (with concern or obedience)" (Strong's Concordance). So, what we exercise our minds with or are mentally disposed toward or are interested in indicates whether or not we are walking after the spirit or the flesh.

Note 11

Romans 8:5-8 explains why only those who walk after the Spirit (see note 10 at Romans 8:4) are seeing the righteousness of the Law fulfilled in their lives (see note 9 at Romans 8:4)). It is because whatever people think on is what they are going to become or do (Proverbs 23:7). Those who are after the flesh think on carnal things and therefore do carnal things. Thinking carnally can only produce death, while thinking spiritually (according to the Word, John 6:63) can only produce life (see note 15 at Romans 8:6).

Note 12

This verse gives us a test so that we can determine if we are walking after the flesh or after the Spirit: We just have to judge what we are thinking about. If we are consistently thinking on the things of the Spirit (John 6:63), then we are walking after the Spirit. If we are dominated with carnal thoughts (see note 13 at Romans 8:6), then we are walking after (see note 20 at Romans 8:6) the flesh (see note 3 at Romans 7:18).

Romans 8:6

For to be carnally minded is death; but to be spiritually minded is life and peace.

LIVING COMMENTARY

Carnal-mindedness doesn't just tend toward death. It equals death. And spiritual-mindedness doesn't just tend toward life. It equals life. I don't have to be with a person to see what he has been thinking. All I have to do is see the dominant fruit of that person's life and I can tell. It's like looking at a person's garden. What was planted is what grows there. Death here is much more than just physical death where our bodies and souls and spirits separate. Sickness, depression, anger, poverty, and anything else that is a result of sin is a form of death (Romans 6:23). The Greek word that was translated "carnally" in this verse is SARX. That's the same Greek word that was translated "flesh" in the previous verse. Therefore, the words "carnal" and "flesh" are being used interchangeably here.

Note 13

The same Greek word, "SARX," that was translated "flesh" in Romans 8:1, 3-5, and 8 was translated "carnally" in this verse and "carnal" in Romans 8:7. So these terms can be used interchangeably.

Note 14

The death that is spoken of here is not just physical death, although that is included. It refers to all the effects, or wages, of sin (see note 3 at Romans 6:23). The Amplified Bible translates this as "[death that comprises all the miseries arising from sin, both here and hereafter]."

Sickness, depression, loneliness, hatred, poverty, fear, and everything else that came as a result of sin would be included in this term "death."

Note 15

This is a powerful statement. Being carnally minded doesn't just tend toward death; it is death. Likewise, being spiritually minded doesn't just tend toward life; it is life and peace. Those who say they are spiritually minded yet are experiencing death (see note 14 at this verse) are deceived. If they would just dominate themselves with the spiritual truths of God's Word, they would receive only life and peace.

Romans 8:7
> *Because the carnal mind is enmity against God: for it is not subject to the law of God, neither indeed can be.*

LIVING COMMENTARY

A mind focused on what can be seen, tasted, heard, smelled, and felt will always oppose God. The New International Version's interpretation of the Greek word "SARX" as "sinful" in this verse is misleading. The King James Version correctly translates this as "carnal." All sin is carnal, but not all carnality is sin. The word "carnal" is describing a mind that is controlled by only physical things as perceived by the five senses. This doesn't limit this mind to just sinful things; a person who is only physically minded (carnal) will also not receive or understand spiritual things. Notice that the carnal mind cannot be subject to God. It is naturally opposed to God and His ways. So, we have to lose our minds (carnal way of thinking) to serve God.

Note 16

This word "carnal" is translated from the same Greek word as "flesh" (see note 13 at Romans 8:6). Just as with the word "flesh" (see note 3 at Romans 7:18), there is more than one way that the word "carnal" is used. All sin is carnal, but not all carnality is sin. The word "carnal" can also refer to human ability or natural things. Trying to live the Christian life from our own ability is carnal. In context, Paul was contrasting the hopeless struggle of the flesh to live holy, which he described in Romans 7:15-24, with the Spirit-filled life that he presented in Romans 8. Therefore, he was portraying that trying to obtain holiness through the flesh is being carnal. It is inaccurate to think that only sin is carnal. All our self-righteousness is carnal too.

Note 17

The carnal mind is hostile or opposed to God. The carnal mind hates the things of God. Therefore, no one just naturally pleases God. It is impossible for the natural mind to think in the ways of God. As Paul said in 1 Corinthians 2:14, "But the natural man receiveth not the things of the Spirit of God: for they are foolishness unto him: neither can he know them, because they are spiritually discerned." We have to deny our natural way of thinking and be led by the Spirit of God in order to walk pleasing to God.

Romans 8:8

So then they that are in the flesh cannot please God.

:8

:8

:8

: Living: :

:8:8:8: :8

LIVING COMMENTARY

According to my note at Romans 8:1, the use of the word "in" here is describing someone who is not born again. A Christian can be "after" the flesh but not "in" the flesh (Romans 8:9). The only ones who are "in" the flesh are those who have not received Jesus as their Lord. Romans 8:9 confirms this. Obviously, being in the flesh is not being in faith (Hebrews 11:6).

Note 18

Hebrews 11:6 says, "Without faith it is impossible to please him," so Romans 8:8 could also read, "So then they that are in the flesh cannot have faith" because faith is the only way to please God. Faith is a fruit of the Spirit (Galatians 5:22-23) and cannot be produced by human effort.

Note 19

This is the sum of what Paul was saying in Romans 7:15-24 and the reason we can never trust in our own holiness to be justified in the sight of God. The Christian life is not just hard to live; it is impossible to live in our own ability. Christianity only works when the Spirit of God indwells and controls us, thereby giving us supernatural ability. Without the quickening power of the Holy Spirit, we can't believe God and receive salvation. Many religions of the world believe in one God—some of them even worship the God of Abraham—but they don't believe in Jesus as their Savior. Without Jesus, they are in the flesh and cannot please God.

They may even live holier lives than those who have put faith in Jesus as their Savior, but their flesh will fail to be holy enough to earn salvation (see note 6 at Romans 3:23).

Romans 8:9

But ye are not in the flesh, but in the Spirit, if so be that the Spirit of God dwell in you. Now if any man have not the Spirit of Christ, he is none of his.

LIVING COMMENTARY

All Christians are "in" the Spirit even if they walk "after" the flesh (see my note at Romans 8:1).

Note 20

Paul made a clear distinction between being "in" the flesh and "after" the flesh, and "in" the Spirit and "after" the Spirit. Born-again people (see note 2 at John 3:3) cannot be "in" the flesh, but they can walk (see note 10 at Romans 8:4) "after" the flesh. Lost people cannot be "in" the Spirit although they seek to walk "after" the ways of the Spirit. The word that was translated "in" here is the Greek word "EN," and it denotes a "(fixed) position (in place, time or state)" (Strong's Concordance). In contrast, the word that was translated "after" in Romans 8:1, 4-5, and 12-13 denotes "according to anything as a standard, agreeably to" (Thayer's Greek-English Lexicon). Therefore, when Paul spoke of being "in" the flesh or Spirit, he was referring to a fixed position or state. When he spoke of being "after" the flesh or Spirit, he was referring to whatever we are using as a standard of conduct or whatever we are agreeing to at any given time. Christians can agree to or conduct their actions according to some standard other than God's and still keep their position in Christ (see note 1 at Romans 6:20). So Christians can walk "after" the flesh, but they are never considered "in" the flesh.

Note 21

According to Jesus' statement in John 14:17, people cannot receive the Holy Spirit unless they have first received Jesus as their Savior (see note 27 at John 14:17). Therefore, those who have the Spirit of God dwelling in them are born again (see note 2 at John 3:3) and are not in the flesh (see note 20 at this verse).

Note 22

This passage makes an emphatic statement that every believer receives the Spirit of Christ at salvation. The supposition that the "Spirit of Christ" and the "Spirit of God" are synonymous terms has led many to believe that every Christian receives the Holy Spirit at salvation. However, this seems to contradict the examples given in the book of Acts (see note 6 at Acts 2:4, note 3 at Acts 8:16, and note 1 at Acts 19:1). It is very likely that the phrase "Spirit of Christ" refers to the born-again spirit that every believer receives at salvation. The phrase "Spirit of God" possibly refers to the Holy Spirit that only indwells the believers if they receive the baptism of the Holy Spirit (see note 6 at Acts 2:4).

Romans 8:10

And if Christ be in you, the body is dead because of sin; but the Spirit is life because of righteousness.

LIVING COMMENTARY

This isn't saying that our physical bodies are literally dead. That's obvious. This is speaking of our physical bodies and un-renewed minds (or flesh) being separated from God. Our bodies and carnal minds cannot relate to God because they can't perceive God through one of the five senses. To contact God, we have to do it through our spirits. God is a Spirit, and we must worship Him in spirit and in truth (John 4:24). Those who are spiritual don't enshrine the body the way unbelievers do. Those without Christ are only carnally minded; therefore, the body is everything to them. But true believers "keep under" their bodies (1 Corinthians 9:27) and are looking forward to their spiritual bodies (1 Corinthians 15:44). So, the believers who are living "after" the spirit should keep under their bodies, not as the unbelievers who think the physical is all there is, but because they are exalting the spirit. Sin kills (Romans 6:23), both emotionally and physically.

Note 23

Based on Romans 8:9, as well as John 14:20, 2 Corinthians 13:5, and Colossians 1:27, Christ is in every born-again believer. Therefore, Paul was saying that for all Christians, our bodies are dead because of sin (see note 24 at this verse).

Note 24

The body is dead "because" of sin, but the Spirit is life "because" of righteousness. The Greek word translated "because" here is "DIA," and it denotes "the channel of an act; through" (Strong's Concordance). Therefore, our bodies are dead through, or because of, the influence of sin in our lives. In the same way that some people who have recovered from the polio virus still have crippled bodies, so Christians who have been delivered from the old sin nature (see note 9 at Romans 5:21) still have to deal with the corruption that the old sin nature released into our physical bodies and minds. That's why no one can please God in the flesh.

The flesh has been corrupted and is therefore dead, or incapable of living up to God's standard. To counter this, the Spirit of God is releasing life because of our new righteous spirits that we received through faith in Jesus. Sin has left its mark on our bodies, but the Spirit of life within us is more than enough to overcome these problems. That's why it is imperative that we Christians learn how to walk after the Spirit and not after the flesh.

Romans 8:11

But if the Spirit of him that raised up Jesus from the dead dwell in you, he that raised up Christ from the dead shall also quicken your mortal bodies by his Spirit that dwelleth in you.

LIVING COMMENTARY

Is this talking about the quickening that will take place when we receive our glorified bodies, or is this talking about the Spirit quickening our mortal bodies right now, as in healing? Maybe this is speaking of both.

Note 25

This verse is speaking of more than just the quickening of our bodies at the second return of Christ, although that is included. In Romans 8:10, Paul spoke of the body being dead because of sin, but the Spirit being life because of righteousness. This is speaking of the current situation we face in this life. Our flesh (see note 3 at Romans 7:18) has been rendered incapable of serving God correctly because of the effect sin has had on us, but our situation isn't hopeless. God has given us His Spirit, and we can overcome this deficit by letting Him live through us (Galatians 2:20). Here in Romans 8:11, Paul was commenting on this quickening power of the Holy Spirit for this life as well as the ultimate victory when our physical bodies will be resurrected.

Romans 8:12

Therefore, brethren, we are debtors, not to the flesh, to live after the flesh.

LIVING COMMENTARY

Since the Spirit is the life-giving part of us as described in the previous verse, then we should give priority to walking "after" the Spirit and not "after" the flesh. The flesh profits nothing. The words of Jesus are Spirit and they are life (John 6:63).

Note 26

Paul was saying that the flesh (see note 3 at Romans 7:18) never helped us. It has been rendered powerless through sin (see note 24 at Romans 8:10). It is only through the indwelling power of the Holy Spirit that we

Christians have any hope of living in victory. Therefore, we are indebted to the Spirit and should yield to Him.

Romans 8:13

For if ye live after the flesh, ye shall die: but if ye through the Spirit do mortify the deeds of the body, ye shall live.

LIVING COMMENTARY

This has to be speaking of spiritual life and death, since everyone will die physically. This is saying that those who put their minds predominantly on spiritual things will have God's kind of life and that those who keep their minds predominantly on the flesh will suffer all the wages sin can pay (Romans 6:23). The word "mortify" means "to kill" (Strong's Concordance). We are to kill our actions that are not consistent with what the Lord wants us to do.

Note 27

Paul was speaking of death in a figurative sense rather than a literal sense. He was addressing believers who had already received eternal life through the new birth (see note 2 at John 3:3), and he was not saying that they would lose their salvation if they walked "after" the flesh (see note 10 at Romans 8:4). As explained in note 3 at Romans 6:23, "death" is a term that not only refers to physical death but also can denote all the effects of sin in our lives. Therefore, Paul was speaking about experiencing defeat as we Christians walk after the flesh compared to experiencing victory when we walk after the Spirit.

Note 28

The word "mortify" was translated from the Greek word "THANA-TOO," and it means "to kill" (Strong's Concordance). The American Heritage Dictionary defines "mortify" as "to discipline (one's body and appetites) by self-denial." If we deaden ourselves to the flesh by self-denial and follow the leadership of the Holy Spirit, we will live.

Romans 8:14

For as many as are led by the Spirit of God, they are the sons of God.

Note 29

Being led by the Spirit of God is the ultimate standard whereby we may know someone is a son of God. This raises the question, "If you aren't led by the Spirit of God, does that mean you are not born again?" It is true that everyone who is not born again is not led by the Spirit of God and that everyone who is born again is led by the Spirit of God, but that requires some explanation. First, there are varying degrees of being led by the Holy Spirit. No believers are following the leading of the Lord as much as they could be, and if an absolute standard was applied to this verse, no believers would qualify to be sons of God. With this in mind, believers have been led by the Spirit to some degree in making Jesus their Lord, if nothing else. Second, being led by the Spirit does not cause people to be sons of God, but being sons of God causes them to be led by the Spirit. All believers do have the Spirit of God to lead them, but that doesn't mean all believers heed His leading (see note 3 at John 10:3). In context, Paul had just spoken about denying the flesh through the power and leading of the Holy Spirit. Here he was simply pointing out that all Christians have the leading of the Holy Spirit available to them to accomplish this.

Note 30

Some people have tried to make a distinction between being a "child of God" and a "son of God." They say a "child of God" is any born-again believer, while a "son of God" refers only to a mature Christian. This looks good on the surface, but further study will reveal there is no difference. In Galatians 4, these same terms are used, and "son" or "sons" is applied to all believers. Galatians 4:6 says, "And because ye are sons, God hath sent forth the Spirit of his Son into your hearts, crying, Abba, Father," and Romans 8:9 says, "Now if any man have not the Spirit of Christ, he is none of his." Since every believer must have the Spirit of Christ (Romans 8:9) and every son of God has the Spirit of God's Son in him, crying, "Abba, Father" (Galatians 4:6), then we can clearly see that every born-again believer is a son of God. Therefore, these terms are used interchangeably, and no doctrine about different levels of maturity can be drawn.

Romans 8:15

For ye have not received the spirit of bondage again to fear; but ye have received the Spirit of adoption, whereby we cry, Abba, Father.

LIVING COMMENTARY

Our new born-again spirits are not like our old sinful natures that were bound by fear (Hebrews 2:15). But we have received the Spirit of adoption that leads us to call God our Father, a term of intimacy unknown to O.T. saints. This signifies the inner witness of the Holy Spirit bearing witness with our spirits that we are the sons of God (next verse). God cannot be seen or perceived by carnal means, but we have an inner witness that assures us of unseen reality.

Note 31

This "spirit of bondage" is a reference to the old sin nature (see note 9 at Romans 5:21). The fact that Paul said, "Ye have not received the spirit of bondage **again** " (emphasis mine), is a further testimony that our old sin nature is not just ceremonially dead but that it is totally gone from our lives (see note 3 at Romans 6:2).

Note 32

We are sons of God by adoption. Jesus was the Son of God by nature. As Jesus said to the Jews, we were of our father, the devil (John 8:44 and Ephesians 2:3), but Jesus purchased us and made us adopted sons of God.

Romans 8:16

The Spirit itself beareth witness with our spirit, that we are the children of God:

LIVING COMMENTARY

God cannot be seen. Sins cannot be seen, and we don't know what they look like when they are forgiven. But we do not have to wonder if God has forgiven our sins. He sends His Spirit who constantly assures us of His reality, forgiveness, and love. Without the Holy Spirit's ministry, salvation would just be blind faith. But with the Holy Spirit's ministry, there is assurance. It's just not carnal.

Note 33

First John 5:10 says, "He that believeth on the Son of God hath the witness in himself." John went on to say in 1 John 5:13, "These things have I written unto you that believe on the name of the Son of God; that ye may know that ye have eternal life." So the Spirit bearing witness with our spirits is to assure us that we are the children of God (1 John 3:19).

Romans 8:17

And if children, then heirs; heirs of God, and joint-heirs with Christ; if so be that we suffer with him, that we may be also glorified together.

LIVING COMMENTARY

Our relationship with Jesus makes us heirs of God. What a statement! We are joint-heirs with Christ of everything God has. The term "joint-heir" signifies a shared inheritance. A joint checking account means two people share the account, and both signatures are needed to cash a check or make a withdrawal. One signature will not release funds from a joint account. Jesus is our joint-heir. Even though we might be tempted to sign our inheritance away as Adam did, Jesus will never cooperate with that. Our inheritance is secure because Jesus will never put His signature on any of our bad choices. Adam was not a joint-heir with Christ; he was a joint-heir with Eve. They shared dominion over the earth. In order for their transgression to be valid, both of them had to participate. They did (Genesis 3:6), and they signed away their authority over the earth to Satan. He became the god of this earth (2 Corinthians 4:4) through what Adam did. In a very real sense, God didn't create Satan. He created Lucifer, a powerful angel. Adam and Eve created Satan when they gave him the power and authority they had been given over the earth.

Note 34

We are not just heirs; we are joint-heirs with Christ. How wonderful it would be to inherit any amount of God's glory and power, but to think that we share equally with the One who has inherited everything God is and has is beyond comprehension. This is an awesome blessing, but it places a tremendous responsibility on us too. In the same way that a check made out to two people cannot be cashed without the endorsement of both parties, so being joint-heirs with Jesus cannot be taken advantage of without people's cooperation.

Unaware of this, many Christians are just trusting that the Lord will produce the benefits of salvation for them. They are acutely aware that they can do nothing without Him but don't realize that He will do nothing without them (Ephesians 3:20). The way we place our endorsement on the check is to believe and act like what God promised in His Word is true. Jesus has already signed His name to every promise in the Word. We aren't waiting for Him; He is waiting for us.

Romans 8:18

For I reckon that the sufferings of this present time are not worthy to be compared with the glory which shall be revealed in us.

LIVING COMMENTARY

What a statement! Just think of some of the terrible things people have suffered in this life. The Holocaust, wars, slavery, shame, sickness, hatred, and all the other tragedies are nothing compared to the wonderful things the Lord has prepared for us. That is not lessening the suffering; it is placing the consolation so high above all tragedy that there is no comparison. The glory God has prepared for us is infinitely greater than all the pain sin has inflicted. Our consolation will be so great that the former things will never come to mind (Isaiah 65:17). Thank You, Jesus! Notice that this glory is going to be revealed IN us. Right now we have all the awesome glory of God on the inside of our born-again spirits; we just can't totally perceive it at this time. As Paul said, "We see through a glass, darkly" (1 Corinthians 13:12). But when we go to be with the Lord, or for those who are alive when He returns, we will receive our glorified bodies and totally renewed minds. Then we will have full revelation of what was in us all along.

Note 1

This is a very important statement. Paul did not say that this glory would be revealed "to us" but rather "in us." The complete glory of God that most dream of receiving in eternity is already in us here on this earth! Paul said in 2 Thessalonians 2:14, "He called you by our gospel, to the obtaining of the glory of our Lord Jesus Christ." And in 1 Peter 5:1, Peter said he was a partaker of this "glory that shall be revealed." Paul also prayed for the Ephesians that the Lord would grant them the spirit of wisdom and revelation in the knowledge of Him so that they would see the glory of His inheritance that was already in the saints (Ephesians 1:17-18). This leaves no doubt that, as Christians, our spirits are already complete. We don't need more faith, more power, or more anointing. We simply need to use more of what we have already received. Many Christians will be shocked when they stand before God and realize that all the things they prayed for were inside them from the time they believed (see note 3 at Matthew 26:41).

Romans 8:19

For the earnest expectation of the creature waiteth for the manifestation of the sons of God.

LIVING COMMENTARY

All of creation is waiting for this glory that is in us (see my note at Romans 8:18) to be manifested; i.e., made visible to our eyes. This will not be completely done until we receive our glorified bodies and totally renewed minds, but we can do it now to the degree that we renew our minds and act accordingly. Phillips New Testament Bible says, "The whole creation is on tiptoe to see the wonderful sight of the sons of God coming into their own." We should not keep them waiting.

Note 2

The two English words "earnest expectation" were translated from the Greek word "APOKARADOKIA." This Greek word was only used twice in the New Testament (here and Philippians 1:20). This is a compound word meaning "intense anticipation" (Strong's Concordance). Other scholars have translated it as "to strain forward," "a watching with outstretched head" (Vine's Expository Dictionary), and "to expect on and on, to the end" (Cremer). Fritz Rienecker says this word "denotes diversion from all other things and concentration on a single object." Therefore, this verse makes it very clear that all of creation is eagerly and intensely anticipating the day when the glory of God that is already deposited within God's saints (see note 1 at Romans 8:18) will be revealed. That day won't completely arrive until the Second Coming of the Lord, but it is logical to think that creation rejoices to some degree every time a saint manifests His glory here on this earth.

Note 3

The Greek word "KTISIS" was translated "creature" in Romans 8:19-21. This same word was translated "creation" in Romans 8:22. It literally means "original formation (properly, the act; by implication, the thing, literally or figuratively)" (Strong's Concordance).

Note 4

The American Heritage Dictionary defines "manifestation" as "an indication of the existence or presence of something." Something that does not already exist cannot be manifested. As the Apostle John said, "Beloved, now are we the sons of God, and it doth not yet appear what we shall be" (1 John 3:2). We are already the sons of God. This is not something that has yet to transpire. All of creation is waiting for us to manifest what is already in us (see note 1 at Romans 8:18).

Romans 8:20

For the creature was made subject to vanity, not willingly, but by reason of him who hath subjected the same in hope,

LIVING COMMENTARY

The animal creation didn't do anything to corrupt themselves. They were placed under man's dominion by God and entered into the fallen state through our transgression. God set it up this way in hope of something better than the animal creation existing separate from us. He will bring the animal creation into our glorious liberty.

Note 5

Many people have thought that the "creature" spoken of here is human beings. However, the contrast made in Romans 8:22-23 clearly exempts the saints from this group. Romans 8:21 speaks of the creature being "delivered from the bondage of corruption into the glorious liberty of the children of God." If "creature" were referring to unsaved people, then this would mean ultimate reconciliation of the human race to God, and that is not the teaching of Scripture. Therefore, it is most probable that the creature being spoken of here is all of creation, living and non-living, excluding humans. Paul was speaking of how all of creation did not choose to rebel against God. It was just mankind that sinned. Yet the Lord brought all the rest of creation, against their choice, into our cursed state with us so that He could also redeem them with mankind. Take for example the animal creation. Genesis 1:30 says that all the animals were given "every green herb" for their food. There were no carnivorous beasts. Yet after man's rebellion, parts of the animal creation began to devour one another, as we see today. This was not God's original plan, and it was not because of a specific sin on the animals' part that this happened. God subjected the animal creation to the same vanity (see note 6 at this verse) that man had come into, in the hope of redeeming them also. The animal creation, as well as the inanimate creation, will be delivered from the corruption that we now see, to walk in the glorious liberty of the children of God. It is not clear that every animal that has ever lived will be resurrected, but it is clear that the animal creation will be represented. The Scriptures declare this freedom for the creation when it speaks of the child playing with the snake; the wolf and the leopard dwelling peacefully with sheep; and the lion and lamb, and cow and bear dwelling together and eating straw like the ox (Isaiah 11:6-8 and 65:25). We know that in heaven, there are animals because the saints ride white horses at the Second Coming of Jesus (Revelation 19:14). In summary, the animal creation was plunged into the same degenerate state as mankind so that they could also be redeemed with us into liberty. Therefore, it can be expected that on the new earth where the saints will live for eternity (Revelation 21:1-7), animals will be living in harmony with each other and mankind as God originally designed in His first creation.

Note 6

The Greek word that was translated "vanity" here is the word "MATAIOTES," and it means "emptiness as to results" (Vine's Expository Dictionary). In this verse it specifically means "failing of the results designed, owing to sin" (Vine's Expository Dictionary). This is speaking of the non-human creation (see note 5 at this verse) being subjected to a corruption (Romans 8:21) that was not God's original design.

Romans 8:21

Because the creature itself also shall be delivered from the bondage of corruption into the glorious liberty of the children of God.

LIVING COMMENTARY

This doesn't necessarily mean that every animal that has ever lived will live again (that is a possibility). But it does mean the animal creation will be saved and exist in the new heaven and the new earth.

Note 7

God made creation involuntarily subject to the same corruption that mankind voluntarily entered into so that He could reunite us through redemption back into the glorious creation He originally intended for us to be.

Romans 8:22

For we know that the whole creation groaneth and travaileth in pain together until now.

LIVING COMMENTARY

Animals fight and kill just like people do. They are corrupted just like people. The Greek word "SYSTENAZO," which was translated "groaneth" in this verse, means "to moan jointly, i.e. (figuratively) experience a common calamity" (Strong's Concordance).

Note 8

Many times we are awestruck at the perfect balance that we see in nature. As glorious as it may seem, it is not God's best. Creation as we see it today has been corrupted and is far less than what God originally intended for it to be. All of creation is groaning and travailing together in pain and will not be relieved until the manifestation of the children of God (see note 4 at Romans 8:19).

Romans 8:23

And not only they, but ourselves also, which have the firstfruits of the Spirit, even we ourselves groan within ourselves, waiting for the adoption, to wit, the redemption of our body.

LIVING COMMENTARY

Paul was certainly enjoying all the benefits of being born again. He is not saying his existence was just a groan and travail. But even though he was rejoicing in his spirit, he was longing for the time when his flesh would be transformed into his glorified body and renewed soul. Then there would be no warfare against the wonderful liberty he had in his spirit. There would be perfect manifestation of life in spirit, soul, and body.

Note 9

The Holy Spirit is called the "firstfruits" of our salvation. Where there are first fruits, there has to be further fruit. Paul spoke of the Holy Spirit as being the earnest, or down payment, of our salvation with more to come (2 Corinthians 5:5 and Ephesians 1:14). As wonderful as our salvation is right here in this life, it is not complete. The flesh (see note 3 at Romans 7:18) is a constant source of trouble, and even victorious Christians groan for the time when we will be delivered from this flesh at the redemption of our bodies (2 Corinthians 5:1-4).

Note 10

The word "adoption" is used five times in the New Testament (Romans 8:15, 23, 9:4; Galatians 4:5; and Ephesians 1:5). People draw many analogies from this term that have merit, but this verse makes it very clear that the term "adoption" is referring to the time when we will receive our glorified bodies.

Note 11

Jesus purchased redemption for us—spirit, soul, and body—but our redemption is not completed yet. Our spirits are the only part of us that have experienced total redemption (see note 3 at Matthew 26:41). The English word "redemption" was translated from the Greek word "APO-LUTROSIS," and this Greek word means "(the act) ransom in full" (Strong's Concordance). However, it is specifying more than just the payment of a ransom; it includes the deliverance that comes as a result (Vine's Expository Dictionary). So Paul was speaking of the time when we will experience in our bodies what Jesus has already purchased for us. This can be illustrated by the way trading stamps are used. First, the stamps have to be purchased, and then they are redeemed for the desired product. The purchase is essential, but so is the redemption. No one really wants the stamps. They want what the stamps can be redeemed for. The purchase for our total salvation has already been made with the blood of Jesus, but our bodies are not redeemed yet. That is to say, we have not yet received all the benefits of that transaction in our physical bodies. That will take place at the Second Coming of the Lord, when we receive our new glorified bodies (see note 3 at Luke 24:39).

Romans 8:24

For we are saved by hope: but hope that is seen is not hope: for what a man seeth, why doth he yet hope for?

LIVING COMMENTARY

Paul had been speaking of the glory that is in us (Romans 8:17) and the day when we would receive glorified bodies and renewed souls that would perfectly manifest that glory. This is the hope to which he was referring. And we can't see the manifestation of that hope as long as we are alive in these bodies. But this is what we are believing for. Hope is seeing something that can't be seen (see my note at 2 Corinthians 4:18). Hope is seeing on the inside what you can't see on the outside. It appears to me like it is a positive imagination.

Imagination is the ability to see things in your heart that you can't see with your eyes, and this is what is being spoken of here. So, I believe you could take all the scriptures on hope and relate them to a positive imagination. See my note on hope at Romans 5:4. See these notes on imagination: Genesis 6:5, 11:6, 30:37 ,39; Joshua 1:8; 1 Chronicles 29:18; Psalms 2:1, 5:1, 42:5, 103:14, 143:5; Proverbs 15:28, 23:7, 29:18; Isaiah 26:3; Matthew 22:37; Luke 1:51; Acts 4:25, 16:19, 27:20; Romans 1:21, 8:24-25, 15:4, 13, 29; 2 Corinthians 10:5; Ephesians 1:18, 2:3, 12, 4:18; 1 Timothy 4:15; and Hebrews 11:1.

Note 12

Ephesians 2:8 says, "For by grace are ye saved through faith." Is there a contradiction between these two scriptures? Not at all. Putting faith in God's provision is what saves us, but hope is an important part of faith (see note 12 at Romans 5:4). This verse makes it very clear that hope is not based on what is seen. Someone who says, "I have no reason to hope," doesn't understand what hope is. Hope comes directly from God (Romans 15:13) through His **Word** (Romans 15:4).

Romans 8:25

> *But if we hope for that we see not, then do we with patience wait for it.*

LIVING COMMENTARY

Patience has a direct relationship to hope. If we don't have a strong hope, we can't have patience. Therefore, to increase our patience, we need to increase our hope. And if hope is a positive imagination, as I wrote in my note at Romans 8:24, then our positive imaginations are a vital part of patience. Patience comes easily to those with a strong hope.

Note 13

This verse definitely links patience and hope together. Hope produces patience. When we are in need of patience, we are in need of hope (see note 10 at Romans 5:3).

Romans 8:26

Likewise the Spirit also helpeth our infirmities: for we know not what we should pray for as we ought: but the Spirit itself maketh intercession for us with groanings which cannot be uttered.

LIVING COMMENTARY

The Greek word that was translated "helpeth" in this verse is "SUNANTILAMBANOMAI," and it means "to take hold of opposite together, i.e. co-operate (assist)" (Strong's Concordance). This means the Holy Spirit doesn't do this for us but with us. Many people have said that this groaning is speaking in tongues. But speaking in tongues can be uttered. This is speaking of a groaning in the spirit that is different than speaking in tongues. The Greek word "ALALETOS," which was translated "which cannot be uttered" in this verse, means "unspeakable" (Strong's Concordance). This is clearly referring to something other than speaking in tongues.

Note 1

The word "likewise" is stressing that in the same way that hope helps us endure until the redemption of our bodies (Romans 8:23), so the Holy Spirit helps us through the frailties of our flesh by interceding for us.

Note 2

The word "helpeth" was translated from the Greek word "SUNANTI-LAMBANOMAI," and it means "to take hold of opposite together, i.e. co-operate (assist)" (Strong's Concordance). It describes a union, not the Holy Spirit doing all the interceding for us. The Holy Spirit helps us as we are interceding, but He doesn't automatically do it for us.

Note 3

The Greek word that was translated "infirmities" in this verse is "ASTHENEIA," and it means "feebleness (of mind or body); by implication, malady; morally, frailty" (Strong's Concordance). This same word was translated "weakness" five times (1 Corinthians 2:3, 15:43; 2 Corinthians 12:9, 13:4; and Hebrews 11:34), so it is easy to see that this word is describing mental and moral weakness, not sickness. Paul went on to describe what these infirmities are when he said, "For we know not what we should pray for as we ought." The infirmities this scripture is speaking of are the weaknesses that come from not knowing how we should pray.

Note 4

This has been an encouraging scripture for countless believers. It is certain that none of us knows exactly how to pray in every situation. Therefore, it is very comforting to know that the Holy Spirit is there to help us. However, as mentioned in note 2 at this Romans 8:26 verse, He helps us; He doesn't do the interceding for us but through us. Even Jesus drew on this ministry of the Holy Spirit. It is written in John 11:33 and 38 that Jesus groaned in the Spirit twice when He raised Lazarus from the dead. What infirmity did Jesus have that He needed this ministry of the Holy Spirit? Jesus had no sin, but He did have an infirmity—His physical mind. Even a sinless human mind could not comprehend raising a man from the grave after four days. If Jesus needed the Holy Spirit to help Him when He didn't know how to pray, then certainly this should be an important ministry of the Holy Spirit in our lives.

Note 5

This intercession of the Holy Spirit is with "groanings which cannot be uttered." Some Spirit-filled Christians have said that this means groaning that cannot be uttered in our normal speech and therefore have said this is referring to speaking in tongues (see note 13 at Mark 16:17 and note 9 at Acts 2:4). Yet this is referring to an intercession that is different from speaking in tongues. In John 11:33 and 38, Jesus groaned in the Spirit twice. This is the exact terminology that is used here in Romans 8:26, and in John 11, it is easy to see that no words were uttered. It was exactly as the Scripture states, a groaning in the Spirit. All those who have the indwelling presence of the Holy Spirit have or will have this happen to them. Paul was referring to this in Galatians 4:19 when he spoke of travailing in birth for the Galatians. As explained in note 16 at John 11:33, this groaning of the Holy Spirit is not just of grief but a groan of anger and resistance against Satan's devices in people's lives. Many times Christians don't discern this, because they think they are the only ones grieved with their situations. But this is the Holy Spirit desiring to get into intercession with people against their problems. Although the groaning is unutterable, it can be discerned, and many times people react to this with audible groans or other outward acts. This has led to religious doctrines and traditions that are offensive to many people and are unscriptural. There is nothing wrong with people reacting to the inner working of the Holy Spirit as long as they don't confuse their reactions with the Holy Spirit's actions. This intercession cannot be uttered. Any counterfeits that religion may have produced only serve to illustrate that there has to be a genuine. The genuine groaning in the Spirit is priceless.

Romans 8:27

And he that searcheth the hearts knoweth what is the mind of the Spirit, because he maketh intercession for the saints according to the will of God.

LIVING COMMENTARY

"He that searcheth the hearts" is speaking of God the Father, and He knows perfectly well what the Holy Spirit is communicating. The Holy Spirit is always leading us and interceding with us for God's perfect will to come to pass in our lives. We don't always say things correctly, but when we intercede, the Holy Spirit translates our hearts' cry to the Father. The Father and the Holy Spirit communicate perfectly.

Note 6

"He that searcheth the hearts" is a reference to God. God knows our hearts, and He knows that the Holy Spirit will only intercede for the will of God to be done. The Holy Spirit is never at a loss as to how to convey our needs to the Father, as we sometimes are. That's the reason this ministry of the Holy Spirit is so important.

There is such oneness between the Father and the Holy Spirit that even His groanings are perfectly understood.

Romans 8:28

And we know that all things work together for good to them that love God, to them who are the called according to his purpose.

LIVING COMMENTARY

This is one of the most abused verses in the Bible. Many people have quoted this to say that whatever happens to us works out for our good. Observation can easily reveal that is not the case. First of all, this verse begins with the conjunction "And." This means everything that is being said here is dependent on the previous verse about the Holy Spirit making intercessions together with us. If we are not letting the Holy Spirit help us with intercession, then all things do not work together for good. Second, notice that this verse does not say that all things come from God, as it is often quoted. It is simply saying that if we are interceding in the power of the Holy Spirit, then we can take whatever the devil throws at us and make it work together for our good. That is a huge difference. If people interpret this verse to say that whatever comes our way is from God, then it makes them yield to their problems and removes them from the deliverance available through Christ (James 4:7). Notice also that this only works for those who love God. That's not everyone.

And it also only works for those who are the called according to His purpose. First John 3:8 says, "For this purpose the Son of God was manifested, that he might destroy the works of the devil." Those who are not resisting the problem but submit to their problems are not operating in the same calling that Jesus did. So whatever comes our way only works together for our good if we are interceding in the power of the Holy Spirit, if we love God, and if we are out to destroy the works of the devil.

> Those are big ifs that people who submit to problems as being God's will do not overcome.

Note 7

This is a very powerful verse with a wonderful promise, but it has been greatly abused and misapplied. This verse is not saying that everything that happens to us is from God and is used by Him to accomplish His purposes in our lives. The Bible doesn't teach that. Second Peter 3:9 makes a clear statement that the Lord is "not willing that any should perish, but that all should come to repentance." However, many men and women are perishing, because they have a choice. So, regarding salvation, God's will is not being done in the lives of many people. Concerning physical healing, the Bible states that Jesus has already provided healing for us (Isaiah 53:5, see note 2 at Matthew 8:17 and my note at 1 Peter 2:24) and that it is God's will for us to be healed (3 John 1:2). Yet not all of us are healed, and our sicknesses are not automatically working some redemptive purpose in our lives (see note 2 at John 9:2 and note 4 at John 11:4). Romans 8:28 begins with the word "and." This means that the statement about everything working together for our good was made after Paul had spoken of the Holy Spirit making intercession for us. If we are not cooperating with the Holy Spirit so that He can make intercession for us (see note 4 at Romans 8:26), then everything will not work together for our good. This verse also says this happens for those "that love God, to them who are the called." That means this doesn't apply to everyone. However, this verse has been used to try to convince even unbelievers that God is controlling the circumstances of their lives. That is not the message of this verse. Also this verse does not say that everything that comes our way is from God but rather that the Lord can work it together for our good through the intercession of the Holy Spirit. Romans 6:16 clearly states that if we yield to the devil, we become his slaves. The false teaching that nothing happens to us but what God wills or allows has caused many of us to yield to Satan's bondage instead of resisting him (James 4:7). People may cite experiences where they learned great lessons through tragedy and argue that these negative experiences are the only way the Lord could have accomplished His will in their lives. Again, that is not what the Bible teaches (see note 7 at Romans 3:4). Second Timothy 3:16-17 says, "All scripture is given by inspiration of God, and is profitable for doctrine, for reproof, for correction, for instruction in righteousness: That the man of God may be perfect, throughly furnished unto all good works." Second Timothy 3:17 says that God's Word will make us perfect, thoroughly furnished unto all good works. That means we don't have to learn through hardships. God's Word is for correction and reproof. Although not ordained by God for their good, people will experience tribulation. Therefore, they can and should learn from trials, but God's Word could have taught them the same thing with less grief. Those who submit to their problems because they believe God has brought them to teach them something are making a great mistake. That mistake is allowing the devil to inflict much pain in their lives.

Romans 8:28 is really promising that when we let the Holy Spirit intercede through us with these groanings that cannot be uttered, then we can rest assured that regardless of what the devil brings across our path, God can turn that situation around and work it together for our good.

Romans 8:29

For whom he did foreknow, he also did predestinate to be conformed to the image of his Son, that he might be the firstborn among many brethren.

LIVING COMMENTARY

This verse is the key to predestination (1 Peter 1:2). God only predestinates those who He foreknew would accept Him. He has never predestinated anyone to hell. Those He knew would accept Him as Savior are predestinated to become just like Jesus. As we renew our minds, this can happen to a degree in this life, but every true believer will be exactly like Jesus when we see Him (1 John 3:1-2).

Note 1

The word "foreknowledge" refers to God knowing who would accept His offer of salvation in advance of them actually doing it. The Scriptures teach that we (believers) were chosen in Christ before the foundation of the world (Ephesians 1:4). That's how infinite God's ability is to know our choices in advance. The Scriptures also reveal that there are some things God does not know. Twice in the book of Jeremiah, God said the fact that people would offer their children as sacrifices to demon gods never even came into His mind (Jeremiah 19:5 and 32:35). There are some things that God Himself said He had never foreseen. It is most probable that the Lord has the ability to know everything in advance, but He simply doesn't choose to exercise that ability in every situation. He told us to be wise concerning that which is good, and simple (or innocent) concerning that which is evil (Romans 16:19). He also told us to think on things that are true, honest, just, pure, lovely, of good report, and things that have virtue and praise (Philippians 4:8). That's the way He desires us to be because that's the way He is. Therefore, when God acted surprised that Adam and Eve had eaten of the forbidden tree, He probably was. As we have already pointed out from Ephesians 1:4, God chose us in Christ before the foundation of the world. He knew there would be a transgression and a need for redemption before man was even created. But apparently, He did not utilize His foreknowledge to the extent that He knew every move that man was making. No reason is given for this, but certainly one reason is that an absolute use of God's foreknowledge would hinder His relationship with man. God sent two angels to Sodom and Gomorrah to see if their actions were really as bad as had been reported to Him (Genesis 18:20-19:29). The Lord tested Abraham (Genesis 22:1-10). After the test, He said, "For now I know that thou fearest God, seeing thou hast not withheld thy son, thine only son from me" (Genesis 22:12). The Lord repented for choosing Saul to be king when He saw the way he turned out (1 Samuel 15:11). The Scripture contains many other examples besides these. God's ability to know all things in advance is limitless, but by His choice, God does not know every detail. Understanding foreknowledge provides the foundation for understanding predestination (see note 2 at this verse), calling (Romans 8:30), and election (1 Peter 1:2).

Note 2

This verse provides the key for unlocking the answer to the doctrine of predestination. Predestination is dependent on foreknowledge (see note 1 at this verse). The word "predestinate" means to predetermine. "Predestinate" and its variant "predestinated" are only used four times in the New Testament (Romans 8:29-30; Ephesians 1:5, and 11). People have interpreted this doctrine as saying that God predetermines everything in people's lives, including whether they will be saved or lost. This interpretation is not consistent with other doctrines or examples in Scripture. This belief will destroy people's motivation to fight evil and do good. If God predetermines everything that happens in people's lives, then everything that happens to them is God's will—even sin. That is not true. This verse limits God's predestination to only those whom

He foreknew. This means that only those people who God knew would accept His offer of salvation have been predestined. He does not predestine people to be saved or lost. Those whom He foreknew in Christ have been predestined to be conformed to the image of Christ. As we can tell by observation, God doesn't even force that to happen.

With some Christians, this will not occur until they receive their glorified bodies, but it will occur. God gave all people free will, and God will not violate that free will except in judgment. Even in judgment, God is only enforcing the choices that people have already made of their own free will. All people have a God-given right to go to hell if they want to. Just as in Romans 8:28, God works everything together for good for those who already love Him. And even then He does not take away their free will. Everything that happens to them is not good, and it is not from God. However, God, in His infinite wisdom, can work it together for good (see note 7 at Romans 8:28). Romans 8:29 is simply continuing to develop the truth that God is for man and has predetermined that those who have come to Him for salvation will be saved to the uttermost. Understood correctly, this verse provides great reassurance to believers that God is for them and working with them to bring them to the complete stature of the Lord Jesus Christ (Ephesians 4:13).

Note 3

This English word "firstborn" was translated from the Greek word "PROTOTOKOS." According to Strong's Concordance, this is a compound Greek word comprised of "PROTOS," which means "foremost (in time, place, order or importance)," and "TIKTO," which means "to produce (from seed…)." Therefore, this word "firstborn" could refer to either first in order or importance. Both of these applications are true of Jesus.

Although others were raised from the dead before Jesus (see note 3 at Mark 16:6), Jesus was the first one to be raised from the dead never to die again. Jesus was also the firstborn in the sense of importance, since His resurrection made all other resurrections possible. In context, Paul was stressing that we believers are predestined to be just like Jesus, then he drew from scripture that prophesied Jesus being the firstborn (Psalm 89:27). Therefore, the point being made is the extent that we will be conformed to the image of Jesus. There are other children who will become just like Jesus, and it is in this sense that "firstborn" is used here.

Romans 8:30

Moreover whom he did predestinate, them he also called: and whom he called, them he also justified: and whom he justified, them he also glorified.

LIVING COMMENTARY

As discussed in my note at Romans 8:29, God's foreknowledge doesn't make anything happen; it just knows what will happen. So, those who the Lord knew would accept Him were all called and justified as they believed on the sacrificial atonement of Jesus, and also glorified. Notice that we are already glorified. This hasn't happened in our flesh yet. That manifestation is still off in the future (1 Corinthians 15:42-43). But our born-again (see my note at John 3:3) spirits are right now just as Jesus is in heaven (see my notes at 1 John 4:17 and 2 Corinthians 5:17).

Romans 8:31

What shall we then say to these things? If God be for us, who can be against us?

LIVING COMMENTARY

God is for us. Who can successfully be against us? No one!

Note 4

Romans 8 came as the answer to the hopelessness of the flesh ever pleasing God that Paul declared in Romans 7. Romans 8 is full of victory through the indwelling presence and power of the Holy Spirit. Paul had just spoken of the Holy Spirit making intercession for us (Romans 8:26-27), God working all things together for our good (Romans 8:28), and us being predestined to be conformed to the image of Jesus (Romans 8:29). Here he was drawing a conclusion from all these things. If God be for us (which is exactly what he had been saying), then no one can successfully be against us. This is an exclamation of victory for the Spirit-controlled life that Paul continued teaching through the end of this chapter.

Romans 8:32

He that spared not his own Son, but delivered him up for us all, how shall he not with him also freely give us all things?

LIVING COMMENTARY

Any need we could have is infinitely inferior to the need we had for the forgiveness of our sins. That was accomplished by God the Father giving His own Son in sacrifice for our debt. If God loved us enough to pay that great price, there should be no doubt that our loving heavenly Father is more than willing to meet all other needs. Notice the phrase "freely give." This was translated from the Greek word "CHARIZOMAI," and this Greek word means "to grant as a favor, i.e. gratuitously, in kindness, pardon or rescue" (Strong's Concordance). This is stressing that this is something the Lord will do by grace, not because of our performance.

Note 5

Paul had already used this same reasoning in Romans 5:6-10.

Romans 8:33

Who shall lay any thing to the charge of God's elect? It is God that justifieth.

LIVING COMMENTARY

The highest judge in the universe (God the Father) has acquitted us; therefore, all other judges have no authority to accuse us of anything. And since we stand forgiven by God, He will never bring any accusation against us. He's the One who forgave us.

Note 6

If Almighty God has dropped all charges against us because of our faith in Christ, then why should we let the accusations of others bother us?

Romans 8:34

Who is he that condemneth? It is Christ that died, yea rather, that is risen again, who is even at the right hand of God, who also maketh intercession for us.

LIVING COMMENTARY

Romans 8:33 said that God had forgiven us, so we can be assured that He won't accuse us. He has wiped our slate clean. Here, Paul assured us that Jesus won't condemn us. He's the one who redeemed us from condemnation. Therefore, we can be certain that any condemnation or accusations against us are not from God the Father or God the Son. Those who interpret Romans 8:1 as saying there is only no condemnation toward us when we are walking in the Spirit don't connect this verse with that one. But if you put them together, you see there is no condemnation from God toward us—period (see my note at Romans 8:1).

Note 7

Jesus is making intercession for us. Therefore, Jesus couldn't be the one ministering condemnation to us. Intercession and condemnation are opposites.

Romans 8:35

Who shall separate us from the love of Christ? shall tribulation, or distress, or persecution, or famine, or nakedness, or peril, or sword?

LIVING COMMENTARY

Pay careful attention to the way this verse is stated. It doesn't say "who can separate us from our love FOR Christ." There are many examples of believers walking away from the Lord because of persecution, famine, nakedness, peril, and sword. But those things will never stop Christ from loving us. That's awesome!

Note 8

Neither people nor external things can separate us from the love of Christ. The only way for believers to be exempted from the love of Christ is to deny their faith in Christ (see note 5 at Acts 5:5 and note 4 at Acts 12:23).

Romans 8:36

As it is written, For thy sake we are killed all the day long; we are accounted as sheep for the slaughter.

LIVING COMMENTARY

This was quoted from Psalm 44:22.

Romans 8:37

Nay, in all these things we are more than conquerors through him that loved us.

Note 9

How can we be more than conquerors? Conquerors have the victory and the spoils of war, but they have to fight to get them. We are more than conquerors because we have victory and all the spoils of war, but we didn't do the fighting. Jesus fought and won this battle for us, and all we have to do is receive the benefits. That's being more than conquerors.

Romans 8:38

For I am persuaded, that neither death, nor life, nor angels, nor principalities, nor powers, nor things present, nor things to come,

LIVING COMMENTARY

It's wonderful that Paul was persuaded of this. I'm happy for him. But you and I must be persuaded of this in order to benefit from it. This is all-inclusive. Death and life cover it all. Also, everything that now exists and anything that ever will exist covers it all too. This is tremendous assurance that nothing can stop Christ from loving us.

Romans 8:39

Nor height, nor depth, nor any other creature, shall be able to separate us from the love of God, which is in Christ Jesus our Lord.

LIVING COMMENTARY

These verses are awesome! But religion makes them of none effect in many Christians' lives (Mark 7:13). Religion says the Lord separates us from His love for a multitude of reasons. Many Christians live in constant dread of doing something that will cause them to lose their salvation and this love of God. That is totally against what these verses are saying. See Romans 3:4.

ROMANS

CHAPTER NINE

Romans 9:1

I say the truth in Christ, I lie not, my conscience also bearing me witness in the Holy Ghost,

---

LIVING COMMENTARY

Paul is about to make such a radical statement that most people would not believe it. So, he guarantees its accuracy before he says it.

Note 1

Paul was going to great lengths to verify that what he was saying was the truth. This needed to be stated because Paul's statement in Romans 9:3 would certainly have been interpreted as a hyperbole (exaggeration) if there had not been some clarification.

Romans 9:2

That I have great heaviness and continual sorrow in my heart.

LIVING COMMENTARY

Paul had just spoken that he was never separated from the love of God. There are also many times where he said he continually rejoiced, and he commanded us to do the same (Philippians 4:4). Here, he spoke of having great heaviness and continual sorrow. So, we see that both of these emotions coexisted in Paul at the same time. Indeed every godly person has great joy and thankfulness for all that God has done and yet, at the same time, has great sorrow for those who don't know that joy.

Note 2

This is not a contradiction to other statements by Paul (2 Corinthians 7:13; Galatians 5:22-23; Philippians 1:4, 18, 2:2, 18, 4:4; Colossians 1:24; 1 Thessalonians 3:9, 5:16; and Philemon 7). Paul did operate in the joy of the Holy Ghost, just as he told others to do. However, there was this continual heaviness and sorrow in his heart when it came to the unbelieving Jews. This is comparable to those who have lost loved ones who were very dear to them. In the process of time, they "get over it" to the point that they may be considered very joyful people, but there is always that vacancy in their hearts. Similarly, Paul was rejoicing in the Lord, but he always had this great longing in his heart for the salvation of the Jews.

Romans 9:3

For I could wish that myself were accursed from Christ for my brethren, my kinsmen according to the flesh:

LIVING COMMENTARY

Jesus said in John 15:13, "Greater love hath no man than this, that a man lay down his life for his friends." Paul is saying that he would not only sacrifice his physical life but his eternal soul if that would produce salvation for the Jews. This degree of love cannot be found in man by himself. This is the love of God that was expressed in Jesus living in Paul (Galatians 2:20).

Note 3

What a statement! Paul was saying that he would go to hell in the place of the Jews if that would accomplish their salvation. This is nothing less than the perfect "AGAPE" love (see note 4 at John 13:35) that Jesus demonstrated when He died for our sins. Although this desire on Paul's part is commendable, there is nothing that he could have accomplished that Jesus hadn't already accomplished completely. Paul was specifically commissioned by the Lord to go to the Gentiles, yet we see him repeatedly going to the Jews, even after he said he wouldn't do that anymore (see note 2 at Acts 13:14). Paul even went to Jerusalem, apparently against the instruction of the Holy Ghost (see note 4 at Acts 21:4), and was more than willing to lay down his life for the sake of the Jews (Acts 21:13). This illustrated his great love for the Jewish people as he was describing here.

Romans 9:4

Who are Israelites; to whom pertaineth the adoption, and the glory, and the covenants, and the giving of the law, and the service of God, and the promises;

LIVING COMMENTARY

The Jews had all the things listed here in Romans 9:4-5 going for them, but their rejection of Jesus and the grace He offered voided all of these advantages. Faith in what Jesus did for us trumps all of the good works we can do. The word "adoption" was never used in the Old Testament, although the concept was there. The Lord told Pharaoh that Israel was His son (Exodus 4:22). Moses reminded the Israelites that they were the children of the Lord their God (Deuteronomy 14:1). Jeremiah said that God was a father to Israel and that Ephraim was His firstborn (Jeremiah 31:9).

Romans 9:5

Whose are the fathers, and of whom as concerning the flesh Christ came, who is over all, God blessed for ever. Amen.

LIVING COMMENTARY

The Jews had a rich, godly history. All the patriarchs were their forefathers. Jesus came to be the Savior of the Jews. They should have been the first to accept Christ, but as a whole, they rejected their Messiah.

Romans 9:6

Not as though the word of God hath taken none effect. For they are not all Israel, which are of Israel:

LIVING COMMENTARY

Paul had presented the pitiful picture of the Jewish nation rejecting the Lord. Now he is quick to add that doesn't mean every Jew had rejected Jesus. Paul himself was a Jew. He shows that the true Jew is not just a physical Jew but a spiritual Jew. This is the same point he made in Romans 2:28-29, which says, "For he is not a Jew, which is one outwardly; neither is that circumcision, which is outward in the flesh: But he is a Jew, which is one inwardly; and circumcision is that of the heart, in the spirit, and not in the letter; whose praise is not of men, but of God."

Note 1

Paul had just expressed a compassion for the Jewish race that was so strong that he was willing to be damned in their place if that would have produced their salvation (see note 3 at Romans 9:3). As he said in Romans 9:2, this produced "great heaviness and continual sorrow." According to Romans 9:4-5, one of the reasons he longed for the salvation of the Jews so intensely was because he himself was a Jew and he was acutely aware that Christ was the Jewish Messiah. How ironic it was that Jesus came unto His own and His own received Him not (John 1:11). Here Paul began to relate the reasoning that had enabled him to cope with the Jews' tragic rejection of Jesus. The promises made to Abraham and his descendants were not made to his physical descendants but to his spiritual seed (Romans 9:6-8). Therefore, the true people of God have not rejected their Messiah. There is a body of believers comprised of believing Jews and Gentiles, and they are the true Israel of God. To back this up, Paul cited the two Old Testament examples of Isaac

(Romans 9:9) and Jacob (Romans 9:10-13) to illustrate how the blessing of God was not passed on through the normal method of inheritance but through election. Paul had expressed some of these same thoughts twice before in this epistle, and he used the same reasoning in his letter to the Galatians (Romans 2:28-29, 4:12-16; Galatians 3:16, and 6:16).

Romans 9:7

Neither, because they are the seed of Abraham, are they all children: but, In Isaac shall thy seed be called.

LIVING COMMENTARY

A true Jew isn't a physical descendant of Abraham but a spiritual one who has the same faith that Abraham had. Isaac wasn't Abraham's firstborn, who traditionally received the greater inheritance. But Isaac was the son of promise and, in God's eyes (which are the only eyes that count), the only covenant child (Genesis 22:2). Genesis 21:12 is the Old Testament verse being cited.

Romans 9:8

That is, They which are the children of the flesh, these are not the children of God: but the children of the promise are counted for the seed.

LIVING COMMENTARY

Isaac, through whom the Jewish nation descended, was not the firstborn of Abraham. But he was the promised son through whom God said He would bless all nations of the earth (Genesis 21:12 and 22:18). Likewise, Abraham's true children are not physical descendants but those who have received the promise. The application of this for us today is that God doesn't count as His children those who are of the flesh; i.e., of their own efforts or righteousness. The only people who are truly His are those who have been born of the Spirit and not the flesh (see my notes at John 3:3-7).

Note 2

Paul cited six Old Testament references to make his point that God's promises to Abraham and his "seed" were made to the spiritual offspring of Abraham, not the physical. First, Isaac was not the firstborn son of Abraham, entitled to the birthright and blessing, yet he obtained both because he was chosen by God. Next, Jacob was not the firstborn either, yet he was chosen by God. These two examples confirm that God's promise was not inherited by birth. Paul also pointed out that before Jacob and his twin brother, Esau, were born, God told Rebekah that the elder would serve the younger. They weren't even born yet, so they had not done any good or evil that caused God to make this choice. This means that the blessing of Abraham was not obtained by individual performance either but was based solely on God's choosing by grace.

Romans 9:9

For this is the word of promise, At this time will I come, and Sara shall have a son.

LIVING COMMENTARY

This is a quote from Genesis 18:10: "And he said, I will certainly return unto thee according to the time of life; and, lo, Sarah thy wife shall have a son. And Sarah heard it in the tent door, which was behind him," and Genesis 18:14: "Is any thing too hard for the LORD? At the time appointed I will return unto thee, according to the time of life, and Sarah shall have a son."

Romans 9:10

And not only this; but when Rebecca also had conceived by one, even by our father Isaac;

LIVING COMMENTARY

This principle of the true heir not being just the firstborn but the son of promise wasn't limited to Isaac. This was also the case with Jacob, Isaac's second-born son. This is showing that the inheritance isn't passed on by just physical or natural selection. It was by God's election. Salvation isn't inherited by our own works. We have to be born again (see my note at John 3:3).

Romans 9:11

(For the children being not yet born, neither having done any good or evil, that the purpose of God according to election might stand, not of works, but of him that calleth;)

LIVING COMMENTARY

The Lord chose Jacob before he was born. Therefore, it wasn't according to any effort of his part that he was chosen. It was just the election of God. This choice stood to illustrate that it is not natural effort that obtains the blessing of God.

Note 3

Paul was citing these Old Testament examples to show that those who were considered the children of Abraham were not his physical descendants, but they were chosen by God, in this case, before they were born. This proves God's election is not based on birth or performance (see note 2 at Matthew 9:8). However, some people have interpreted this verse and the quotation from Malachi 1:2-3 in Romans 1:13 as an example of extreme predestination. They reason that Esau was hated by God before he was born (see note 5 at Romans 9:12). Therefore, some people are predestined by God for damnation, while some are elected to salvation before they are ever born. This means people have no choice in the matter. That is not what these verses are saying. As explained in note 2 at Romans 8:29, God's predestination is based on His foreknowledge (see note 1 at Romans 8:29). Only those whom God foreknew would accept Him have been elected and predestinated. God did not force Jacob and Esau to make the choices they made. But through His foreknowledge,

He was able to foresee who would respond to Him, and that is the one He chose.

Note 4

The doctrine of election is based on God's foreknowledge (see note 1 at Romans 8:29) the same way that predestination is based on His foreknowledge (see note 2 at Romans 8:29). This can be clearly seen in 1 Peter 1:2, which says we are "elect according to the foreknowledge of God the Father." God does not choose people independent of their free will. Instead, through His foreknowledge, He knows who will choose Him, and those are the individuals He elects to be His own.

Romans 9:12

It was said unto her, The elder shall serve the younger.

LIVING COMMENTARY

Rebecca had problems during her pregnancy. She asked the Lord what was happening, and the Lord said to her, "Two nations are in thy womb, and two manner of people shall be separated from thy bowels; and the one people shall be stronger than the other people; and the elder shall serve the younger" (Genesis 25:23). This shows God's calling and election is according to grace and not performance. But it does not show, as some teach, that the Lord predestines some to blessing and others to cursing. That is not so. All people have the right to choose for themselves (Deuteronomy 30:19). Jacob was selected to continue the blessing of Abraham through his lineage, but Esau wasn't chosen to be cursed. He chose to despise his birthright (Genesis 25:29-34), thereby bringing God's curse on him. See my note at Romans 9:13.

Note 5

There is no record in Scripture that the individual Esau ever served the individual Jacob. However, Esau's posterity (Edomites, Genesis 32:3) did serve Jacob's posterity (1 Chronicles 18:13). Although Paul was making reference to the actual birth of these two individuals, the prophecy given to Rebekah and its fulfillment were referring to the nations that came from these men.

Romans 9:13
As it is written, Jacob have I loved, but Esau have I hated.

LIVING COMMENTARY

This verse and Romans 9:10-12 are often used to say that individuals have no choice in whether they serve God or not. Some are predestined to salvation and others to damnation. Nothing could be further from the truth. All people have a choice as to their relationship with the Lord (Romans 10:13). It is true that each of us has callings and gifts different from each other that we have from birth. We don't have a choice as to what the Lord calls us to do. Jacob was chosen before his birth to be the one through whom Abraham's blessing would continue. But Esau wasn't predestined to be hated. God had plans for him. They just weren't plans to be the one through whom the blessing of Abraham passed on. But Esau rebelled at God. He despised his birthright (Genesis 25:29-34) and married outside of God's commands (Genesis 26:34-35). Esau hated Jacob (Genesis 27:41), who was the blessed of the Lord, thereby bringing the curse of Genesis 12:3 on himself. The Old Testament passage this verse is quoting is from Malachi 1:2-3. The Lord didn't say he loved Jacob and hated Esau when they were still in Rebecca's womb. This was spoken hundreds of years after their deaths. The Lord had different callings on these twins' lives that were according to His grace and not their works. But the Lord didn't predestine Esau to be hated. This came as the result of Esau's choices and actions. This was spoken about Esau and his descendants hundreds of years after Esau's death to show that the one God chose did excel. God chose the right one. See my note at Malachi 1:3.

Note 6

God did not hate Esau and love Jacob while they were still in their mother's womb. He did choose Jacob over Esau as the inheritor of Abraham's blessing before they were born, but Esau could have walked with God and have been blessed by God if he had chosen to do so. Malachi 1:2-3 says, "I loved Jacob, and I hated Esau." This was written in approximately 557-525 B.C., thousands of years after the birth of Esau and Jacob, so this is not speaking of God hating Esau at birth. There is no mention in Scripture that God hated the individual Esau. This reference to Esau was referring to the nation of Edom (Esau's descendants) in the same way that the term Israel often referred to the entire nation of Israel, not the individual (Genesis 32:28). God was saying that He had rejected the nation of Edom and had chosen the nation of Israel. Paul quoted from Malachi, not to show that God hated Esau and loved Jacob while they were still in their mother's womb, but rather to confirm that the choice God made before they were born, based on His foreknowledge (see note 1 at Romans 8:29), was the right choice. Jacob went on to become a mighty man of God, and Esau despised the things of God.

God's choice of Jacob didn't cause this to happen. This quotation from Malachi simply confirms that God's foreknowledge was accurate. Jacob was called to a higher position than his brother, Esau, before they were born, but that does not display any rejection of Esau on God's part. That is comparable to God choosing certain people to be pastors while others are called to be deacons. The deacons are not inferior to the pastors. They are simply called to different positions. Jacob and Esau were called to different positions before they had done any good or evil, to illustrate that election was not based on performance but choice.

Romans 9:14

What shall we say then? Is there unrighteousness with God? God forbid.

Note 7

Paul was seeking to stop anyone from interpreting his statements in a way that would make it look like God was unfair in His dealings with man. God can extend mercy to an individual without treating others unjustly. Just as in the parable that Jesus gave in Matthew 20:1-16, God treats everyone fairly, but to some He chooses to give extra mercy. Does that mean He is unjust? Not at all. If God chooses to call individuals to account for their actions and choices they have made of their own free will, He is completely justified to do that at any time. In Luke 13:1-9, Jesus mentioned the people whom Pilate had killed and mingled their blood with the sacrifices, and the people on whom the tower in Siloam fell and were killed. He raised the question (Luke 13:2 and 4), "Were these people worse sinners than others to suffer this judgment?" He answered His own question by saying that all of them deserved such judgment, but God in His mercy had spared them (see note 2 at Luke 13:2). He then immediately followed that with the parable about the man with an unproductive tree in his vineyard. He was going to cut down this dead tree and replace it, but the vinedresser interceded for the tree. The owner then gave him some extra time to see if he could revive it (see note 1 at Luke 13:6).

Likewise, people all deserve judgment, but through things such as the intercession of others, God will sometimes show extra mercy to certain individuals. However, if He chose not to extend mercy to anyone and He called everyone's accounts due, He would be completely justified in doing so. It's His choice. God has never brought judgment on anyone without being righteous in doing so. Likewise, He has never extended mercy to any individual that made His treatment of someone else unfair.

Romans 9:15

For he saith to Moses, I will have mercy on whom I will have mercy, and I will have compassion on whom I will have compassion.

LIVING COMMENTARY

The Lord is totally within His rights to show mercy to whom He wills. That's what this verse is saying. But it doesn't say the Lord curses whomever He chooses.

That's not so. No one has ever come under God's judgment unjustly.

Romans 9:16

So then it is not of him that willeth, nor of him that runneth, but of God that sheweth mercy.

Note 8

There is a very subtle trap that many people who have been used of God fall into. They see what God has accomplished through them, and they begin reasoning, "God must use me because of my great faithfulness." But that is not the case. God has never had anyone qualified working for Him yet. God is a lot more merciful than we are faithful.

Romans 9:17

For the scripture saith unto Pharaoh, Even for this same purpose have I raised thee up, that I might shew my power in thee, and that my name might be declared throughout all the earth.

LIVING COMMENTARY

This verse is referencing Exodus 9:16. The Scripture does say that God hardened Pharaoh's heart. But it also says Pharaoh hardened his own heart toward God (Exodus 8:15, 32; and 9:34). I believe Pharaoh hardened his heart first, and after he had chosen that path, God just enforced his decision. Pharaoh proclaimed himself to be a god and demanded worship. I know the Spirit of the Lord convicted him about this. But when he hardened his heart and persisted in that deception, the Lord used his own choice to bring glory to Himself. But He wasn't unjust. Pharaoh chose this of his own free will.

Note 9

Some people have taken this word from God about Pharaoh and made a paragraph out of it. They have drawn conclusions that God predetermines everything in people's lives to the degree that free will doesn't exist.

That is not what the Lord was speaking of here. We can be assured that Pharaoh had already had ample opportunity to respond to God prior to the time that God began to harden his heart. Since Pharaoh had already made his choice, even to the point that he proclaimed himself to be a deity and commanded the Egyptians to worship him, God was not unrighteous in bringing him into judgment for this. God did not make Pharaoh the way he was, but God used, for His glory, the way Pharaoh had chosen to be. God exalted Pharaoh and gave him leadership of the nation, knowing full well how he would respond to His demands to let His people go.

Since Pharaoh had already hardened his heart toward God, God was not unjust in continuing to harden his heart further until His glory was manifest completely. This verse is depicting God as using Pharaoh's hardened heart for His glory, but Pharaoh had already had his chance. God simply upheld his choice and received glory through His triumph over Pharaoh and all his host.

Romans 9:18

Therefore hath he mercy on whom he will have mercy, and whom he will he hardeneth.

LIVING COMMENTARY

The Lord only hardens people's hearts after they have chosen that path. See my note at Romans 9:17.

Romans 9:19

Thou wilt say then unto me, Why doth he yet find fault? For who hath resisted his will?

Note 10

The argument that Paul was refuting here is not a correct interpretation of what he had said. This is comparable to his statement in Romans 6:1 where he said, "What shall we say then? Shall we continue in sin, that grace may abound?" Paul knew someone would interpret his teaching on grace to be advocating sin; therefore, he spoke their wrong conclusion and then refuted it. Likewise here, he stated an abusive interpretation of his statements and then proceeded to counter it.

Romans 9:20

Nay but, O man, who art thou that repliest against God? Shall the thing formed say to him that formed it, Why hast thou made me thus?

Note 11

The truth that Paul was expressing here is the overall point that was made in the book of Job. God never did explain Himself to Job as Job had insisted that He do. Instead, God rebuked Job for his "know-it-all" attitude (Job 38:18). God basically asked Job what right he had to maintain his own integrity at the expense of God's (Job 40:8). Job got the message when God spoke to him from a whirlwind, and he humbled himself (Job 42:2-6). Paul's message should draw the same response from us.

Romans 9:21

Hath not the potter power over the clay, of the same lump to make one vessel unto honour, and another unto dishonour?

Note 12

Paul was drawing an illustration from an Old Testament passage of Scripture, Jeremiah 18:3-6. In that passage, God sent Jeremiah to the potter's house to learn a lesson. The potter was making a vessel; it was marred, so he remade it. The Lord spoke to Jeremiah and said, "O house of Israel, cannot I do with you as this potter?...Behold, as the clay is in the potter's hand, so are ye in mine hand, O house of Israel" (Jeremiah 18:6). From this illustration, some people have drawn a wrong conclusion that the Lord creates some people evil and predestined to a life of damnation, not by their choice, but by God's. However, a closer look at the passage in Jeremiah and its context will show that is not the case. First of all, the potter started to create a good vessel, but the clay was marred. Whose fault was that? It wasn't the potter's fault. The clay was faulty. The potter took this imperfect clay, and instead of discarding it, he refashioned it into another vessel that may not have been worth nearly as much as his original design but was still useful. Likewise, the Lord does not create certain individuals for destruction. However, some do become marred by their own choices, not due to any fault of the Creator. Instead of just removing them from the earth, the Lord will endure (Romans 9:22) their atrocities. He may even put them in great positions of authority, such as He did with Pharaoh, so that He may manifest His great power through His victory over them and their devices. God can still use someone who has rejected Him, in the same way that a potter can take a marred piece of clay and find some use for it. By continuing to read the context of Jeremiah's experience with the potter, it can be clearly seen that the Lord does not do these things against the will of the individual. In Jeremiah 18:7-10, the Lord said that when He purposes evil or good against a nation, if that nation repents, then God will change His plans for them. That undeniably states that man's choice influences God's choice.

Romans 9:22

What if God, willing to shew his wrath, and to make his power known, endured with much longsuffering the vessels of wrath fitted to destruction:

LIVING COMMENTARY

Notice that this verse says God endured with much long-suffering these individuals. That shows that He didn't just damn some godly people and choose this course for them against their wills. They were already in rebellion toward God before the Lord established their own choices and turned them into vessels of wrath to accomplish His will.

Romans 9:23

And that he might make known the riches of his glory on the vessels of mercy, which he had afore prepared unto glory,

LIVING COMMENTARY

This can be clearly seen in the story of the Exodus. The Lord endured with much long-suffering the Egyptian Pharaohs who oppressed His people, Israel. And by allowing Pharaoh to put His people in such a bad situation, it was even more glorious when the Lord used Moses to bring Egypt to its knees.

Romans 9:24

Even us, whom he hath called, not of the Jews only, but also of the Gentiles?

Note 13

Paul had started explaining in Romans 9:6 that there was a true people of God, not based on nationality, but on faith in God. Here he gave four quotes (Romans 9:25-29) from two Old Testament prophets to show that this was not a new concept but had been prophesied hundreds of years before.

Romans 9:25

As he saith also in Osee, I will call them my people, which were not my people; and her beloved, which was not beloved.

LIVING COMMENTARY

This is a quotation from Hosea 2:23.

Romans 9:26

And it shall come to pass, that in the place where it was said unto them, Ye are not my people; there shall they be called the children of the living God.

LIVING COMMENTARY

This is a quotation from Hosea 1:10. This is speaking of the Gentiles (who had not been God's people) becoming the children of the living God. Thank You, Jesus.

Romans 9:27

Esaias also crieth concerning Israel, Though the number of the children of Israel be as the sand of the sea, a remnant shall be saved:

LIVING COMMENTARY

Most scholars believe this is quoting Isaiah 10:20-23.

Note 14

This verse could read, "**only** a remnant shall be saved." That is the point Paul was making. His next reference from Isaiah (Romans 9:29) complements this one, and it is clearly stressing that there will be very few Jews who are truly God's people.

Romans 9:28

For he will finish the work, and cut it short in righteousness: because a short work will the Lord make upon the earth.

LIVING COMMENTARY

If I had been reading this in Paul's day, I would have thought this meant that the return of the Lord was imminent. We now know that there were at least 2,000 years before the return of the Lord. But if Paul was saying it would be a short work 2,000 years ago, then it certainly is a lot closer now than it was when he wrote it.

Romans 9:29

And as Esaias said before, Except the Lord of Sabaoth had left us a seed, we had been as Sodoma, and been made like unto Gomorrha.

LIVING COMMENTARY

This is a quotation from Isaiah 1:9. If the Lord hadn't shown mercy upon Israel, they would have been destroyed as completely as Sodom and Gomorrah were (Genesis 19:24-25). That would be true of all of us if we only got what we deserved. Praise God we don't get justice. Through Jesus we get mercy and grace.

Romans 9:30

What shall we say then? That the Gentiles, which followed not after righteousness, have attained to righteousness, even the righteousness which is of faith.

Note 1

Paul was saying that this was the conclusion or the summary of his point in this chapter.

Note 2

This is another one of Paul's radical statements. How can it be that people who are not seeking to be righteous can become righteous? The answer to this question lies in God's grace. By grace, God has provided righteousness for all people, regardless of their actions. If people will believe and receive this gift, God will reckon them righteous. This is what happened to the Gentiles. They had a reputation for not seeking God (Ephesians 4:17-19 and 1 Peter 4:3), yet the Gentiles as a whole accepted God's gift of salvation, while the Jews as a whole, who were seeking after God, rejected His gift. The reason for this was given by Paul in Romans 9:32-33 (see note 5 at Romans 9:32). People who don't understand God's grace will always be confused and unbelieving that a person who hasn't lived a morally good life can be righteous in the sight of God, while a morally good person can be unrighteous in His sight. Righteousness is based on faith, not actions.

Romans 9:31

But Israel, which followed after the law of righteousness, hath not attained to the law of righteousness.

LIVING COMMENTARY

There are two different approaches to obtaining right standing (righteousness) with God. One approach is to try and earn right standing with God through our performances. That's what this verse is saying the nation of Israel as a whole had tried to do. That approach will always fail because we fail. We might do things better than someone else, but all of us have sinned and come short of the glory of God (Romans 3:23). Therefore, the only approach to righteousness that works is that of faith. We can't earn God's favor; we just have to receive it as a gift by faith (Ephesians 2:8-9).

Romans 9:32

Wherefore? Because they sought it not by faith, but as it were by the works of the law. For they stumbled at that stumblingstone;

Note 3

Why is it that a person who is seeking so hard to please God can be rejected, while a person who has not sought God at all can come into a righteous relationship with Him? This is an important question, and its answer is one of the most profound doctrines in Scripture. Paul gave the answer to his own question. The answer is faith and its object. The Jews were zealous (Romans 10:2) for the things of God, but their faith was in themselves. They were trusting that they could earn God's favor by their acts of righteousness. On the other hand, the Gentiles had no holiness to trust in. So when they heard the Gospel that Jesus paid man's debt, they readily accepted His "gift" of salvation, while the religious Jews could not abandon their trust in themselves for salvation. This same problem exists today. Millions of church people are trying to live holy lives, but they do not have a true faith in Jesus as their Savior. If they were to stand before God and He was to ask them what they had done to deserve salvation, they would immediately start recounting all their acts of holiness: church attendance, financial giving, etc. Regardless of how good their actions are compared to others, they always come short of the perfect standard of God (see notes 5-6 at Romans 3:23). The only response to this kind of question that would grant them entrance to heaven is for them to say that their only claim to salvation is faith in Jesus as their Savior. Anything more or less is damned.

Note 4

There is a difference between works of faith (1 Thessalonians 1:3 and 2 Thessalonians 1:11) and works of the Law (Galatians 2:16; 3:2, 5, and 10). The difference is not in the action but in the attitude. A work of the Law is some act of righteousness or holiness that is being done to earn the favor of God. A work of faith may be the same act of righteousness or holiness, but it is done as a labor of love (1 Thessalonians 1:3). It is done not to obtain favor but in gratitude for the favor that has already been extended to us in Christ. Works of the Law and faith in Jesus are opposites (Romans 11:6).

Note 5

Jesus is the "stumblingstone" that Paul was speaking of. God has placed Jesus directly in the path of every person. Those who fail to put their complete trust in Jesus because they are trusting in themselves will stumble and fall into hell, while those who believe in Him will never be ashamed (Romans 9:33).

Romans 9:33

> As it is written, Behold, I lay in Sion a stumblingstone and rock of offence: and whosoever believeth on him shall not be ashamed.

LIVING COMMENTARY

Compare with Isaiah 8:14-15.

Note 6

Those who are offended at Jesus are the ones who are trusting in themselves. They feel they will be accepted with God because they think they are holy enough on their own. It is humbling to admit that all of our righteousness is as filthy rags (Isaiah 64:6). This is why the religious people have always been the persecutors of true Christians (see note 6 at Mark 15:10).

Note 7

This quotation does not appear in the Old Testament in these exact words. It is most probable that Paul was quoting the last part of Isaiah 28:16. If so, Paul substituted the words "be ashamed" for Isaiah's words, "make haste." In the context of war, making haste is descriptive of a person who has been shamed in battle.

ROMANS

CHAPTER TEN

Romans 10:1

Brethren, my heart's desire and prayer to God for Israel is, that they might be saved.

LIVING COMMENTARY

Compare with Romans 9:3.

Romans 10:2

For I bear them record that they have a zeal of God, but not according to knowledge.

Note 1

This scripture goes contrary to many religious teachings. Many people believe that it's not necessary to believe the right thing—just as long as people believe something, they'll be all right. However, Paul disproved this kind of thinking by saying in this passage that their zeal was without knowledge and therefore they were not saved. The Jews were very zealous about their religion, but that wasn't enough. It's not enough just to believe; people have to believe the truth. Even those who are sincere can be sincerely wrong. Jesus said, "And ye shall know the truth, and the truth shall make you free" (John 8:32).

Romans 10:3

> For they being ignorant of God's righteousness, and going about to establish their own righteousness, have not submitted themselves unto the righteousness of God.

Note 2

This verse describes the condition of much of the church today. Most people are unaware that there are two kinds of righteousness. Only one type of righteousness is acceptable to God. One form of righteousness that Paul described here is one's own righteousness (Philippians 3:9). These are the acts of holiness that we do in an attempt to fulfill the commands of the Old Testament Law. This is an imperfect righteousness because human nature is imperfect and incapable of fulfilling the Law (see note 7 at Romans 8:3). Therefore, our own righteousness, which is according to the Law, is inadequate. Isaiah said it this way in Isaiah 64:6, "All our righteousnesses are as filthy rags." In contrast, God's righteousness is perfect. Also, God's righteousness is not something that we do but something that we receive as a gift through faith in Christ (see note 5 at Romans 10:5). Paul made it very clear in this verse that it's not possible to trust in our own righteousness and in God's righteousness also. If we believe that we must earn God's acceptance by our holy actions, we cannot be believing in God's righteousness, which is a gift. It has to be one or the other; we cannot mix the two.

Righteousness is not what Jesus has done for us plus some minimum standard of holiness that we have to accomplish (Romans 11:6).

Romans 10:4

For Christ is the end of the law for righteousness to every one that believeth.

Note 3

The Greek word that was translated "end" here is "TELOS," and it means "the point aimed at as a limit, i.e. (by implication) the conclusion of an act or state (termination...)" (Strong's Concordance). This verse does not say that Christ is the end of the Law but rather that Christ is the end of the Law for the purpose of righteousness. This means that people no longer become righteous, or justified in the sight of God, by how well they perform the deeds of the Law (see note 2 at Luke 1:6). However, the Law still has useful purposes for New Testament believers. The Old Testament Law still reveals to us God's holiness, which we should seek to emulate. It must be understood, however, that our failure to comply does not bring the punishments pronounced in the Law since Jesus bore those for us (Galatians 3:13). Our compliance does not earn the blessings of God either; those only come by faith in Christ (Romans 4:8-13). We also need to be acquainted with the Old Testament Law so that we will better understand our New Covenant and God's historical dealings with mankind. Also, Paul said to Timothy, "But we know that the law is good, if a man use it lawfully" (1 Timothy 1:8). He then said that the Law was not made for a righteous person (i.e., a Christian, 2 Corinthians 5:21) but rather for an unbeliever (1 Timothy 1:9-10). So, a Christian can still use the Law when ministering to unbelievers to show them their sin and their need for a savior (see note 4 at Romans 3:19). As Christians, we should not discard the Old Testament Law. When understood in the light of the New Covenant, the Old Covenant provides us with invaluable revelation of God. Paul was simply stressing that the time when people sought to be justified through the keeping of the Old Testament Law is over. Now, people must put their faith in Christ, and Christ alone, for salvation. Someone might ask, "Was anyone ever justified by the keeping of the Law?" The answer is yes. One person did become righteous through His keeping of the Old Testament Law. That person was Jesus. One of the reasons the Old Testament Law was given was so that Jesus could legally earn man's redemption. Now that the purchase has been completed, that function of the Law is over.

Note 4

The phrase "to every one that believeth" limits this benefit only to believers (Christians). To those who do not receive God's gift of salvation, the Law is still in effect (see note 4 at John 3:36). Those who fail to believe on Jesus will have to answer to God for each and every one of their transgressions of the Law.

Romans 10:5

For Moses describeth the righteousness which is of the law, That the man which doeth those things shall live by them.

LIVING COMMENTARY

This quotation from Leviticus 18:5 is another way of saying we will get what we deserve. We don't want that, but that is what the Law did. Praise God for the New Covenant (Hebrews 8:12).

Note 5

In Romans 10:5-9, Paul contrasted those who seek righteousness by the Law with those who seek the righteousness of God as a gift (see note 2 at Romans 10:3). Those who seek to earn righteousness through keeping the Law are consumed with "doing" (this verse), while those who receive righteousness by faith are simply confessing what has already been done (Romans 10:9). This is a simple yet profound difference. If we are still "doing" acts of holiness to get God to move in our lives, then we are still operating under a "Law" mentality that is not faith (Galatians 3:12). When we simply believe and confess what has already been provided through Christ, that's grace. Those who are living under the Law and those who are living under grace should have very similar actions of holiness, but their motivations are completely opposite. Legalists have their attention on what they must do, while those living by faith have their attention on what Christ has already done for them. For instance, the Scriptures teach us to confess with our mouths and believe with our hearts and we will receive from God (Romans 10:9-10 and Mark 11:23-24). Legalists think that means they can get God to heal them by confessing that by His stripes, they are healed. However, those who understand God's grace will not confess the Word to get healed. They will confess that by His stripes, they are healed, because they really believe it has already been done. Analyzing our mindsets is the simplest way of discerning whether we are operating in true Bible faith or a legalistic counterfeit. If the motive for our actions is to be accepted by God, then that's legalism. If we live holy out of faith and gratefulness for what God has already done, then that's grace.

Note 6

The Greek word that was translated "live" here is "ZAO," and it means "to live" (Strong's Concordance). However, that definition by itself doesn't fully convey Paul's intent in quoting this Old Testament passage from Leviticus 18:5. It is clear from the context that Paul was contrasting the effort to keep the Old Testament Law with the New Testament faith in Christ. He was concluding that the observance of the Old Testament

Law for producing righteousness (see note 3 at Romans 10:4) is inferior to the New Testament method of obtaining righteousness by putting faith in Jesus as our Savior. This quote from Moses is intended to illustrate the harshness of living by the Old Testament Law. Paul quoted this same Old Testament passage in Galatians 3:12, and so did Nehemiah in Nehemiah 9:29. In each case, the context clearly reveals that the writer was quoting this verse to speak of the negative effects of living by the Law. The word "live" in the English language can mean many different things, as can be seen by the multiple definitions of this word in any dictionary. In the American Heritage Dictionary, there is one definition that communicates Paul's meaning here. The word "live" can mean "to continue to be alive." Using this definition, this quote from Leviticus 18:5 is saying that once people start trying to fulfill the Law to earn righteousness, they will have to subsist, or continue to be alive, by their ongoing adherence to the precepts of that Law. In other words, once they decide to "earn" right standing with God, then God is going to give them what they deserve. The thing that is dreadfully wrong with this thought is that people don't really deserve righteousness. They don't need justice. They need mercy! This is what Paul was communicating when he quoted this scripture from Leviticus.

Trying to achieve righteousness by keeping the Law doesn't bring peace, because it puts the burden of salvation on our shoulders (see note 2 at Romans 5:1). In contrast, salvation by grace through faith places the burden on Jesus and allows us to walk free.

Romans 10:6

But the righteousness which is of faith speaketh on this wise, Say not in thine heart, Who shall ascend into heaven? (that is, to bring Christ down from above:)

Note 7

Paul was saying that failure to understand justification by grace produces an attitude that, in effect, denies Christ's substitutionary work for us. Those who still believe that their performance is essential for salvation are denying that Christ is in heaven, making intercession for man (Romans 8:34). That dethrones Christ from His present position. It is like denying that Christ has ascended into heaven for us. Likewise, a belief that we have to bear the punishment for our sins is like denying that Christ's death was sufficient by itself. If we are to be punished for our sins, then Christ might as well not have died for us. All of this is continuing what Paul began in Romans 10:5, contrasting the doing of the Old Testament Law and the believing of the New Testament grace (see note 5 at Romans 10:5). The Law mentality puts us under an unbearable load of performance to obtain righteousness; faith just receives the righteousness that has already been provided through Christ.

Romans 10:7

Or, Who shall descend into the deep? (that is, to bring up Christ again from the dead.)

LIVING COMMENTARY

Jesus went to hell for us (Ephesians 4:9) so that we don't have to. But in effect, those who believe they still have to suffer punishment from God for their sins—even after they are born again—are denying that Jesus has already suffered for them. In a sense, they are descending into hell and suffering for their sins, and that negates what Jesus did. Jesus paid it all so that we don't have to pay any at all.

Romans 10:8

But what saith it? The word is nigh thee, even in thy mouth, and in thy heart: that is, the word of faith, which we preach;

LIVING COMMENTARY

This doesn't just apply to our initial salvation; everything we receive from the Lord comes this same way (Colossians 2:6). We don't have to ascend into heaven or go down to the depths to get our needs met. It's not by our effort. Jesus purchased for us everything we will ever need. All we have to do is believe in our hearts and confess with our mouths. It's that simple and easy. But, sadly, our tendency is to look at what we don't have and think it is too hard to get from where we are to where we need to go. That is not what these verses are saying. It's a done deal. The Lord has provided everything we need to get the job done. We don't have to do it. We just need to rest in what He has already done (see my notes at Hebrews 4:3-11).

Note 8

In Romans 10:6-8, Paul was again quoting Moses, this time from Deuteronomy 30:11-14. However, in this verse, Paul added, "that is, the word of faith, which we preach," and that provides us with a commentary on Moses' statements. A reading of Deuteronomy 30:11-14 by itself might lead some to suggest that Moses was saying that the Law was not hard to keep. Yet that is against everything that Paul taught and the context of this verse in particular. Paul was saying that Moses' statements in this quotation were actually prophesying the day of justification by faith that Paul was preaching. Paul revealed in Galatians 3:22-25 that the purpose of the Old Testament Law was to shut us up "unto the faith which should afterwards be revealed" (Galatians 3:23). The Law was our schoolmaster to bring us unto Christ. From Paul's use of Moses' statements to make his point, it can be supposed that Moses had a revelation of the day when faith in Christ would supersede the Law (Deuteronomy 18:15-18).

Romans 10:9

That if thou shalt confess with thy mouth the Lord Jesus, and shalt believe in thine heart that God hath raised him from the dead, thou shalt be saved.

Note 9

Remember that, in context, Paul had been contrasting two types of righteousness (see note 2 at Romans 10:3). The righteousness of the Law binds a person up in "doing," while the righteousness of faith just receives what Christ has already done (see note 5 at Romans 10:5). This verse is stressing the simplicity of receiving righteousness by faith, as opposed to the bondage of trying to produce our own righteousness that is by the Law (Philippians 3:9). An attempt to amplify too much on the conditions of this verse would counter the point that Paul was making. However, in light of other scriptures, some explanation needs to be given. This verse is not saying that anyone who just says the words, "Jesus is Lord," and believes that He rose from the dead is born again (see note 2 at John 3:3). As explained in note 1 at Mark 1:24, the Greek word "HOMOLOGEO," translated "confess" here, means more than just saying words. It literally means "to assent, i.e. covenant, acknowledge" (Strong's Concordance). By looking at Jesus' statement in Luke 6:46, a true confession of Jesus as Lord has to be heartfelt enough to involve a person's actions. There are some groups that interpret the word "Lord" in a way that denies the deity of Jesus (see note 3 at Luke 1:43 and note 8 at John 5:23). This confession of Jesus as Lord has to be a declaration of faith in Jesus as God manifest in the flesh (1 Timothy 3:16). A Jesus who is less than God could not provide salvation for the whole human race. Therefore, this verse is a promise to those who believe on Jesus to the extent that they are willing to change their actions accordingly and confess Him as Lord (God) with their mouths so that they might be saved.

Romans 10:10

For with the heart man believeth unto righteousness; and with the mouth confession is made unto salvation.

Note 10

For true salvation to take place, there must be confession with the mouth and belief from the heart. People tend to major on one or the other of these requirements, but that fails to obtain the desired results. Confession is scriptural, but it is a result of faith in the heart. Only when people have already believed with their hearts will confession release the power of God. Confession without sincere belief in the heart is dead works (Hebrews 9:14). Likewise, faith without works is dead (James 2:17). When people really believe in their hearts, they will speak what they believe (Matthew 12:34 and Luke 6:45). A faith that won't confess what is believed is not God's kind of faith (see note 6 at Romans 4:17). Failure to properly combine these two truths has caused some people to fail in their attempts to receive from God, and reject "faith teaching" or "confession teaching." However, if one of these truths was presented without the proper emphasis on the other, then it wasn't scriptural teaching. The truths of faith and confession will work when used according to the instructions in this verse.

Romans 10:11

For the scripture saith, Whosoever believeth on him shall not be ashamed.

LIVING COMMENTARY

This Old Testament scripture was also quoted in Romans 9:33 and 1 Peter 2:6. The scripture being quoted is Isaiah 28:16. The Isaiah passage says those who believe on the Lord "shall not make haste," while Peter said "shall not be confounded."

Note 11

The emphasis here, as well as in Romans 10:13, is on the word "whosoever." In the first chapter of Romans, Paul started making the point that Gentiles did not have to become Jews to be saved (Romans 1:16). He had developed that truth all the way through this epistle and was declaring it once again.

Romans 10:12

For there is no difference between the Jew and the Greek: for the same Lord over all is rich unto all that call upon him.

Note 12

The differences between Jew and Gentile do not mean much to the Christian church today. Therefore, many church people may feel that they agree with this verse. However, Paul was speaking of more than just racial differences. Paul was saying that there is no difference between moral and immoral people. There is no difference in the sight of God between the religious and the nonreligious. All people are sinners and in need of the same salvation. This point still aggravates the religious people today as much as it did in the days of Paul.

Romans 10:13

For whosoever shall call upon the name of the Lord shall be saved.

LIVING COMMENTARY

Notice that "whosoever" calls on the name of the Lord shall be saved. Those who preach that some are predestinated to salvation while others are predestinated to damnation are wrong (see my note on predestination at Romans 8:29). "Whosoever" means anyone can be saved. All they have to do is believe (Romans 5:2).

Note 13

Paul was quoting from Joel 2:32. Paul interchanged the word "saved" for the word "delivered" that Joel used. There is no contradiction. Salvation includes deliverance (see note 7 at Acts 2:21).

Romans 10:14

How then shall they call on him in whom they have not believed? and how shall they believe in him of whom they have not heard? and how shall they hear without a preacher?

Note 1

Paul had just conclusively proven that salvation was not according to people's performance but according to their acceptance of God's grace by faith in Christ Jesus. This was great news! Yet this great news will not do people any good if they don't know it. The Gospel has to be heard to release its power (Romans 1:16).

Note 2

Romans 10:14-15 shows a number of things that must happen in order for people to be born again. Individuals must believe, but they need to have something or someone to believe in. Therefore, ministers have to share the Gospel with them. But in order for that to happen, others have to send the ministers to the uttermost parts of the earth. So there are three areas of responsibility for salvation: individuals have to believe, ministers have to preach, and others have to send. Satan works on all three of these areas to stop people from receiving God's gift of salvation. Satan tries to harden people's hearts through the deceitfulness of sin (Hebrews 3:13) to the point that the Gospel will not penetrate. If people are faithful to the two other responsibilities, salvation still will not occur if the individuals reject the good news. Yet many times, people are hungry and ripe for salvation, and still there is no one to share the good news with them. If Satan can stop people from preaching the Gospel through a lack of preachers or a lack of people who will send them, then he can stop people from being saved. As Christians, we cannot take responsibility for people's reactions to the Gospel, but we must take the responsibility of preaching the Gospel and giving so that others can preach the Gospel.

Romans 10:15

And how shall they preach, except they be sent? as it is written, How beautiful are the feet of them that preach the gospel of peace, and bring glad tidings of good things!

LIVING COMMENTARY

Two hundred of David's men who were too faint to go to the battle stayed with the supplies, but David shared the spoil of victory with them equally as with those who actually fought (1 Samuel 30:21-25). Likewise, those who give to support the preaching of the Gospel will share equally with those who actually delivered the message. Those who have supported the preaching of the Gospel will literally have people whom they've never seen come up to them in heaven and thank them for their gifts, which enabled them to be saved (see my note at Luke 16:9).

Note 3

When people understand that sharing the Gospel is just as important a part of salvation as others accepting the message, then they will rejoice with Isaiah about the beauty of those who share this good news.

Romans 10:16

But they have not all obeyed the gospel. For Esaias saith, Lord, who hath believed our report?

LIVING COMMENTARY

This verse quotes Isaiah from Isaiah 53:1.

Note 4

Contrary to popular belief, an anointed messenger with an anointed message is not always well received. This quotation from Isaiah shows that not everyone received his message about the coming Messiah. The same thing was true of many other prophets that the Lord sent to Israel, including Jeremiah, Ezekiel, and even Jesus. An incorrect belief that if we really minister in the power of the Holy Spirit, we will always succeed in converting the hearers has brought undeserved condemnation on many of us Christians. We cannot take responsibility for other people's actions.

Romans 10:17

So then faith cometh by hearing, and hearing by the word of God.

LIVING COMMENTARY

This verse starts with the phrase, "so then." That means this statement about faith coming through God's Word is a conclusion or result of what was said before. Romans 10 is speaking about a faith righteousness versus a works righteousness. So it's this message of righteousness by grace that causes faith to come. It's specifically saying that the message of grace causes faith to come. See my note at Acts 14:9.

Note 5

Faith comes by hearing God's Word because God's Word is His faith (see note 4 at Romans 3:3). People cannot be born again (see note 2 at John 3:3) through human faith. They have to use God's supernatural faith (see note 2 at Matthew 8:10, note 4 at John 20:29, and note 6 at Romans 4:17) to receive God's supernatural gift of salvation. The only place to obtain God's kind of faith is from God's Word. Therefore, we cannot compromise God's Word. It must be proclaimed boldly to make God's faith available to those who choose to believe.

Note 6

Notice that this verse says faith comes by "hearing," not by "having heard." People cannot rest on revelation they received from God years ago, unless they are still hearing the Lord speak those same truths to them now. The Lord doesn't fail to speak; we fail to hear. Therefore, we can keep our faith in the present tense if we will open our spiritual ears to hear what God's Word is saying (Proverbs 4:20-22, see note 10 at Mark 6:52 and note 3 at Mark 8:17).

Romans 10:18

But I say, Have they not heard? Yes verily, their sound went into all the earth, and their words unto the ends of the world.

LIVING COMMENTARY

Romans 10:16 shows that not everyone will receive the Gospel. Then, Romans 10:17 shows that people can't believe without hearing God's Word. This verse shows that everyone has heard. How can that be? Not everyone has heard a man or woman preach the Gospel, but everyone has heard the witness of the Holy Spirit in their hearts (see my notes at Romans 1:18-20). Regardless of what someone might claim, they know in their heart that there is only one God and they are not Him.

Romans 10:19

But I say, Did not Israel know? First Moses saith, I will provoke you to jealousy by them that are no people, and by a foolish nation I will anger you.

Note 7

What was it that Israel knew? Paul was saying that Israel knew the Gospel of salvation by faith, which he had expounded on in this epistle. One way this truth was revealed in the Old Testament was through the prophecies concerning the Gentiles becoming the people of God. If God was going to embrace nationalities that didn't adhere to the rites and ceremonies that were delivered to the Jews, then it should have been evident that these things were not prerequisites to salvation. Paul quoted a prophecy from Moses and two additional passages from Isaiah to verify that this truth was revealed in the Old Testament. The truth was there, but the Jewish hearts had become so hardened through legalism that they couldn't perceive this truth (see note 3 at Mark 8:17).

Romans 10:20

But Esaias is very bold, and saith, I was found of them that sought me not; I was made manifest unto them that asked not after me.

LIVING COMMENTARY

This is a quotation from Isaiah 65:1. The Isaiah passage adds "I said, Behold me, behold me unto a nation that was not called by my name," which was not quoted here.

Romans 10:21

But to Israel he saith, All day long I have stretched forth my hands unto a disobedient and gainsaying people.

LIVING COMMENTARY

This is a quotation from Isaiah 65:2. The Isaiah passage used the term "rebellious," which was translated "disobedient and gainsaying" here. The Houghton Mifflin American Heritage Electronic Dictionary defines "gainsaying" as "to contradict, deny."

ROMANS

CHAPTER ELEVEN

Romans 11:1

I say then, Hath God cast away his people? God forbid. For I also am an Israelite, of the seed of Abraham, of the tribe of Benjamin.

Note 1

Paul's message of grace and his announcement that Gentiles could become a part of the true Israel of God through the new birth without becoming Jews was a startling revelation. Paul had systematically dealt with objections that a legalistic Jew would have to such a message. Here he answered the criticism that this would mean God has forsaken the Jewish nation. Basically, Paul was saying that Jews are not excluded, but that they just aren't favored over the Gentiles. He cited himself as an example of a believing Jew and compared the status of Israel to that of the Jewish nation in the days of Elijah. In the same way that there were 7,000 true worshipers of God left in Israel in Elijah's day (1 Kings 19:18), so there was a remnant of believing Jews in Paul's day. The rest of this chapter is Paul's explanation of Israel's current relationship to God during the church era.

Romans 11:2

God hath not cast away his people which he foreknew. Wot ye not what the scripture saith of Elias? how he maketh intercession to God against Israel, saying,

LIVING COMMENTARY

Elijah's complaining about all the things the Israelites had done (killing God's prophets and tearing down God's altars) was called making intercession to God against Israel. It is true they had done these things, but Elijah was pleading with God to execute judgment for these things while God was wanting to extend mercy to them. Likewise, we live in a day where nations are turning from God. It's true. But we need to be careful that our speech about this isn't murmuring and complaining like Elijah, which God called making intercession against them. This cost Elijah his ministry (see my note at 1 Kings 19:14).

Romans 11:3

Lord, they have killed thy prophets, and digged down thine altars; and I am left alone, and they seek my life.

LIVING COMMENTARY

This is referencing what Elijah said to the Lord twice, in 1 Kings 19:10 and 14. Elijah was complaining that he was the only servant of the Lord left in Israel. This was not true, and Elijah knew it (see my note at 1 Kings 18:13). But it's what he felt. We must never let our feelings overrule what we know to be true in our hearts. This cost Elijah his ministry (see my note at 1 Kings 19:14).

Romans 11:4

But what saith the answer of God unto him? I have reserved to myself seven thousand men, who have not bowed the knee to the image of Baal.

LIVING COMMENTARY

The Lord said this to Elijah in 1 Kings 19:18. Elijah knew this but was going by how he felt, not what he knew (see my note at 1 Kings 18:13).

Romans 11:5

Even so then at this present time also there is a remnant according to the election of grace.

LIVING COMMENTARY

The situation that Elijah found himself in was terrible. The king and queen were the most corrupt rulers Israel had ever had (1 Kings 21:25). Jezebel had killed many of the Lord's prophets (1 Kings 18:13). This had driven the true followers of the Lord underground. It looked bad. But there were still 7,000 true believers of the Lord left (1 Kings 19:18). Likewise, as bad as things look today, there are still millions who are true worshipers of God. Anytime we get to feeling we are the only ones truly serving the Lord, we need to remember Elijah and God's answer to him. This Elijah syndrome of thinking you are the only one is a sure sign of error. This "election of grace" is not talking about God predestinating some to salvation and some to damnation (see my note at Romans 8:29). God chooses those who choose grace. But His grace is open to all (Titus 2:11). All we have to do to enter into His grace is believe (Romans 5:2).

Romans 11:6

And if by grace, then is it no more of works: otherwise grace is no more grace. But if it be of works, then is it no more grace: otherwise work is no more work.

Note 2

Paul stated the doctrine of justification by grace through faith so clearly in his writings that any person who claims to believe the Bible has to acknowledge this truth. However, one of Satan's cleverest deceptions is to take a truth and add to it until it is no longer the truth. Lest that happen with this doctrine of grace, Paul stated emphatically that we cannot combine anything with God's grace as a requirement for salvation. In the same way that gasoline and water don't mix, so grace and works will not mix. Justification has to be all works or all grace, but not a combination of the two. In this epistle, Paul repeatedly made his point of justification by grace through faith. He repeatedly stressed that faith is the only requirement on our part. Here he was repeating that point once again in perhaps his clearest words yet. Still, an abundance of religious people today cannot accept the fact that all we have to do is to believe to receive God's grace (Romans 5:2). This verse leaves no alternatives.

Romans 11:7

What then? Israel hath not obtained that which he seeketh for; but the election hath obtained it, and the rest were blinded

LIVING COMMENTARY

The nation of Israel was seeking the right thing. They wanted relationship with God, but they didn't obtain it, because they sought it the wrong way. They sought to be right with God through their keeping of the commandments (Romans 10:1-4). Therefore, this conclusively proves that just wanting the right thing is not enough. There is a right way and a wrong way to obtain salvation.

Romans 11:8

(According as it is written, God hath given them the spirit of slumber, eyes that they should not see, and ears that they should not hear;) unto this day.

Living Commentary

Second Peter 3:9 clearly says that the Lord is "not willing that any should perish, but that all should come to
repentance." So, we can rest assured that the Lord didn't
prevent these people from being saved. No! They had
already rejected God and His wooing, so He just upheld
their choice and hardened their hearts even further so
that they couldn't believe. It's like it says in 2 Thessalonians 2:11-12.

Note 1

This appears to be a paraphrase of a Bible truth that is expressed in
many scriptures. See Deuteronomy 29:4; Isaiah 6:9, 29:10; Jeremiah
5:21; Ezekiel 12:2; Mark 4:11-12; Luke 8:10; and Acts 28:26.

Romans 11:9

*And David saith, Let their table be made a snare, and a trap, and
a stumblingblock, and a recompence unto them:*

Note 2

This quotation from David comes from Psalm 69:22-23. In that psalm,
David was prophesying about the suffering of Christ in the first person,
as if David himself was actually describing his own suffering. However,
there are seven very clear references to Christ in this psalm that were
quoted in the New Testament as having a direct fulfillment through
Jesus: (1) Psalm 69:4, fulfilled in John 15:25; (2) Psalm 69:9a, fulfilled
in John 2:17; (3) Psalm 69:9b, fulfilled in Romans 15:3; (4) Psalm 69:21

a, fulfilled in Matthew 27:48, Mark 15:23, and Luke 23:36; (5) Psalm 69:21b, fulfilled in Matthew 27:48, Mark 15:36, and John 19:28-30; (6) Psalm 69:22, fulfilled in Romans 11:9; and (7) Psalm 69:25, fulfilled in Acts 1:20. Also, Psalm 69:8 was certainly fulfilled in Jesus (John 7:5), although this passage was not quoted in the New Testament. Therefore, Psalm 69 is a prophetic psalm where Christ, through David, was describing His earthly ministry and crucifixion. The denunciation of Psalm 69:22-23 was given by Christ against those who crucified Him. When understood in this context, it is easy to see that this blindness and deafness didn't cause the Jews' rejection, but it was the Jews' rejection that caused this pronouncement. All of this is to say that God is not unjust and has never taken away people's freedom of choice unless they had already exercised that choice against Him (see note 9 at Romans 9:17).

Romans 11:10

Let their eyes be darkened, that they may not see, and bow down their back alway.

LIVING COMMENTARY

This is from Psalm 69:23. "Bow down their back alway" is referring to bearing a heavy load. The Amplified Bible translated this as "Let their eyes be darkened (dimmed) so that they cannot see, and make them bend their back [stooping beneath their burden] forever."

Romans 11:11

I say then, Have they stumbled that they should fall? God forbid: but rather through their fall salvation is come unto the Gentiles, for to provoke them to jealousy.

Note 3

The Greek word translated "fall" here is "PIPTO," signifying "a complete irrevocable fall" (Rienecker). Paul was saying, "Is this rejection of Jesus by the Jews irrevocable?" The answer is no. The Amplified Bible reads, "So I ask, have they stumbled so as to fall [to their utter spiritual ruin, irretrievably]? By no means!" The New International Version reads, "Again I ask: Did they stumble so as to fall beyond recovery? Not at all!" Paul then began to relate how the Jews can still be saved during this "church age," and he cited Old Testament scriptures to declare a future time when the whole nation of Israel will once again come back into God's fold (Romans 11:26-27).

Romans 11:12

Now if the fall of them be the riches of the world, and the diminishing of them the riches of the Gentiles; how much more their fulness?

LIVING COMMENTARY

The Message's interpretation of the previous verse is interesting. It says, "The next question is, 'Are they down for the count? Are they out of this for good?' And the answer is a clear-cut no. Ironically when they walked out, they left the door open and the outsiders walked in. But the next thing you know, the Jews were starting to wonder if perhaps they had walked out on a good thing." If things are as good as they are in this church age, which started with the overall rejection of Christ by the Jews, then how much better will it be when the Jews accept their Messiah?

Romans 11:13

For I speak to you Gentiles, inasmuch as I am the apostle of the Gentiles, I magnify mine office:

LIVING COMMENTARY

Paul was commissioned directly by the Lord to be an apostle to the Gentiles (see my note at Acts 22:21). Yet he was continually seeking for the Jews to be saved (Romans 9:1-3). But this love for the Jews got him in a lot of unnecessary trouble (see my note at Acts 21:26). We need to stick to what God has called us to do.

There is a special anointing when we abide in our calling. The Greek word "DOXAZO," which was translated "magnify" in this verse, was translated "glorified" in Romans 1:21. Therefore, to glorify also could be rendered to magnify. See my note at Romans 1:21.

Romans 11:14

If by any means I may provoke to emulation them which are my flesh, and might save some of them.

LIVING COMMENTARY

The church is supposed to make the Jews jealous (Romans 11:11).

Romans 11:15

For if the casting away of them be the reconciling of the world, what shall the receiving of them be, but life from the dead?

Note 1

Paul had conclusively proven that the Jews did not have a monopoly on God. The Gentiles could now come directly to God without becoming Jews. He had also stated that the Jewish nation as a whole had rejected God because they denied the concept of a savior. They had become their own savior (see note 3 at Romans 9:32). This could leave some Jews wondering if the Jews had been forsaken by God. Paul answered this question in this chapter (see note 1 at Romans 11:1). There was still a remnant of Jews who were heirs through faith (Romans 11:5). In this passage of Scripture, Paul drew a conclusion: "If the Jews' rejection of Christ opened up salvation to the rest of the world, then what will happen when the Jews turn back to God? It will be resurrection from the dead!" Paul's statement that the return of the Jews to their God will be life from the dead could be an analogy. That is, Paul could be comparing the Jews' return to God to the joy and blessing that would come from seeing a friend raised from the dead. Or Paul could be speaking literally that the time the Jews return to God will be at the end of the world and the return of Christ when the dead shall be raised. In either case, Paul was stressing that there will be a future spiritual restoration of Israel (see note 3 at Romans 11:26) and great blessing on the world as a result.

Romans 11:16

For if the firstfruit be holy, the lump is also holy: and if the root be holy, so are the branches.

LIVING COMMENTARY

Christianity is like the first fruit, or the branch, out of Judaism. Look at the wonderful things that have come through the church. Just think what it will be like when the root of that tree also receives salvation. It's going to be glorious.

Romans 11:17

And if some of the branches be broken off, and thou, being a wild olive tree, wert graffed in among them, and with them partakest of the root and fatness of the olive tree;

LIVING COMMENTARY

The branches that were broken off were the children of Israel who rejected their Messiah. So, they were broken off, and the Christians were grafted in their place. But the roots of Christianity go all the way back to the Old Testament and Abraham as the father of us all (Romans 4:16).

Romans 11:18

Boast not against the branches. But if thou boast, thou bearest not the root, but the root thee.

Note 2

Paul was warning the Gentiles against gloating in the fact that salvation had been opened unto them as though it happened because of some goodness on their part. It wasn't earned. It was God's grace. Paul explained that the Jews' unbelief (Romans 11:20) caused them to be broken off and that the same thing could happen to the Gentiles (Romans 11:21) if they didn't stand strong through faith.

Romans 11:19

Thou wilt say then, The branches were broken off, that I might be graffed in.

LIVING COMMENTARY

This is classic! Some people think all the good things that happen to them are because of some superior virtue on their part. As often as not, it's rather because others whom God wanted to bless rejected the blessing. So, we cannot boast in our goodness as the reason for our favor. It might be that we simply were next in line.

Romans 11:20

Well; because of unbelief they were broken off, and thou standest by faith. Be not highminded, but fear:

LIVING COMMENTARY

This verse shows that salvation isn't because of a person's actions. This didn't say that it was because of their badness or our goodness. Instead, it was the Jews' unbelief that caused them to be rejected, and it is only our faith that has grafted us into their tree.

Romans 11:21

For if God spared not the natural branches, take heed lest he also spare not thee.

LIVING COMMENTARY

If the Jews' unbelief caused them to fall from grace, then the same thing could happen to us. We need to humble ourselves and only believe.

Romans 11:22

Behold therefore the goodness and severity of God: on them which fell, severity; but toward thee, goodness, if thou continue in his goodness: otherwise thou also shalt be cut off.

LIVING COMMENTARY

This is not speaking on a personal level. This chapter speaks about the Jewish nation and the Gentiles. This is not saying that an individual who has the promise that the Lord will never leave them nor forsake them (Hebrews 13:5) will be rejected by the Lord. But just as the Jews rejected their Messiah and therefore, as a whole, have fallen from the favored status they once occupied, if the Gentile church totally rejected Him, they could likewise be rejected and salvation passed on to some other group.

Note 3

Even in the midst of God's judgment, there is mercy. The people who suffered destruction during the Flood and the overthrow of Sodom and Gomorrah experienced the severity of God, but these judgments were actually acts of mercy upon the world as a whole. During those times, sin was so rampant in the earth that it was like a cancer. God did radical surgery on mankind by removing these vile sinners and therefore allowed the human race as a whole to survive. Likewise, God's turning from the Jewish nation to the Gentiles had both severity and goodness in it. It had severe consequences for the Jews, but it blessed the rest of the world.

Romans 11:23

And they also, if they abide not still in unbelief, shall be graffed in: for God is able to graff them in again.

Note 1

God is not only "able" to restore the Jewish nation, but Paul went on to say in Romans 11:26 that all Israel "shall" be saved (see note 3 at Romans 11:26).

Romans 11:24

For if thou wert cut out of the olive tree which is wild by nature, and wert graffed contrary to nature into a good olive tree: how much more shall these, which be the natural branches, be graffed into their own olive tree?

LIVING COMMENTARY

If God could take Gentiles, who were aliens from the covenants of promise (Ephesians 2:12), and graft them into His vine, then how much more could the original branches (the Jews) be grafted back into their native tree?

Romans 11:25

For I would not, brethren, that ye should be ignorant of this mystery, lest ye should be wise in your own conceits; that blindness in part is happened to Israel, until the fulness of the Gentiles be come in.

Note 2

This phrase, "fulness of the Gentiles," is only used here. A similar expression, "times of the Gentiles," is used in Luke 21:24. There are two obvious ways this phrase could be interpreted. First, the fullness of the Gentiles could be referring to all the Gentiles who are foreordained (see note 2 at Romans 8:29) to come to Christ, experiencing salvation. Then there would be a wonderful move of God among the Jews in which the Jewish nation as a whole would come to the Lord (Romans 11:26). The Amplified Bible's translation would lend itself to this interpretation: "a hardening (insensibility) has [temporarily] befallen a part of Israel [to last] until the full number of the ingathering of the Gentiles has come in." This phrase could also be referring to the time when the Gentiles would no longer be dominating the Jewish nation, and specifically referring to the occupation of Jerusalem by the Gentiles. This is apparently what Luke 21:24 is referring to. If so, then there will have to be a future fulfillment of the scriptures that prophesied the end of Gentile control of Jerusalem, since Israel has physically possessed Jerusalem since the Israel-Arab War of 1948, yet the nation as a whole has not come to God.

Romans 11:26

And so all Israel shall be saved: as it is written, There shall come out of Sion the Deliverer, and shall turn away ungodliness from Jacob:

Note 3

An abundance of Old Testament prophecies speak of the Jewish nation being restored to its former status, both physically and spiritually. It must be understood that when Paul said "all" Israel will be saved, he was using a figure of speech (see note 6 at Mark 1:5). The Jewish nation as a whole will return to God, but there will be individual Jews who do not.

Romans 11:27

For this is my covenant unto them, when I shall take away their sins.

Romans 11:28

As concerning the gospel, they are enemies for your sakes: but as touching the election, they are beloved for the fathers' sakes.

LIVING COMMENTARY

The unbelieving Jews persecuted the Gospel (Acts 14:2). So, in that sense, they were the enemies of the Gospel message. But from God's point of view, the whole Jewish nation is elected by God for salvation. This is the promise made to their forefathers.

Romans 11:29

For the gifts and calling of God are without repentance.

Note 4

In context, this is speaking about the future restoration of the Jewish nation. Paul was saying that even though the Jews had rejected God, the Lord was still going to bring His promises to the Jews to pass. This is an act of total grace on the Lord's part (see note 5 at Romans 1:5). This scripture has a broader application too. Any calling, or gift to accomplish that calling, that the Lord gives an individual is without repentance. It means that regardless of what an individual does, God doesn't withdraw His gifts and callings. This is why some ministers who fall into sin can still see the supernatural gifts of God flow in their ministries. That is not to say that living a life separated unto God is not important. It is very important. People who are living in sin are going to have their faith made shipwreck through their consciences (1 Timothy 1:19). They will begin to lose effectiveness. However, as much as they can operate in faith, the gifts and callings of God that they have received are still there and they will function. Anything that you've ever received from God is still there; it just needs to be activated by faith.

Romans 11:30

For as ye in times past have not believed God, yet have now obtained mercy through their unbelief:

LIVING COMMENTARY

This is speaking of the Gentiles to whom Paul was writing. There was a time when the Gentiles were not the people of God. But since the Jews rejected their Messiah, the opportunity for salvation passed on to the Gentiles.

Romans 11:31

Even so have these also now not believed, that through your mercy they also may obtain mercy.

LIVING COMMENTARY

There was a time when we, the Gentile believers, were not the people of God. But through Christ, we are now a royal priesthood, a holy nation, and His peculiar treasure (1 Peter 2:9). And we are to extend mercy—not judgment—to the Jews so that they, too, may be part of His bride.

Romans 11:32

For God hath concluded them all in unbelief, that he might have mercy upon all.

LIVING COMMENTARY

This is not only true of the Jewish nation. This is true of the whole human race. The Law made us all guilty (Romans 3:19 and 23) so that one sacrifice would cleanse us all (Galatians 3:22-24).

Romans 11:33

O the depth of the riches both of the wisdom and knowledge of God! how unsearchable are his judgments, and his ways past finding out!

LIVING COMMENTARY

Isaiah 55:8-9 reveals that God's thoughts are not our thoughts and His ways are not our ways. God's ways are as high above our ways as the heavens are above the earth. Now it's like we are looking through a dirty glass (1 Corinthians 13:12) that hinders our view.

Because of the frailties of our human minds, we don't totally comprehend God's wisdom in our natural minds (1 Corinthians 2:14), but through the Holy Spirit we can understand much more and much better than humanly possible (see my notes at 1 Corinthians 2:9-10).

Romans 11:34

For who hath known the mind of the Lord? or who hath been his counseller?

LIVING COMMENTARY

Obviously, no one has any knowledge or instruction for the Lord. He is infinitely greater in all these things than anyone else. See 1 Corinthians 2:16.

Romans 11:35

Or who hath first given to him, and it shall be recompensed unto him again?

LIVING COMMENTARY

The Lord is the original giver (John 3:16). God gave us all life (John 1:4) and everything that pertains to life (2 Peter 1:3). He doesn't owe anyone anything.

Romans 11:36

For of him, and through him, and to him, are all things: to whom be glory for ever. Amen.

LIVING COMMENTARY

God is the source of all life (John 1:3-4). He is the means by which all life functions (Acts 17:28), and all life is ultimately accountable to Him (Philippians 2:10-11).

ROMANS

CHAPTER TWELVE

Romans 12:1

I beseech you therefore, brethren, by the mercies of God, that ye present your bodies a living sacrifice, holy, acceptable unto God, which is your reasonable service.

LIVING COMMENTARY

Romans 12:1-2 are the first scriptures the Lord ever supernaturally quickened to me. They changed my life. They are a recipe for finding and fulfilling God's perfect will for your life. Notice the word "therefore." That means this is a continuation and conclusion from the previous statement in Romans 11:36. God is all in all and therefore deserves our total submission to Him. This is our reasonable service. Paul pleaded with the people, by the mercies of God, to do these things. This reflects the fact that God's plans for our lives are better than our plans for ourselves (Jeremiah 29:11). We have to present our own bodies to the Lord as living sacrifices. The problem is that living sacrifices keep crawling off the altar. This isn't just a one-time decision. It may start with a one-time commitment, but then we have to follow through with that decision every day for the rest of our lives. That's why it's called a living sacrifice. The English word "acceptable" was translated from the Greek word "EUARESTOS," which means "fully agreeable" (Strong's Concordance). See 1 Corinthians 10:31. And notice that this isn't asking too much. This is only our reasonable (Greek - "rational ("logical")" [Strong's Concordance]) service. Jesus died for us; the least we can do is live for Him.

Note 1

Paul was speaking to us Christians. It is possible to commit our lives to the Lord for the purpose of salvation and yet not be yielded to the Lord in our daily lives. It is only when we make the total sacrifice of every area of our lives that we begin to see God's perfect will manifest through our lives.

Note 2

Paul used the mercies of God to encourage these Romans to give themselves totally to God. Today, most preachers use the wrath of God to try to drive people to God. Some people need the condemnation of the Law to make them aware of their need for a Savior, but as a whole, we could "draw more flies with honey than with vinegar." It's the goodness of God that leads people to repentance (Romans 2:4).

Note 3

Notice that we are the ones who have to make this presentation of our bodies to the Lord. He will not do it for us. Some of us might pray, "Lord, You do what You have to do to make us serve You." That is not a proper prayer. We cannot have someone lay hands on us to impart this commitment to us. We cannot just rebuke the flesh and expect it to disappear. We have to give our bodies to God as living sacrifices daily (see note 4 at this verse).

Note 4

This sounds like a contradiction in terms. How can we be living sacrifices when sacrifices are always dead? This is speaking of the fact that offering ourselves to God is not just a one-time deal. We have to die to our own desires daily. This has to be a living, ongoing commitment to the Lord. The Apollo spacecraft traveled to the moon, but it was not just as simple as blasting off and landing on the moon. Course corrections were made every ten minutes or so for the entire trip. And then, they only landed a few feet inside the targeted landing area of 500 miles. Yet the mission was a success. Likewise, there has to be a starting place for this decision to be a living sacrifice. We have to "blast off," or start our journey, sometime, but we don't ever "arrive" in this life. We just leave and start toward the goal (Philippians 3:12-13). We may be making course corrections every ten minutes for the rest of our lives. You see, living sacrifices have a tendency to keep crawling off the altar. Every minute of every day, we have to reaffirm this decision to be totally separated unto God. This is what Paul was referring to by the term "living sacrifice."

Note 5

Many Christians think that living lives totally consecrated to God is something that only preachers or a few laypeople do. They see it as "extra" and not "normal" Christianity. However, Paul said this level of commitment is our reasonable service. Jesus died for each one of us. Each one of us ought to live for Him.

Romans 12:2

And be not conformed to this world: but be ye transformed by the renewing of your mind, that ye may prove what is that good, and acceptable, and perfect, will of God.

Note 6

Many of us would think that if we fulfill the conditions of Romans 12:1, then everything else would automatically work out. Yet Paul went on to state that we also have to renew our minds. Many of us who have made genuine commitments to the Lord but haven't renewed our minds through God's Word, have needlessly suffered many problems.

Note 7

The Greek word that was translated "conformed" here is the word "SUSCHEMATIZO," and it means "to fashion alike, i.e. conform to the same pattern" (Strong's Concordance). This scripture is telling us that we should be different than the unbelievers. Most of us as Christians recognize this, but we seem at a loss as to how to accomplish it. This verse goes on to give us the answer. The key is our minds. "For as he thinketh in his heart, so is he" (Proverbs 23:7). If we think on the same things that the world thinks on, we are going to get the same results. If we keep our minds stayed upon God through the study of His Word and fellowship with Him, then we'll have perfect peace (Isaiah 26:3). It's that simple.

Note 8

The Greek word that was translated "transformed" here is the word "METAMORPHOO" and is the same word that we get our word "metamorphosis" from. It is describing a complete change, like that of a caterpillar changing into a butterfly. This word is also the same word that was used to describe Jesus' transformation when His face shone and His garments became white as the light (Matthew 17:2). Making our thinking line up with God's Word will affect this complete transformation in our lives.

Note 9

When people are born again (see note 2 at John 3:3), they become totally new creations in their spirits. Their spiritual salvation is complete. They don't need any more faith, joy, or power. They are complete in Him (Colossians 2:9-10, see note 3 at Matthew 26:41). However, it is not God's will that we only be changed on the inside. He wants to manifest this salvation in our physical lives also. That takes place through the renewing of our minds. We each have a spirit, soul, and body (1 Thessalonians 5:23). As born-again believers, our spirits are as perfect as they will ever be in heaven (see note 1 at Romans 8:18). If we will change our thinking so that we believe what God says in His Word about who we are and what we have, then this agreement between our spirits and souls forms a majority, and our flesh will experience the life of God that has been deposited in our spirits. If we fail to renew our minds, we can live our entire time on this earth without experiencing the abundant life that Jesus provided for us (John 10:10).

Note 10

The American Heritage Dictionary defines "prove" as "to establish the truth or validity of by argument or evidence...to be shown to be such; turn out." Therefore, this is speaking of how to physically display God's will in our lives. This is a promise that if we fulfill the requirements of these two verses, we will prove (not might prove, but will prove) the good and acceptable and perfect will of God. Finding God's will for our lives is not hard when we do what these verses instruct us to do. As a matter of fact, it would be impossible to miss God's will once we commit ourselves to God as living sacrifices and begin to renew our minds. Finding God's will for our lives only becomes hard if we are not totally committed to God.

Note 11

There is a difference of opinion among scholars as to whether Paul was using "good, and acceptable, and perfect" to describe the will of God or if he was saying that there are stages in walking in the will of God (i.e., good, then acceptable, then perfect). Either of these cases would be doctrinally correct. God's will certainly is good and acceptable and perfect. It is also true that people don't move immediately into everything that God has for them, but there is always growth into the things of God.

Note 12

This is a wonderful promise that we can prove God's will in our lives (see note 10 at this verse). The first step is to make a total commitment of our lives to the Lord ("living sacrifice," Romans 12:1). Actually this is the will of God for us all. Our vocation is secondary. God's will for all of us is to be living sacrifices to Him. Once that is accomplished, more specific direction will come as we renew our minds. If we try to find God's vocation for us but don't present ourselves to God as living sacrifices, then we are frustrating God's plan. God doesn't just want our service; He wants us. Once He gets us, He'll get our service.

Romans 12:3

For I say, through the grace given unto me, to every man that is among you, not to think of himself more highly than he ought to think; but to think soberly, according as God hath dealt to every man the measure of faith.

LIVING COMMENTARY

Notice that God hath (already been done) dealt to every man THE measure of faith, not A measure of faith. There is a big difference. If I was serving soup to a line of people and I used a ladle for one person, a soupspoon for another, a tablespoon for one, and a teaspoon for another, those would all be different measures. But if I used only one ladle to serve every person, then that would be THE measure of soup. God didn't give some Christians a large measure of faith and others just a tiny bit of faith. We were all given THE faith of Christ. We know that because the Apostle Paul said the faith he lived by was THE faith OF Christ (Galatians 2:20). It's possible for Christians to only use a small portion of what God has given them or possibly even none of the faith the Lord has given them. But it's there. It's a fruit of the Spirit (Galatians 5:22). We first have to acknowledge what we have (Philemon 6) and then learn how to use it.

Note 13

Paul began this sentence with the conjunction "for." That means the point he was making in Romans 12:3 was a continuation or result of what was said in Romans 12:2. Many times the word "because" can be used interchangeably with "for." Paul had just admonished them about humility and submission (living sacrifices) being the way to true success. He here continued that thought by giving these people another reason for humility: the fact that every person has been dealt "the measure of faith" (see note 16 at this verse). In other words, we all, as believers, have perfect plans for our lives that we can "prove" (see note 10 at Romans 12:2) if we will totally yield ourselves to God. We may have different gifts, but they are not better than someone else's. Paul then continued in Romans 12:4 with the word "for" again, and drew a comparison from the way our bodies have different parts but they all work together to make one body.

Note 14

Religion has interpreted this verse to say that we should think of ourselves in a lowly manner, but that is not what Paul was saying. It would be proper to say that we shouldn't think of ourselves more highly or more lowly than we ought to. We need to remember that any good thing we have is a gift from God (1 Corinthians 4:7). Paul was admonishing us to have the correct viewpoint, not a lowly viewpoint.

Note 15

The dictionary defines "according as" as "in proportion to." Paul was saying we need to remember that God has given every believer "the" measure of faith (see note 16 at this verse). This sobers us up because we recognize that what we have is a gift from God that every child of God possesses. Some of us live up to more of our potential than others, but it's only God's mercy that makes it possible for any of us to accomplish anything.

Note 16

God has dealt to every person "the" measure of faith, not "a" measure of faith. There are not different measures with God. The Lord doesn't give one person great faith while another person is given small faith. We were all given an equal amount of faith at salvation. The problem is not that we don't have faith, but rather we don't know how to use our faith, because of a lack of renewing our minds. Peter said we had "like precious faith" with him (2 Peter 1:1). The same faith that he used to raise Dorcas from the dead (Acts 9:36-42) is in us too. The same faith that Peter used is the same faith that we have. Paul said he was living his Christian life by the faith of the Son of God (Galatians 2:20). Since we all have been given "the" measure of faith, then that means we all have the faith of the Son of God in us. Our faith is sufficient. The problem we're experiencing is a result of our minds not knowing what we have. In the same way that a car battery transfers its power to the starter through battery cables, so our minds are what allows this faith of God that is in our spirits to flow into our bodies. If our minds are not renewed, then it's like having corroded cables. The power is there, but it won't flow. Likewise, we believers have the same faith that Jesus has, but it won't flow through us until we renew our minds through the Word of God.

Romans 12:4

For as we have many members in one body, and all members have not the same office:

Note 1

This verse starts with the word "for"; i.e., a conjunction, just as in Romans 12:3 (see note 13 at that verse). This is linking Paul's following statements with his previous ones. Paul had encouraged these people to experience the perfect will of God (Romans 12:2) by humbling themselves (being living sacrifices). This was vastly different than the world's formula for success and needed some further explanation. Therefore, in Romans 12:3, Paul explained that every believer has been given the same opportunity for success through "the" measure of faith. Here in Romans 12:4, Paul continued to explain that although every believer has been given "the" measure of faith, not every believer has been given the same job in the body of Christ. He used the physical body to illustrate this. We have many different parts of our bodies, and they all have different purposes or functions. Yet it takes all the parts operating in unity to make one body. Likewise, it takes all the different people in the church performing their different functions to make up Christ's body. So, in Romans 12:1-2, Paul gave a "foolproof" formula for success. However, to keep anyone from gloating at the tremendous potential of these promises, he made it clear in Romans 12:3 that everyone has been given the same potential. And in Romans 12:4-8, he revealed that people all have different functions, and all need each other.

Romans 12:5

So we, being many, are one body in Christ, and every one members one of another.

LIVING COMMENTARY

The foot is very different than the hand or the head. Yet, all these parts are members of one body. Likewise, every believer has different giftings and jobs, yet we all make one body. It's important to embrace the God-given differences and try not to make everyone just like us. A person with only feet and no hands would be considered "handicapped." Even so, the body of Christ has performed in a handicapped way because all the different parts don't function as one.

Romans 12:6

Having then gifts differing according to the grace that is given to us, whether prophecy, let us prophesy according to the proportion of faith;

LIVING COMMENTARY

There is a grace for salvation that has come to all (Titus 2:11). But there are other graces that the Lord gives as He chooses (1 Corinthians 12:4-7). Seven of them are listed here in Romans 12: prophecy, ministry, teaching, exhorting, giving, ruling, and showing mercy.

Note 2

It must be remembered that Paul was not teaching on the function and administration of these seven gifts that he mentioned here like he taught on the nine gifts of the Spirit in 1 Corinthians 12-14. He was simply mentioning these gifts to illustrate his point that different people in the body of Christ have different positions or functions. However, there are some truths concerning these gifts that can be gleaned from these scriptures. First, it needs to be pointed out that all believers can operate in the gifts listed here, but that doesn't mean that is their ministry. For instance, they can and should be able to teach others, but that doesn't make them teachers. Paul said "ye may all prophesy one by one" (1 Corinthians 14:31), but he also made it clear that not all are called to be prophets (1 Corinthians 12:29). It is definite that believers should all show mercy and be givers, but some people are given supernatural gifts in these areas. Paul was describing that here. Concerning the gift of giving, Paul said that giving should be done with simplicity (see note 7 at Romans 12:8).Those that rule should be diligent about it (see note 8 at Romans 12:8, and those who have the gift of mercy should administer it with cheerfulness.

Note 3

The Greek word that was translated "prophecy" here is "PROPHETEIA," and it "signifies the speaking forth of the mind and counsel of God" (Vine's Expository Dictionary). This originally applied to Old Testament prophets who predicted future events, but it came to be applied to any messengers who were inspired by God as they spoke. This would apply to preachers today if they are speaking under the anointing of the Holy Spirit. This verse is saying essentially the same thing that Peter said in 1 Peter 4:11. If we are going to prophesy, let's do it according to the ability that God gave us—the measure of faith (see note 16 at Romans 12:3).

Romans 12:7

Or ministry, let us wait on our ministering: or he that teacheth, on teaching;

Note 4

The Greek word that was translated "ministry" here is "DIAKONIA," and it means "attendance (as a servant, etc.)" (Strong's Concordance). It is a variation of the Greek word "DIAKONOS" from which we get our English word "deacon." This same Greek word was translated "serving" in Luke 10:40, "service" (referring to charitable giving) in Romans 15:31, "relief" in Acts 11:29, and "office" in Romans 11:13. The Amplified Bible translates this verse as "[He whose gift is] practical service, let him give himself to serving." Therefore, we can surmise from these things that this is referring to those who have been given a ministry of serving others, as Paul described the house of Stephanas (1 Corinthians 16:15). This gift is not often recognized and even more often not appreciated, but it is listed in good company. Paul mentioned this between prophecy and teaching, two gifts that are recognized and accepted.

Note 5

The ministry gift of a teacher was placed third in authority in the church, behind the ministry of the apostle and the prophet (1 Corinthians 12:28). The basic difference between a teacher and a preacher is that a preacher proclaims and a teacher explains.

Romans 12:8

Or he that exhorteth, on exhortation: he that giveth, let him do it with simplicity; he that ruleth, with diligence; he that sheweth mercy, with cheerfulness.

LIVING COMMENTARY

All members of the body of Christ can exhort others, give, rule, and show mercy, but there are certain individuals who are called to these things as their ministry. Just as the previous verse spoke of those who are gifted with a teaching ministry (see my note at Romans 12:7), so some members are supernaturally gifted in these areas.

Note 6

The Greek word for "exhorteth" is "PARAKALEO." It was translated "beseech" in Romans 12:1, 15:30, and 16:17. It was also translated as "comfort," and it is probably used that way here. Our English word "exhort" comes from the Latin "EXHORTARI." This is a compound word comprised of "EX," meaning "completely" (www.wordinfo.info) and "HORTARI," meaning "encourage" (Merriam-Webster Dictionary). Therefore, the word "exhort" literally means to "completely encourage." One of the purposes of prophecy is exhortation (1 Corinthians 14:3). Exhortation is also a part of preaching the Word (2 Timothy 4:2). However, this verse shows that there are individuals who have a special ministry of encouraging people. This is a supernatural gift.

Note 7

The Greek word used here for "simplicity" is "HAPLOTES." According to Vine's Expository Dictionary, this word denotes "simplicity, sincerity, unaffectedness," but it can also mean "simplicity as manifested in generous giving." Most scholars agree that in this case, it is expressing generosity. Therefore, Paul was saying that those who have a ministry of giving should be generous in their giving.

Note 8

The Greek word translated "ruleth" here is "PROISTEMI," and it means "to stand before, i.e. (in rank) to preside" (Strong's Concordance). The Amplified Bible translates this phrase as "he who gives aid and superintends, with zeal and singleness of mind." This could be speaking of any one of many positions of authority in the church. This does reveal that although everyone has some degree of authority, there are individuals who are given a ministry gift of ruling, or what might be commonly called "administration" today.

Note 9

The Greek word that was translated "cheerfulness" here is "HILAROTES," and it means "alacrity" (Strong's Concordance). "Alacrity," according to the American Heritage Dictionary, means "cheerful willingness; eagerness." HILAROTES comes from the Greek word "HILAROS," which is where we get our word "hilarious." Therefore, Paul was admonishing those who show mercy to be hilarious in their administration of this gift.

Romans 12:9

Let love be without dissimulation. Abhor that which is evil; cleave to that which is good.

Note 1

The American Heritage Dictionary defines "dissimulate" as "to disguise under a feigned appearance." The Greek word that was used for "without dissimulation" was "ANUPOKRITOS," and it means "unfeigned, undisguised" (Thayer's Greek-English Lexicon). This Greek word was only used six times in all the New Testament. In James 3:17 it was translated "without hypocrisy," and four times it was translated "unfeigned" (2 Corinthians 6:6, 1 Timothy 1:5, 2 Timothy 1:5, and 1 Peter 1:22). Paul was still talking about love when he said, "Abhor that which is evil; cleave to that which is good." Part of true love is hatred (see note 2 at this verse). If we don't hate the things that oppose the one we love, then it is not God's kind of love. If we don't hate evil, then our love for God is with dissimulation. It is hypocritical. It has become customary in our society to conceal our real feelings behind a hypocritical mask. Although we should be tactful and not purposely say things to offend people, there is a time and a place for speaking the truth, even if it isn't popular. In Leviticus 19:17, the Lord said, "Thou shalt not hate thy brother in thine heart: thou shalt in any wise rebuke thy neighbour, and not suffer sin upon him." That verse is saying that if we fail to rebuke our brethren when we see sin approaching, then we hate them. Many people have concealed their true feelings about evil under the pretense of "I just love them too much to hurt their feelings." The truth is, they just love themselves too much to run the risk of being rejected. That's hypocrisy. This scripture commands us to abhor (see note 2 at this verse) that which is evil. We need to love the sinner, but hate the sin. We need to be outspoken on what is right and wrong. Jesus illustrated this scripture when He drove the moneychangers out of the temple (John 2:14-17).

Note 2

The Greek word that was translated "abhor" here is "APOSTUGEO," and it means "to detest utterly" (Strong's Concordance). Sometimes people have misunderstood and misapplied God's kind of love so that they no longer hate evil. However, Proverbs 8:13 says, "The fear of the LORD is to hate evil." Those who love the Lord hate evil (Psalm 97:10). Only the wicked don't abhor evil (Psalm 36:4). Jesus got angry (see notes 5-6 at Mark 3:5), and the Scriptures say His hatred for sin was the reason God anointed Him with gladness above His fellows (Psalm 45:7 and

Hebrews 1:9). It is impossible to truly love someone with God's kind of love without hating anything that comes against that person. There is a righteous type of anger that is not sin (Ephesians 4:26).

Romans 12:10

Be kindly affectioned one to another with brotherly love; in honour preferring one another;

Note 3

The word that was translated brotherly love" here is "PHILADELPHIA." It means "fraternal affection" (Strong's Concordance) and comes from the Greek word "PHILOS" ["dear, i.e. a friend" (Strong's Concordance)]. The Greek word that was translated "kindly affectioned" here is "PHILOSTORGOS," a compound of PHILOS and "STORGE" ("cherishing one's kindred") (Strong's Concordance). There is much confusion on the subject of love today because we have only one English word ("love") to describe a broad range of meanings. For example, if I said, "I love my wife, I love apple pie, and I love my dog," obviously I am not talking about love in the same degree or definition. In the New Testament, three major Greek words described the various kinds of love. One of these words, "EROS," was not actually used in the New Testament, but it was alluded to. The following is a brief definition of these three major words. EROS - sexual passion; arousal, its gratification and fulfillment. This Greek word is not used in the New Testament, probably because its origin came from the mythical god Eros, the god of love. It is inferred in many scriptures and is the only kind of love that God restricts to a one-man, one-woman relationship within the bounds of marriage (Song of Solomon 1:13, 4:5-6, 7:7-9, 8:10; 1 Corinthians 7:25; Ephesians 5:31; and Hebrews 13:4). PHILEO - friendly love based on feelings or emotions. We could describe "PHILEO" love as tender affection, delighting to be in the presence of someone, or a warm or good feeling toward someone that may come and go with intensity. This verb and its other related Greek words are found over seventy times in the New Testament. Although PHILEO-love is encouraged in Scripture, it is never a direct command. God never commands us to PHILEO (love) anyone, since this type of love is based on feelings. Even God did not PHILEO the world. He operated in "AGAPE" love toward us. The following are some scriptures in which PHILEO or a form of it is used: John 5:20, 11:3,36, 12:25, 16:27, 20:2; Acts 28:2; Romans 12:10; 1 Timothy 6:10; 2 Timothy 3:4; Titus 2:4, 3:4; Hebrews 13:1; 3 John 9; and Revelation 3:19. AGAPE - God's type of love; the highest kind of love. AGAPE is seeking the welfare or betterment of others even if there is not affection felt (paraphrase based on "Happiness Explained" by Bob Rigdon). AGAPE does not have the primary meaning of affection nor of coming from one's feelings. Jesus displayed this AGAPE kind of love by going to the cross and dying even though He didn't feel like dying. He prayed, "O my Father, if it be possible, let this cup pass from me: nevertheless not as I will, but as thou wilt" (Matthew 26:39, Mark 14:36, Luke 22:41-42, and John 18:11). Jesus sought the betterment of mankind, regardless of His feelings. We, too, can AGAPE (love) our enemies, even though we don't have any warm feelings of affection for them (Luke 6:35). If they are hungry, we can feed them; if they thirst, we can give them a drink (Romans 12:20-21). We can choose to seek the betterment and welfare of others regardless of how we feel. The Apostle John said, "Let us not love in word, neither in tongue; but in deed and in truth" (1 John 3:18). Jesus referred to His love for others (John 13:34; 15:9, and 12), but He never directly told anyone, "I love you."

Note 4

The American Heritage Dictionary defines "prefer" as "to choose as more desirable." That means this verse is admonishing us to desire the welfare of others more than our own. That is an awesome command that is only obtainable through God's supernatural love. If this very simple yet very profound truth could be understood and applied, then strife would cease (Proverbs 13:10), the world would see Christianity as never before (see note 3 at John 13:35), and we would discover the true joy that comes from serving someone besides ourselves (Matthew 10:39 and 16:25).

Romans 12:11

Not slothful in business; fervent in spirit; serving the Lord;

Note 5

There are many scriptures against slothfulness, or laziness. Paul even went so far as to say, "This we commanded you, that if any would not work, neither should he eat" (2 Thessalonians 3:10). It is interesting that Paul spoke about not being slothful right after he mentioned brotherly love and preferring one another. This adds a very important balance to brotherly love, a balance that many today are missing. While it is true that we have a responsibility to help others, it is also true that a handout doesn't help a lazy person. When we support those who are living in direct disobedience to God's instructions regarding slothfulness, we are hurting those people. Charity should be reserved for those who need it, not those who abuse it.

Note 6

The Amplified Bible's translation of this verse indicates that the "spirit" being spoken of here is the Holy Spirit ("Never lag in zeal and in earnest endeavor; be aglow and burning with the Spirit, serving the Lord"). The New American Standard Bible ("not lagging behind in diligence, fervent in spirit, serving the Lord") and the New International Version ("Never be lacking in zeal, but keep your spiritual fervor, serving the Lord") refer to "spirit" as our attitude. The Greek word that was translated "spirit" is "PNEUMA." This word was used to distinguish the Holy Spirit many times (Matthew 3:16, 10:20, 12:28; Luke 4:18, 11:13; John 7:39; and Acts 2:4), but it was also translated "spirit" when the context clearly indicates it is speaking of attitude (Matthew 5:3; 1 Corinthians 4:21; 2 Corinthians 4:13; Ephesians 1:17, 4:23; Philippians 1:27; 1 Timothy 4:12; and Revelation 19:10). PNEUMA can mean "mental disposition" (Strong's Concordance). In this application, "spirit" is speaking of our attitude. The American Heritage Dictionary defines "spirit" as "a predominant mood or attitude."

Note 7

This same point was made in Ephesians 6:6-7 where Paul said, "Not with eyeservice, as menpleasers; but as the servants of Christ, doing the will of God from the heart; With good will doing service, as to the Lord, and not to men." Paul was emphasizing that even in our business endeavors, we are serving the Lord and not man. He repeated this same thought in Colossians 3:23 when he said, "And whatsoever ye do, do it heartily, as to the Lord, and not unto men."

Romans 12:12

Rejoicing in hope; patient in tribulation; continuing instant in prayer;

LIVING COMMENTARY

Hope causes a person to rejoice. No rejoicing = no hope. See my notes on hope at Romans 8:24 and Hebrews

11:1. The English word "instant" in this verse came from the Greek word "PROSKARTEREO," which means "to be earnest toward, i.e. (to a thing) to persevere, be constantly diligent, or (in a place) to attend assiduously all the exercises, or (to a person) to adhere closely to (as a servitor)" (Strong's Concordance). So, this is speaking of being earnest, persevering, and constantly diligent to attend and adhere to prayer.

Romans 12:13

Distributing to the necessity of saints; given to hospitality.

LIVING COMMENTARY

Christian charity isn't limited to helping only our brothers and sisters in the Lord, but there is a special care that we are supposed to show toward fellow believers, as this verse describes. See also Galatians 6:10, Hebrews 6:10, and 1 John 3:17. It was a qualification for elders that they had to be given to hospitality (1 Timothy 3:2 and Titus 1:8). Many have entertained angels without knowing it as they gave hospitality. All of us are commanded to be hospitable to each other (this verse and 1 Peter 4:9).

Romans 12:14

Bless them which persecute you: bless, and curse not.

Living Commentary

This verse needs to be interpreted in the light of other scriptures that Paul wrote (such as 1 Corinthians 16:22 and Galatians 1:8-9). In those verses, Paul placed a terrible curse on those who didn't love the Lord and those who were perverting the true Gospel. So, which is it? Do we curse others, or don't we? The answer is yes to both. We don't retaliate with curses to those who persecute us. The Lord told us to turn the other cheek (Matthew 5:39), bless those who curse us, and do good to those who despitefully use us and persecute us (Matthew 5:44). But all of these admonitions are about us not avenging ourselves when we are persecuted (Romans 12:19). It's a totally different thing when it comes to a minister defending his flock and the true faith. The Lord told the pastor of the church at Pergamos that he had failed to rebuke the people in his church that held the doctrine of Balaam and the doctrine of the Nicolaitans (Revelation 2:12-15). If he didn't take his authority and rebuke these people, the Lord would fight against them (Revelation 2:16). A similar rebuke was given to the pastor of the church of Thyatira (Revelation 2:18-23). Paul also turned people over to Satan for the destruction of their flesh (see my notes at 1 Corinthians 5:5 and 1 Timothy 1:20). So, if it is just a matter of persecution, we bear it and bless those who persecute us. Our persecutor could be the next Apostle Paul (Acts 7:58). But if it is a matter of someone perverting the Truth and leading others into error, we must take a stand against that, even to the

point of bringing judgment on them as Paul did in Galatians 1:8-9 and 1 Corinthians 16:22. But this should not
be done lightly or by someone who is not in a position
of authority to do so. Paul suffered a demon-possessed
girl who mocked his message for many days before
he turned and rebuked the devil in her (Acts 16:17-
18). Paul placed a curse on Elymas the sorcerer (Acts
13:9-12) because he was withstanding the preaching of
the Gospel. But this is not an excuse for an immature
Christian to bring a curse on someone they don't like
or someone who has hurt them. One test we can place
on this is to examine our motives. Are we coming out
against someone because of personal hurt or selfish
motives? Then that's wrong. But if we are taking a stand
for the Truth, then there may be times when a minister
has to do as Paul did and even Jesus did (Matthew 23)
when He rebuked and cursed the Pharisees, scribes, and
lawyers.

Note 8

Many people think of a curse only in relation to witchcraft. It should
go without saying that Christians should not practice witchcraft against
those who have done them harm. However, that is not the type of curse
that is being spoken of here. The Greek word used for "curse" here is
"KATARAOMAI," and it means "to execrate; by analogy, to doom"
(Strong's Concordance). The word "execrate" means "to protest vehe-
mently against; denounce" (American Heritage Dictionary). Vine's
Expository Dictionary says KATARAOMAI means "to pray against,
to wish evil against a person or thing." Therefore, vicious talk about

others is actually a curse. Without realizing it, many Christians curse others and thereby allow the devil access to the lives of those they are denouncing. Proverbs 18:21 says, "Death and life are in the power of the tongue: and they that love it shall eat the fruit thereof." Every word we speak releases either life or death. Our negative talk releases death. When we speak against others, we are actually releasing Satan against them. Once we understand this, it should make us pray this prayer with David, "Set a watch, O LORD, before my mouth; keep the door of my lips" (Psalm 141:3).

Romans 12:15

Rejoice with them that do rejoice, and weep with them that weep.

Note 9

Self-centered people will not rejoice at someone else's prosperity. They will be jealous instead. Likewise, selfish people will not weep with those that weep, because they really don't care about anyone but themselves. Paul was continuing the thought about preferring one another (see note 4 at Romans 12:10).

Romans 12:16

Be of the same mind one toward another. Mind not high things, but condescend to men of low estate. Be not wise in your own conceits.

Living Commentary

Notice that Paul commanded the Romans to be of the same mind toward each other. People today don't even have that as a goal, much less something they have attained unto. But unity among believers is commanded in Scripture. The only way to attain that is to let the mind of Christ be in us (see my notes at Philippians 2:3-11). This command not to mind high things is saying "Don't be a snob." There is no room for such a thing in Christianity.

Note 10

This is not saying that Christians should never occupy prominent positions. If that were true, then Paul would not have needed to admonish these people to be willing to associate with those of low estate. They wouldn't have any other choice. Many Bible people were people of renown, even among the unbelievers [examples: Abraham, Isaac, Joseph, David, Solomon, Paul (Acts 28:7), and John (John 18:15)]. Paul was just saying that we shouldn't seek out prestigious people and snub those whom the world doesn't consider important. God doesn't evaluate people the way that the world does. Those who are greatest in His kingdom are the greatest servants. We will miss some of the most beautiful people who could bless our lives if we judge people by the world's standards. We also run the risk of destroying our faith when we seek the honor that comes from man (see note 22 at John 5:44).

Romans 12:17

Recompense to no man evil for evil. Provide things honest in the sight of all men.

LIVING COMMENTARY

Paul was preaching the same message Jesus gave in Matthew 5:39-44. Paul repeated this in 1 Thessalonians 5:15. Peter said the same thing in 1 Peter 3:9.

Note 11

There is an unwritten but widely understood code in human relations that says we should treat people the way they treat us. Jesus taught just the opposite (see note 1 at Luke 23:34), and Paul was reaffirming that same teaching here. If we are to be Christlike, then we cannot give people what they deserve.

Note 12

It is not enough just to be honest in the sight of God. This scripture commands us to also have integrity in the sight of man. This corresponds to "abstain from all appearance of evil" (1 Thessalonians 5:22). We not only need to be right, but we also need to appear right as much as possible.

Romans 12:18

If it be possible, as much as lieth in you, live peaceably with all men.

Note 13

This verse is advocating living peaceably with all people, yet the very wording reveals that this is not always possible. We are not responsible for other people's actions. We must pursue peace, even when we are not at fault, but the other people do have a choice. We should be sure that we are at peace with all people. Whether or not they are at peace with us is their decision.

Romans 12:19

Dearly beloved, avenge not yourselves, but rather give place unto wrath: for it is written, Vengeance is mine; I will repay, saith the Lord.

LIVING COMMENTARY

This is a loose quotation from Deuteronomy 32:35. Many commentators believe that the phrase "give place unto wrath" means we are to allow the Lord to work His wrath on those who do us wrong instead of trying to inflict it ourselves. It is evident that this whole verse is saying that the Lord will fight for us. This reveals that the Lord takes what happens to His saints personally, just as he spoke to Saul on the road to Damascus (see my note at Acts 9:4). If we will leave vengeance to the Lord, He will deal with those who hurt us. If we take the matter into our own hands, then we only get what we can do. The Lord is much more capable of dealing with those who trouble us than we are.

Note 14

Romans 12:19-21 is humanly impossible. It takes the supernatural power of God's faith at work in our hearts to fulfill these scriptures. Letting God be the one who defends us is a matter of faith. If there is no God who will bring people into account for their actions, then turning the other cheek would be the worst thing we could do (see note 22 at Matthew 5:44). But if there is a God who promised that vengeance is His and He will repay, then taking matters into our own hands shows a lack of faith in God and His integrity.

Romans 12:20

Therefore if thine enemy hunger, feed him; if he thirst, give him drink: for in so doing thou shalt heap coals of fire on his head.

LIVING COMMENTARY

Paul was quoting from Proverbs 25:21-22. It's a near verbatim quote, except Paul left out the closing phrase "and the LORD shall reward thee." He did get that point across, though, by his statements in Romans 12:19 about the Lord avenging His people. See my notes at Proverbs 25:21-22.

Note 15

These coals of fire are not coals of punishment or torment, but rather conviction. If this was urging us to be kind to our enemies because that would hurt them more than anything else, then that would be violating the context of this verse. Paul was telling us to live peaceably with all people (Romans 12:18) and to render to no one evil for evil (Romans

12:17). God's kind of love is being promoted, not some scriptural way to hurt those who hurt us. When we walk in love toward those who hurt us, it heaps conviction on them. They know what their reaction would be if they were in our place, and to see us walk in love under adverse circumstances shows them that we have something special that they don't have. Paul should know. He saw Stephen forgive and pray for the very people who stoned him to death. When Jesus appeared to Paul on the road to Damascus, He told him that it was hard "to kick against the pricks." The Lord was saying it was hard for Paul to resist the conviction that had come to him through Stephen's witness (see note 6 at Acts 9:5).

Romans 12:21

Be not overcome of evil, but overcome evil with good.

Note 16

We cannot fight evil with evil. Evil has to be overcome with good. It is frustrating to see the schemes of Satan and his kingdom; however, we must never let our frustration drive us to using their tactics. The wrath of man does not accomplish the righteousness of God (James 1:20). Instead of cursing the darkness, turn on a light.

ROMANS

CHAPTER THIRTEEN

Romans 13:1

Let every soul be subject unto the higher powers. For there is no power but of God: the powers that be are ordained of God.

Note 1

The subject of submission to authority is a very basic Bible doctrine. Some of the major areas of submission commanded in the Scriptures are (1) submission to God (Ephesians 5:24 and James 4:7), (2) submission to civil or governmental authority (Romans 13:1-7), (3) submission to the church or religious authority (Hebrews 13:17), (4) wives submitting to their husbands (Ephesians 5:22-24 and Colossians 3:18), (5) children submitting to their parents (Ephesians 6:1 and Colossians 3:20), (6) slaves submitting to their masters (today's equivalent would be employees submitting to employers, 1 Peter 2:18), (7) the younger submitting to the older (1 Peter 5:5), and (8) all of us submitting to each other in love (Ephesians 5:21 and 1 Peter 5:5). The Greek word translated "subject" here, as well as thirteen other times in the New Testament, is "HUPOTASSO." This was a military term meaning "to rank under" (Vine's Expository Dictionary).

Although, in most cases, obedience is a part of submission, these terms are not synonymous. Just as those enlisted in the army have limits to their obedience to an officer, so we only obey others as long as their commands do not oppose God. A failure to understand the difference between submission and obedience has given birth to many false teachings that have caused some people to obey others in matters of sin. That is never commanded in the Word of God. One of the easiest ways to see that a person can submit without obeying an ungodly command is to look at the life of Peter. Peter made some striking statements in 1 Peter 2:13-14 when he said, "Submit yourselves to every ordinance of man for the Lord's sake: whether it be to the king, as supreme; or unto governors, as unto them that are sent by him for the punishment of evildoers, and for the praise of them that do well." This was the same Peter who refused to obey the chief priests when they commanded him not to speak or teach anymore in the name of Jesus (Acts 4:18-19). When Peter and the other apostles continued their teaching and preaching about Jesus, the high priest and the Jewish elders imprisoned them. However, they were supernaturally freed from prison by an angel of the Lord who told them to go back to the temple and preach again (Acts 5:17-20). This command was a direct contradiction to the commands of the Jews. The Jews again arrested Peter and the other apostles and said (Acts 5:28), "Did not we straitly command you that ye should not teach in this name?" Peter responded by saying, "We ought to obey God rather than men" (Acts 5:29). This is always the bottom line. We never obey any person if that would cause us to disobey God. And yet, we are to submit to every ordinance of man (1 Peter 2:13).

Submission is an attitude, not an action. It will express itself through actions, but we can have a submissive attitude and yet disobey an ungodly command. If government officials commanded us not to preach Jesus, we should follow the example of Peter, and not obey them. But we should also not rebel at their authority, in the same way that Peter and the other apostles did not rebel at the authority of the Jews. When the apostles were beaten for their obedience to God, they didn't criticize or form a revolt. They praised God and kept right on preaching the Gospel (Acts 5:41-42). They didn't obey ungodly commands, but they didn't become ungodly, either, by cursing those who had hurt them (see note 8 at Romans 12:14). They submitted to the authority over them to the point that they took a beating without one complaint, but they never did do what the Jews commanded them. If a man commanded his wife not to go to church anymore, she should not obey that command. The Bible clearly says not to forsake the assembling of ourselves together (Hebrews 10:25).

However, there is a submissive way and a rebellious way of doing that. If she said, "You old reprobate. You never have liked me going to church. Well, I'm going to show you that you can't tell me what to do. I'm going anyway, and I don't care what you say," that would be a rebellious attitude. Yet, a woman in the same circumstance could affirm her love to her husband and state that she really wants to comply as much as possible, but in this instance, she has to obey God over her husband. If that was her attitude, she would be in submission to her husband even though she wouldn't do what he said. Submission is also a voluntary thing. You cannot make another person submit. You can make people obey you, but that doesn't mean they've submitted. Their attitude is totally a matter of choice on their part. This is the reason that a man cannot hear a teaching on submission and go home and make his wife submit. She has to choose to submit. The book of Daniel has two examples of civil disobedience done through a commitment to God's higher laws (Daniel 3:8-18 and 6:10-17), yet this disobedience was accomplished with respect and submission to the civil authority. When Pharaoh commanded that the male Hebrew babies were to be killed at birth (Exodus 1:16), Moses' parents did not obey, and God blessed them for their actions. Submission is an essential part of true Christianity. However, it is a missing ingredient in most of our lives. The root of all lack of submission in our lives lies in pride (1 Peter 5:4-6).

Note 2

This sentence—"For there is no power but of God: the powers that be are ordained of God"—has perplexed many people. Was Paul saying that God wills that there be oppressive governments like the Nazis or even the Roman government that Paul was under? Definitely not. Even though He has used corrupt rulers and governments to punish offenses, their governmental authority was not created by God to be oppressive. They were ordained to be ministers of God to us for good (Romans 13:4). In the same way that God ordains people to the ministry yet they fail to fulfill that call as God intended, likewise, God ordains governments but doesn't ordain everything that they do. There are countless scriptural examples of rebukes and punishments by God upon civil leaders because they did not submit to His will. God's original government over mankind was directly administered by God Himself. People answered only to their Creator. Even after the Fall, God worked in cooperation with people's consciences to restrain them from evil. In the beginning, this was effective, as can be seen through Cain's statement, "My punishment is greater than I can bear" (Genesis 4:13). However, people seared their consciences (1 Timothy 4:2) through repeated sin. Therefore, since people were no longer responsive to their Creator, God ordained people to begin to police themselves. He told Noah, "Whoso sheddeth man's blood, by man shall his blood be shed: for in the image of God made he man" (Genesis 9:6). This responsibility of a corporate body to avenge the wrongs of an individual continued to develop until, through the giving of the Old Testament Law, God gave detailed instructions on how mankind was to treat each other and prescribed punishments for failure to do so. So, in that context, God did ordain all government. But in more cases than not, governments are not any more responsive to Him than are individuals. However, we are to submit to them and obey them as long as we don't have to violate a clear command of God. Even bad government is superior to anarchy. The governors themselves may not be of God, but civil government is definitely of God.

Romans 13:2

Whosoever therefore resisteth the power, resisteth the ordinance of God: and they that resist shall receive to themselves damnation.

Note 3

Notice specifically Paul's choice of words here. "Whosoever therefore **resisteth the power**" (emphasis mine). The word "resist" implies actively fighting against. As discussed in note 1 at Romans 13:1, we can refuse to comply with ungodly edicts without resisting the government that issued them. And the word "power" is referring directly to the authority of the government itself, not just its directives. Therefore, Paul was instructing us not to fight against the authority of the government we live under. That doesn't mean we have to comply with any law that is in direct opposition to God's laws, but when we oppose the order of government, we are opposing God's order. The early Christians were great examples of this. They lived under one of the most corrupt and ruthless governments of all time. The Roman emperors even proclaimed themselves as gods. Yet nowhere in Scripture was there any instruction given to the believers to subvert that government and replace it. On the contrary, Paul commanded the believers to pray for their governmental leaders (1 Timothy 2:1-4). Peter commanded the believers to submit to every ordinance of the king and governors (1 Peter 2:13-14). The early Christians never brought any political pressure to bear on the Roman government or encouraged revolt. Yet in a relatively short period of time, Christianity overwhelmed the pagan Roman government and was adopted as the official state religion. Although this was one of the worst things that ever happened to Christianity, it does illustrate how we can overcome evil with good (Romans 12:21).

Note 4

The word that was translated "damnation" here is the Greek word "KRIMA." This word was translated "judgment" twelve times, "damnation" seven times, "condemnation" five times, "be condemned" once, "judgments" once, "go to law" once, and "avenged" once. It means "'judgment'; i.e. condemnation of wrong, the decision (whether severe or mild) which one passes on the faults of others...in a forensic sense, the sentence of a judge" (Thayer's Greek-English Lexicon). In this case, this is not speaking of the eternal damnation or judgment of God. This is saying that if people resist the power of government, they will come under the judgment of that government.

Romans 13:3

For rulers are not a terror to good works, but to the evil. Wilt thou then not be afraid of the power? do that which is good, and thou shalt have praise of the same:

Note 5

There are certainly scriptural exceptions to this statement. The Egyptian government turned on the Israelites (Exodus 1:8-22) not because of any sin on their part but because of the insecurities and fears of the Pharaoh. James the apostle was killed by Herod just because it pleased the Jews (Acts 12:2-3). John the Baptist was imprisoned and beheaded by Herod, and Jesus Himself commented on the innocence of John (Matthew 11:9-11). However, there is a truth that, as a whole, even corrupt governments do not bother those who are doing good. Paul was an example of this. Many times the Roman government actually came to his defense (Acts 18:12-16, 19:35-41, 21:31-36, 23:23-24, 25:1-5, and 27:42-44). In the book of Daniel, Daniel and his three friends were repeatedly honored even though the governmental system was corrupt and unjust. Joseph prospered in Egypt despite the injustices done to him. With few exceptions, governments are established to protect the good and punish the evil. If we do good, we have nothing to fear.

Romans 13:4

For he is the minister of God to thee for good. But if thou do that which is evil, be afraid; for he beareth not the sword in vain: for he is the minister of God, a revenger to execute wrath upon him that doeth evil.

Note 6

The Greek word that was translated "minister" here was also translated "deacon" and "servant." Government officials, including the police and army, were ordained by God to minister to us. The Lord uses this civil authority to protect us and execute His wrath on the ungodly. Knowing this gives us added assurance when we pray for justice to be done through the judicial system (1 John 5:14-15). When people fail to respond to the conviction of the Holy Spirit, we can pray that the Lord will use the legal system to stop their evil ways.

Those in the legal system are ministers of God. Many thousands of prisoners have praised God for the prison term that finally stopped them and made them come to grips with the real problems of their lives.

Note 7

The sword that is being spoken of here is symbolic of power to restrain or kill. That is what swords were used for. God has delegated some of His power to rule to governments, even to the extent of taking life. The Lord told Noah that any person who murdered another had to die at the hand of mankind (Genesis 9:5-6, see note 2 at Romans 13:1). Likewise, this verse shows that God has given government the right to use force and execute His wrath, which would include capital punishment. Even some wars can be justified on the basis of this scripture (see note 6 at John 18:36). Therefore, Christians can serve as police officers or soldiers as long as they are enforcing what is right.

Romans 13:5

Wherefore ye must needs be subject, not only for wrath, but also for conscience sake.

Note 8

In Romans 13:1-4, Paul gave two reasons for being subject to civil government, which he summarized here. First, we need to be subject to it because the government has the power to punish us if we aren't. Second, since God has ordained government, we have to submit or our consciences will condemn us for violating the instruction of God. Therefore, even if we could break the laws of government and get away with it, we shouldn't, because we are also violating God's Word. So laws that are not in direct opposition to God's Word should be kept, whether or not we will get caught and whether or not we think they are important. In the next verse (Romans 13:6), Paul specifically mentioned taxes as one of those laws that we should comply with (see note 9 at Romans 13:6). This could be updated to include speed limits, local ordinances, and a host of other things that many of us may disagree with but cannot say are directly against God's Word. The government has a God-given right and responsibility to regulate and establish order, and we should comply for consciences' sake. Our submission to government and our submission to God are intertwined.

Romans 13:6

For for this cause pay ye tribute also: for they are God's ministers, attending continually upon this very thing.

Note 9

Paul had commanded being subject to the laws of the government we live under as long as they don't cause us to sin against God (see note 1 at Romans 13:1). In Romans 13:5, Paul said we need to do this not just because of the power of government to punish us, but even if we never got caught, we need to submit because of our submission to God (see note 8 at Romans 13:5). Then he mentioned taxes. Many Christians feel that taxes and serving God are two different things. But the Lord commanded us to pay our taxes. We cannot be true servants of God and refuse to obey Him in this area. Jesus, as the Creator, was not obligated to pay taxes to His creation, but He did (see note 1 at Matthew 17:25). He paid taxes to a corrupt system where much of the tax money went straight into the pockets of the tax collectors. In the United States of America, we are given certain tax deductions for charitable gifts and other exemptions. There is nothing wrong with taking advantage of these or even using the political process to try to change taxation laws that we feel are wrong.

Our government guarantees us those rights. But no Christian has any scriptural ground for refusing to pay taxes. Whether or not we can get away with it is immaterial. God commands us to submit, even in the area of taxes. Failure to do so is rebellion against God.

Romans 13:7

Render therefore to all their dues: tribute to whom tribute is due; custom to whom custom; fear to whom fear; honour to whom honour.

LIVING COMMENTARY

Many Christians fail to follow these commands, but their reasoning is wrong. Just because a government is corrupt or an individual is corrupt is no reason not to comply with these instructions.

Romans 13:8

Owe no man any thing, but to love one another: for he that loveth another hath fulfilled the law.

Note 1

In context, Paul was speaking about paying our taxes, respect, and honor (Romans 13:7). However, this principle holds true in every area of our lives. We are to pay our bills. Some people have interpreted this verse as forbidding Christians to go in debt. It can be shown in Scripture that purchasing on credit is not a blessing but a curse (Deuteronomy 28:12 and 44); therefore, it is not God's best. However, it is not a sin to borrow money. Many scriptures speak of lending money and place restrictions on whom we should lend to. The Lord would not have us help someone sin. Therefore, being in debt is not a sin. Failure to pay our bills or make payments on loans that we have given our word on, however, is wrong.

Note 2

Notice that Paul spoke of love for others as a debt. This is not optional. We are commanded to love one another. Indeed, this is the royal law of God (James 2:8).

Note 3

Mankind as a whole had misunderstood the purpose of the Law. They thought that God was giving a list of what people must do to be accepted by Him. But the Law was given to convince people that they didn't have a chance of saving themselves; they needed a savior (see note 4 at Romans 3:19). However, the Law was accurate and a perfect description of what God created man to be. The Law portrayed what those who were walking in God's kind of love would do. Man still can't keep the Law perfectly in the flesh (see note 9 at Romans 8:4), but the New Testament believers can now fulfill the spirit of the Old Testament Law as those in the Old Testament never could.

Romans 13:9

For this, Thou shalt not commit adultery, Thou shalt not kill, Thou shalt not steal, Thou shalt not bear false witness, Thou shalt not covet; and if there be any other commandment, it is briefly comprehended in this saying, namely, Thou shalt love thy neighbour as thyself.

LIVING COMMENTARY

This lists the seventh, sixth, eighth, ninth, and tenth commandments of the Ten Commandments (Exodus 20:13-17). See my notes at Matthew 22:39-40. This was quoted from Leviticus 19:18. Loving our neighbor as ourselves would cause us to fulfill the last five of the Ten Commandments, which all deal with our relationships with others. However, we have an even better commandment under the New Testament. Jesus said in John 13:34 that we were to love others as He has loved us. That's even better. Jesus loved us more than any of us have loved ourselves. He died for us when we were yet sinners (Romans 5:8). This is far better than loving our neighbor as ourselves.

Romans 13:10

Love worketh no ill to his neighbour: therefore love is the fulfilling of the law.

LIVING COMMENTARY

Love would never kill anyone or steal from them or slander them or do anything wrong to them. Anyone who commits one of these acts is not walking in love toward their neighbor.

Note 4

Instead of focusing on all the dos and don'ts, all we have to do is let God's kind of love rule in our hearts and we will automatically meet the requirements of the Law.

Romans 13:11

And that, knowing the time, that now it is high time to awake out of sleep: for now is our salvation nearer than when we believed.

Note 1

Paul had commanded submission to government, and he used two reasons for compliance (see note 8 at Romans 13:5). The most important reason was not just to avoid being caught and punished by the government but to have a good conscience toward God. He was continuing that thought in this verse. He was saying that the time left before the Lord's return is growing short and that we must therefore be even more sensitive to God. This is the same reasoning that the Lord Jesus used in the parable of the ten virgins and the parable of the stewards and their talents (Matthew 25). The message of these four verses (Romans 13:11-14) can be summed up in the words of Jesus from Luke 21:34. The issue of the Lord's imminent return adds even more importance to us walking in love.

Romans 13:12

The night is far spent, the day is at hand: let us therefore cast off the works of darkness, and let us put on the armour of light.

LIVING COMMENTARY

This is a parable comparing the short time we have before the Lord's return to the way darkness comes after late evening. If this was true 2,000 years ago, then it is even truer today. We don't know if the Lord is coming back in our lifetime; but He is going to return, and it's soon.

Romans 13:13

Let us walk honestly, as in the day; not in rioting and drunkenness, not in chambering and wantonness, not in strife and envying.

LIVING COMMENTARY

The English word "chambering" was translated from the Greek word "KOITE," and this Greek word means "a couch; by extension, cohabitation; by implication, the male sperm" (Strong's Concordance). This is speaking of sex without marriage. The Amplified Bible translated this verse as "Let us live and conduct ourselves honorably and becomingly as in the [open light of] day, not in reveling (carousing) and drunkenness, not in immorality and debauchery (sensuality and licentiousness), not in quarreling and jealousy." The New International Version says, "Let us behave decently, as in the daytime, not in orgies and drunkenness, not in sexual immorality and debauchery, not in dissension and jealousy."

Note 2

The American Heritage Dictionary defines "wanton" as "1. Immoral or unchaste; lewd. 2. Gratuitously cruel; merciless. 3. Unrestrainedly excessive. 4. Luxuriant; overabundant. 5. Frolicsome; playful. 6. Undisciplined."

Romans 13:14

But put ye on the Lord Jesus Christ, and make not provision for the flesh, to fulfil the lusts thereof.

LIVING COMMENTARY

This verse starts with the word "but." It is contrasting this verse with the previous verse (Romans 13:13). So, instead of the immoral life denounced in the previous verse, we are supposed to live the godly life described in this verse. The English word "provision" was translated from the Greek word "PRONOIA," and this Greek word means "forethought, i.e. provident care or supply" (Strong's Concordance). So, this provision that we are not supposed to make for the desires of the flesh is speaking of thoughts. All sin starts in our thoughts (see my notes at James 1:14-15). We cannot be tempted with something that we haven't thought (see my note at Hebrews 11:15).

Note 3

Paul was using the term "flesh" here as referring to the part of us that has not been changed by Christ; i.e., our sinful appetites and desires (see note 3 at Romans 7:18). These sinful lusts cannot dominate us if we don't make provision for them. Paul was saying to cut off the flesh's rations and starve it to death. Many of us Christians have mistakenly believed that during our lives here on the earth, we are doomed to have ungodly lusts and desires. However, it doesn't have to be that way. The sin nature that enslaved our flesh is gone, and to the degree that we renew our minds through God's Word, we can experience victory over the flesh (see note 9 at Romans 5:21). The reason that the flesh seems so strong in many of our lives is because we are continually feeding it. Temptation is linked to what we think on. If we don't think on things that engender temptation, we won't be tempted and won't sin (see note 9 at Romans 4:19).

ROMANS

———⚬⚬⚬⚬———

CHAPTER FOURTEEN

Romans 14:1

Him that is weak in the faith receive ye, but not to doubtful disputations.

Note 1

Paul wrote this epistle to the saints in Rome. There was a big argument between the Jewish Christians and the Gentile Christians over the issue of grace versus works. Paul spent the majority of this letter dealing with the mistaken teaching that Gentiles who became Christians had to keep the Old Testament laws in order to be saved. The main Old Testament requirement Paul dealt with up to this point was circumcision (Romans 4).

He conclusively proved that circumcision, or any other part of the Law, was unnecessary for salvation (see note 1 at Romans 4:9, notes 2-3 at Romans 4:10, note 4 at Romans 4:11, and note 5 at Romans 4:12). The only thing that God requires for the born-again experience is faith in what Jesus Christ did for us (see note 2 at Romans 4:14). In this chapter, Paul brought up two more points of the Law that were real stumbling blocks to Jewish Christians. The first was the issue of eating meats that the Law declared unclean, and the second was the issue of observing special days such as the Sabbath and the feast days. The

Jewish Christians were saying that the Gentile Christians had to keep these laws. The Gentile Christians felt no obligation to old Jewish rituals. Paul stated that the Gentile Christians were correct doctrinally (Romans 14:20), but he warned them against despising their weak Jewish brethren who could not, in good conscience, eat meat or skip the observance of special days. Therefore, Paul established a principle that those who have the greater revelation of their freedom in Christ have an obligation to try not to display that freedom in a way that offends their weak brethren.

Note 2

Who was the weak brother referred to here? It was the religious Jew who was converted to Christianity. Romans 14:2 refers to the weak one as the one who was eating herbs. This was a reference to the Jewish Christians who had not totally realized their freedom from the Old Testament dietary laws. The Old Testament Law forbade Jews from eating certain meats (Leviticus 11) and blood (Genesis 9:4; Leviticus 3:17, 7:26-27, 17:10-14; Deuteronomy 12:16, 23-25, and 15:23). Because the Jews who were in Rome could not always be certain of what type of meat they were buying or if it had been killed properly to drain the blood, many of them had become vegetarians to avoid any possible contamination. It is very interesting that Paul cited the religious person as the weak brother. Most religious people think that all their religious convictions make them superior to those who come to Christ without any religious background, but that wasn't Paul's assessment. There is no bondage like religious bondage. A simple pagan background is easy to overcome in comparison to a heritage of legalistic religion. Paul ought to know; he was the Pharisee of the Pharisees.

Note 3

Paul was saying that we shouldn't be critical of or discriminate against those who are weak in their convictions. This has been interpreted by some as inconsistent with some of Paul's actions. Right here, in this epistle, Paul had called the legalistic Jewish Christians impenitent and hardhearted (Romans 2:5). In dealing with the same subject in the letter to the Galatians, Paul was very uncompromising, saying that they had been bewitched (Galatians 3:1) and that they were fallen from grace if they trusted in circumcision (Galatians 5:2- 4). He also said, in Galatians 2:5, that he didn't give any place to the legalistic Jews who were advocating circumcision for salvation. How do Paul's actions harmonize with what he was teaching here? There are some doctrinal points that are nonnegotiable and others that are not. When it comes to the doctrine of grace for salvation, Paul didn't compromise. He even said, "But though we, or an angel from heaven, preach any other gospel unto you than that which we have preached unto you, let him be accursed" (Galatians 1:8). If these Jewish believers had taught that abstinence from meats and observance of special days are essential for salvation, Paul would not have tolerated it. However, if these Jewish Christians were professing righteousness with God solely based on the work of Christ yet had a personal conviction about these other things, that was okay. The thought or the motive behind the action is what must be judged. Paul didn't object to circumcision; Paul objected to faith in circumcision instead of faith in Christ. He even circumcised Timothy to keep from offending the Jews (Acts 16:3). Yet when the legalistic Jews tried to pressure Paul about the circumcision of Titus (Galatians 2:3-5), Paul would not bend. Likewise, we cannot compromise on the matter of salvation by grace through faith (Ephesians 2:8). But there should be room for Christians to dwell together yet have different ways of conduct.

Romans 14:2

*For one believeth that he may eat all things: another, who is weak,
eateth herbs.*

Note 4

This verse is speaking of the Gentile Christian who didn't have any
convictions about eating certain meats and the Jewish Christian who
would only eat herbs for fear of breaking an Old Testament dietary law
(see note 2 at Romans 14:1).

Romans 14:3

*Let not him that eateth despise him that eateth not; and let not
him which eateth not judge him that eateth: for God hath received
him.*

Note 5

Paul was preaching about having a tolerance for other believers who
had differing views that may have appeared contradictory to his own
actions. However, as explained in note 3 at Romans 14:1, these were
not believers who were putting faith in these actions for salvation;
they wouldn't have been true Christians if they had. These people were
justified by faith, but they had a personal conviction about keeping the
ceremonial law of their Jewish heritage. These people were different
from the ones that Paul spoke of in his letter to Timothy. In 1 Timothy 4:1-3, Paul said those who commanded others to abstain from
meats were speaking a doctrine of devils. The key difference is the word
"commanding" (1 Timothy 4:3). Those in 1 Timothy 4 were demanding
compliance for salvation. The people that Paul was saying to receive in

this verse were people who were not judging others for their own personal convictions.

Note 6

Notice that Paul instructed those who have the revelation of their freedom in Christ not to despise those who don't. He also instructed those who are still emphasizing works not to judge those who aren't. Paul was revealing that the danger for those who have a revelation of God's grace is to become insensitive to and impatient with their brethren who haven't yet come to that knowledge. Those believers have to temper their freedom in Christ with love for their fellow Christians. "Knowledge puffeth up, but charity edifieth" (1 Corinthians 8:1). Those who have not yet renewed their minds to their freedom from the Old Testament Law tend to be judgmental of others who don't have their same standard of holiness. Passing judgment on others is a sure sign of a legalistic mentality (see note 46 at Matthew 7:1).

Romans 14:4

Who art thou that judgest another man's servant? to his own master he standeth or falleth. Yea, he shall be holden up: for God is able to make him stand.

Note 7

We are all servants, not judges. We should let the Lord be the judge. All that we are supposed to judge is ourselves, to make sure that we aren't stumbling blocks to anyone (Romans 14:13).

Romans 14:5

One man esteemeth one day above another: another esteemeth
every day alike. Let every man be fully persuaded in his own mind.

Note 8

On other occasions, Paul called it bondage to observe special days
(Galatians 4:9-10). Once again, this must be denoting people who were
observing certain days as a mere conviction and not a command (see
note 3 at Romans 14:1). Personal conviction and doctrinal truth are two
different things.

Romans 14:6

He that regardeth the day, regardeth it unto the Lord; and he that
regardeth not the day, to the Lord he doth not regard it. He that
eateth, eateth to the Lord, for he giveth God thanks; and he that
eateth not, to the Lord he eateth not, and giveth God thanks.

Note 9

This verse verifies that these observances of certain days and abstinence
from meats were not done in a legalistic manner that caused people to
think they were earning salvation. They were doing these things as unto
the Lord.

Romans 14:7

For none of us liveth to himself, and no man dieth to himself.

LIVING COMMENTARY

This will come as news to many people. In their eyes, nobody else matters. We've all heard people say, "It's my life. I'm not hurting anyone but myself." But that is certainly not true. Our lives are inextricably intertwined with others'. Those who love us suffer with us when we make poor decisions. Those who don't even know us suffer by having to pay for our mistakes. But the main reason that is explained in Romans 14:8 is that God loves us and is touched with everything we feel (Hebrews 4:15).

Romans 14:8

For whether we live, we live unto the Lord; and whether we die, we die unto the Lord: whether we live therefore, or die, we are the Lord's.

LIVING COMMENTARY

The child of God is just that—a child of God. And as our heavenly Father, the Lord is touched with everything that touches us. In life or death, the Lord never leaves us or forsakes us (Hebrews 13:5). I think The Message captures the thrust of what Paul was saying: "It's God we are answerable to—all the way from life to death and everything in between—not each other."

Romans 14:9

For to this end Christ both died, and rose, and revived, that he might be Lord both of the dead and living.

LIVING COMMENTARY

Jesus became one of us, died for us, and rose again that He might be Lord, or Master, of every part of our lives. Therefore, we answer to Him, not our critics.

Romans 14:10

But why dost thou judge thy brother? or why dost thou set at nought thy brother? for we shall all stand before the judgment seat of Christ.

LIVING COMMENTARY

Keeping in mind that we will someday stand side by side with the person we have judged before the great judgment of God will soften our judgments. The Lord will have judgment without mercy on those who have shown no mercy (James 2:12-13).

Romans 14:11

For it is written, As I live, saith the Lord, every knee shall bow to me, and every tongue shall confess to God.

LIVING COMMENTARY

Isaiah 45:23 is the closest Old Testament scripture to this that I could find. Think of this: Every God-hater, every tyrant, every evil person who has ever lived will bow their knee and confess that Jesus is Lord (Philippians 2:9-11). Those who lived their lives in total rebellion to the Lord will come to the same place of submission to the Lordship of Jesus as those of us who served Him in this life. But it will be too late. Their confession and submission will be too late to grant them salvation. They will spend eternity in remorse over their folly. It's much better to do it now rather than later. It not only grants us the greatest life possible now but also guarantees our eternal blessings in the next life.

Note 10

Paul was citing this Old Testament verse to show that each one of us is accountable to God (Romans 14:12). Therefore, we don't have to judge our brethren; God will do it.

Romans 14:12

So then every one of us shall give account of himself to God.

LIVING COMMENTARY

It's a full-time job for each of us to take care of ourselves, much less police everyone else. We should leave that up to the Lord and mind our own business.

Romans 14:13

Let us not therefore judge one another any more: but judge this rather, that no man put a stumblingblock or an occasion to fall in his brother's way.

LIVING COMMENTARY

See my notes on judging at Matthew 7:1-4. Instead of judging others, we should judge ourselves so that we aren't a stumbling block to others.

Note 11

We are not supposed to judge others (see note 46 at Matthew 7:1). Instead, we are supposed to judge ourselves to make sure that we are not causing them to stumble in their faith through our actions.

Romans 14:14

I know, and am persuaded by the Lord Jesus, that there is nothing unclean of itself: but to him that esteemeth any thing to be unclean, to him it is unclean.

LIVING COMMENTARY

Paul wasn't making a statement about all sin. He was specifically speaking about clean and unclean animals (Romans 14:2-3). There isn't any animal that is unclean of itself (1 Timothy 4:3-4). It's only our consciences that make eating certain animals wrong. Although our consciences aren't the perfect guide and can be wrong, it's not wisdom to violate our consciences or anyone else's. Those who believe eating certain animals is sin should not be ridiculed or forced to do what they think is wrong. We have to win them over with the truth, and only then are they free to eat without sin (Romans 14:23).

Note 12

This is quite a statement! Nothing is unclean. It is how we use a thing that makes it unclean. The Old Testament Law declared many animals unclean (Leviticus 11), not because there was anything wrong with the animals, but because the Lord was making a point. In the New Testament, Paul revealed that every creature of God is good and that nothing is to be refused if it is received with thanksgiving (1 Timothy 4:4). Every creature of God has always been good, even during Old Testament times. However, the Lord wanted His people to be a holy people, separated unto Him even in the things they ate. Therefore, He gave them dietary laws that pronounced certain animals as unclean so that they would be reminded, even as they ate, that they were not free to do whatever they wanted to do. They were bought with a price (1 Corinthians 6:20), and they were to glorify God in every area of their lives (1 Corinthians 10:31). Colossians 2:16-17 makes it very clear that these dietary laws were shadows of things that are now realities in Christ. Yet, just as with so many other Old Testament truths, the Jews had become engrossed in the observance of the ritual with no understanding as to what it symbolized. Likewise today, some Christians still hold to Old Testament ritual without any idea that the ritual has become reality in Christ (see note 1 at John 5:16). In Colossians 2:16-17, Paul said that these things were shadows of things to come. If I were walking toward you but the corner of a building blocked your view, then my shadow could be very significant. It could show you that I was coming and how close I was, but once I came around the corner and was in view, it would be unthinkable that you would fall down and embrace my shadow. My shadow is meaningful only because it represents me. Once you could talk to me, my shadow would be meaningless. Likewise, Old Testament rituals were significant before Christ came. They illustrated truths that were not yet in full view. But now that Christ has come, the rituals are meaningless and can be oppressive if they are wrongfully thought to be requirements for acceptance by God.

Romans 14:15

But if thy brother be grieved with thy meat, now walkest thou not charitably. Destroy not him with thy meat, for whom Christ died.

LIVING COMMENTARY

First Timothy 4:1-4 makes it very clear that New Testament believers are free to eat any animal. The Old Testament dietary laws do not apply to us (see my notes at Colossians 2:16-17). But not all Christians have stepped into their liberty in Christ. So, what are we to do when we are around Christians who don't share our knowledge and liberty? We are not to flaunt our freedom in a way that will be misinterpreted by those who don't understand (Romans 14:20-21). Paul said in 1 Corinthians 8:13, "Wherefore, if meat make my brother to offend, I will eat no flesh while the world standeth, lest I make my brother to offend." See my note at Romans 14:14.

Note 13

This verse ties all of this teaching back in with Romans 13:8-10. Paul had summarized all our duty to mankind as loving our neighbors as ourselves (see note 4 at Romans 13:10). If we ignore the influence our actions have on others, we are not walking in this law of love.

Romans 14:16

Let not then your good be evil spoken of:

LIVING COMMENTARY

This is not something that can be done perfectly. Jesus was all good, yet He was constantly condemned and criticized by the religious hypocrites. This verse is saying we shouldn't live only by our own consciences, but we should take into account what the standards of others are and not openly live in a way that would violate their weak consciences. This is what Paul was saying in 1 Corinthians 9:20-22. However, there is a balance here. Paul took Timothy and circumcised him, because he knew the Jews wouldn't understand it if he didn't (Acts 16:3).

But Paul specifically refused to circumcise Titus, because the legalistic Jews were demanding circumcision for salvation (Galatians 2:3-5). See my note at Romans 14:1.

Romans 14:17

For the kingdom of God is not meat and drink; but righteousness, and peace, and joy in the Holy Ghost.

LIVING COMMENTARY

The kingdom of God isn't about keeping rules and regulations; it's about relationship with God the Father and Jesus through the power of the Holy Spirit (see my note at John 17:3). Those who are enjoying right standing with God (righteousness), peace that only comes from God, and the true joy that the Holy Spirit gives are the true children of the kingdom. Those who are bogged down in rituals are just religious. Out of all the things Paul could have used to characterize the kingdom of God, he chose righteousness, peace, and joy in the Holy Spirit. Many people would have put faith, authority, power, miracles, being separate, and other things in that list. But Paul boiled it down to right standing with God that produces peace (Romans 5:1) and joy in the Holy Spirit. Truly, if our Christian activities don't produce peace and joy, they are not true New Testament Christianity but just religious calisthenics.

Note 14

People usually focus their attention on external things, such as meat and drink, but God is always concerned with the heart (1 Samuel 16:7). God deals with people's actions because they indicate the condition of their hearts. However, it is always the spiritual condition of the inner being that God is seeking to change. Paul was saying that we need to be like God and focus on the inner condition of our brothers and sisters in Christ. Then we will be able to tolerate minor differences in their actions.

Romans 14:18

For he that in these things serveth Christ is acceptable to God, and approved of men.

LIVING COMMENTARY

"These things" are the righteousness, peace, and joy of Romans 14:17. The Lord looks on our hearts (1 Samuel 16:7). Our actions are important but only as a byproduct of how we are inside (Proverbs 23:7). We don't change from the outside in; we change from the inside out (see my note at Matthew 23:26). The Lord accepts us on the basis of how we are in our hearts (see my note at 2 Corinthians 5:17), and then our actions reflect that inward change.

Romans 14:19

Let us therefore follow after the things which make for peace, and things wherewith one may edify another.

LIVING COMMENTARY

Paul had been changing their focus from outward actions to inner condition. This is similar to what he said in 2 Corinthians 5:16. If a person has been born again (see my note at John 3:3) and therefore is a new creature in their spirit (see my note at 2 Corinthians 5:17), then give them mercy over their actions. Live in peace instead of judging them.

Romans 14:20

For meat destroy not the work of God. All things indeed are pure; but it is evil for that man who eateth with offence.

LIVING COMMENTARY

Some things are worth fighting for. What we eat is not one of those things (see my notes at Romans 14:1, 14-16; and 1 Corinthians 8).

Note 15

Prior to this verse, Paul had encouraged the believers to consider their weaker brothers based on their obligation to love one another (see note 2 at Romans 13:8). Here Paul strengthened that argument by revealing how damaging it could be if the weaker brethren follow our actions with defiled consciences. It is evil for them (this verse); it will offend them and make them weak (Romans 14:21); it will damn them, and it is sin for them (Romans 14:23).

Romans 14:21

It is good neither to eat flesh, nor to drink wine, nor any thing whereby thy brother stumbleth, or is offended, or is made weak.

Note 16

A casual reading of Paul's instructions here might leave people with the impression that Paul was only suggesting that we not offend the weak brethren in this area. However, this is not the case. The Jerusalem church had already issued a command to the Gentile Christians that they abstain from meat that had been offered to idols (Acts 15:20 and 28-29). Paul agreed with this mandate and became one of the messengers who delivered this decree to the churches (Acts 15:25 and 30). Paul also commented on this same subject in 1 Corinthians 8 and 10: "But when ye sin so against the brethren, and wound their weak conscience, ye sin against Christ" (1 Corinthians 8:12). That doesn't sound optional. He also gave a direct command in 1 Corinthians 10:28 not to eat meat sacrificed to idols, for the sake of the weak brethren. However, the greatest proofs that this abstinence from meat offered to idols was not optional are the comments of Jesus Himself. In Revelation 2:14 and 20, the Lord rebuked two churches for allowing individuals to teach in those churches that the people could eat meats sacrificed to idols. Therefore, even though these scriptures do explain that the actual eating of meats sacrificed to idols is not wrong in itself, it does not give believers the right to indulge. They are to abstain strictly because of the effect their actions would have upon the weaker Christians' consciences.

Romans 14:22

Hast thou faith? have it to thyself before God. Happy is he that condemneth not himself in that thing which he alloweth.

Note 17

This is specifically speaking of having faith that they could eat meat sacrificed to idols. "The Life and Epistles of Paul" by W. J. Conybeare and J. S. Howson renders this verse, "Hast thou faith [that nothing is unclean]? keep it for thine own comfort before God." Therefore, Paul was stating that those who have clear consciences about eating meat that has been sacrificed to idols, they should keep that faith to themselves and not practice it openly lest they offend the weaker brethren.

Romans 14:23

And he that doubteth is damned if he eat, because he eateth not of faith: for whatsoever is not of faith is sin.

LIVING COMMENTARY

The Amplified Bible translated this verse as "But the man who has doubts (misgivings, an uneasy conscience) about eating, and then eats [perhaps because of you], stands condemned [before God], because he is not true to his convictions and he does not act from faith. For whatever does not originate and proceed from faith is sin [whatever is done without a conviction of its approval by God is sinful]."

Note 18

The Greek word that was translated "damned" here is "KATAKRINO," and it means "to judge against, i.e. sentence" (Strong's Concordance). This differs from the Greek word "KRINO" that is used in 2 Thessalonians 2:12 to designate eternal damnation. KATAKRINO, as used in this verse, actually means, "to condemn" (Vine's Expository Dictionary), and it was translated as "condemn" and "condemned" fifteen times in the New Testament. In contrast, KRINO was only translated as "condemn" once (John 3:17), "condemned" twice (John 3:18), and "condemning" once (Acts 13:27). Therefore, this verse is not saying that Christians who do something with defiled consciences are eternally damned. Paul was stating that Christians who violate their consciences are going to come under condemnation.

Note 19

This verse provides us with a definition of sin that is applicable to all people of all cultures and different religious backgrounds. Any action is sin for us if we don't have faith in its correctness. Thus, until we can settle our doubts, we aren't to do it. This provides an infallible system for determining right and wrong for any individual.

ROMANS

CHAPTER FIFTEEN

Romans 15:1

We then that are strong ought to bear the infirmities of the weak, and not to please ourselves.

Note 1

This verse is the summary of Paul's teaching in Romans 14. He explained that the Christian who is strong in grace and realizes that it is all right to eat meat sacrificed to idols is technically correct. However, just because it's lawful doesn't mean it is the correct thing to do (1 Corinthians 6:12 and 10:23). He clearly stated that the strong believer is supposed to bear the infirmities of the weak Christian brother.

Note 2

This word "bear" was translated from the Greek word "BASTAZO," and it means "to lift" (Strong's Concordance). This gives us a picture of Christians with weak consciences being burdened down with guilt or condemnation. We that are strong are supposed to help them lift that load. We do that by not offending their weak consciences.

Note 3

The word that was translated "infirmities" here is the Greek word "ASTHENEMA," and it means "a scruple of conscience" (Strong's Concordance). This is saying that the stronger believer needs to help lift the burden (see note 2 at this verse) of the one who has a weak conscience.

Note 4

Here Paul was summing up his instructions given in Romans 14 on how to get along with those who have differing convictions (see note 1 at this verse). It all comes back to love. Love thinks of the other person first. Love is not selfish (1 Corinthians 13). If people would seek the pleasure of others more than their own, strife would be killed. "Only by pride cometh contention" (Proverbs 13:10).

Romans 15:2

Let every one of us please his neighbour for his good to edification.

Living Commentary

This is the same thing Paul said in Philippians 2:3. We are to love others and not just ourselves.

Romans 15:3

For even Christ pleased not himself; but, as it is written, The reproaches of them that reproached thee fell on me.

LIVING COMMENTARY

This verse quotes from Psalm 69:9.

Note 5

As always, Jesus is the supreme example of God's kind of love. Jesus submitted to things that He, as God, didn't have to. However, He became a man and submitted Himself (Matthew 17:27), lest He should offend people. If Jesus did this for us, how can any of us justify not bearing the infirmities of our weak brethren?

Romans 15:4

For whatsoever things were written aforetime were written for our learning, that we through patience and comfort of the scriptures might have hope.

LIVING COMMENTARY

Just as it says in 1 Corinthians 10:6 and 10:11, all the actions of people in the Old Testament, both good and bad, were recorded for our instruction so that we can learn what's acceptable to God. Those who don't pay attention to these examples, but choose to learn everything by hard knocks, are making a huge mistake.

Notice that hope comes from the Scriptures. Hope is a positive imagination (see my note at Romans 8:24). Therefore, the Scriptures quicken our imaginations to see positive things instead of the negative things that tend to dominate most people. See these notes on imagination: Genesis 6:5, 11:6, 30:37, 39; Joshua 1:8; 1 Chronicles 29:18; Psalms 2:1, 5:1, 42:5, 103:14, 143:5; Proverbs 15:28, 23:7, 29:18; Isaiah 26:3; Matthew 22:37; Luke 1:51; Acts 4:25, 16:19, 27:20; Romans 1:21, 8:24-25, 15:4, 13, 29; 2 Corinthians 10:5; Ephesians 1:18, 2:3, 12, 4:18; 1 Timothy 4:15; and Hebrews 11:1.

Note 6

All the Old Testament scriptures were written for our instruction so that we would not make the same mistakes. If we do not heed the lessons of the Old Testament, we are trying to reinvent the wheel. People have already made mistakes, and the Old Testament scriptures were faithful to report the consequences of those sins. We don't have to learn the same lessons by "hard knocks." We can learn at their expense instead of our own.

Note 7

Patience, comfort, and hope do not come to us by begging and pleading with God. We cannot have a lasting measure of these things just by having others lay hands on us. These things come through the Scriptures (see note 12 at Romans 8:24 and note 13 at Romans 8:25). Some people have also mistakenly thought that problems produced patience because of a misunderstanding of scriptures like Romans 5:3 and James 1:3.

However, this verse makes it clear that patience is a product of the Scriptures. If tribulations produced patience, every Christian would be patient. Everyone has experienced tribulation. Patience comes through God's Word, but problems cause us to exercise or use our patience and thereby become stronger (see note 8 at Romans 5:3).

Romans 15:5

Now the God of patience and consolation grant you to be like-minded one toward another according to Christ Jesus:

Note 8

Paul was referring back to Romans 15:3 where he used Christ as an example of bearing the infirmities of those who are weak. He was praying that the Lord would work in us the same grace that was displayed in Christ Jesus.

Romans 15:6

That ye may with one mind and one mouth glorify God, even the Father of our Lord Jesus Christ.

LIVING COMMENTARY

Most Christians don't think we can glorify God with one mind and one mouth (speaking the same thing). But this isn't the only scripture that commands it (see also 1 Corinthians 1:10). This always has been and always will be God's standard.

Romans 15:7

Wherefore receive ye one another, as Christ also received us to the glory of God.

LIVING COMMENTARY

How does God love us? Certainly, it is by grace. We should love others the same way. Back in Romans 14:1-3, Paul spoke to the Romans about how to treat those who didn't believe exactly the way they did. He said not to dispute with them or to despise or judge them. So, since this verse tells us to receive others the way Christ has received us, we can take from this that Christ doesn't dispute with us or despise or judge us.

Note 9

How do we determine what doctrines are negotiable and which ones are not? If individuals have truly been born again by Christ receiving them, then we should receive them also, regardless of our differences. If Jesus is able to overlook the doctrinal errors of those people, who are we to refuse them?

Romans 15:8

Now I say that Jesus Christ was a minister of the circumcision for the truth of God, to confirm the promises made unto the fathers:

LIVING COMMENTARY

Notice that Paul said Jesus was a "minister of the circumcision," not a "minister of circumcision." This is significant. This was referring to Jesus being a minister to the Jews. Jesus did not preach or enforce the Old Testament command of circumcision.

Note 1

In Romans 15:7, Paul concluded his remarks about walking in love toward brethren who had different convictions. He judged that on certain issues that were not critical to salvation (see note 3 at Romans 14:1), the stronger should bear with the weak (see note 1 at Acts 15:1). Here in case someone should try to cite Jesus' exclusion of the Gentiles during His earthly ministry as proof that we can reject those who don't conform to Jewish traditions, Paul explained why Jesus ministered nearly exclusively to the Jews. He was fulfilling God's promises to the Jews. Jesus could not become the Savior of the Gentiles until He had been the Messiah to the Jews. Paul then went on to cite a number of Old Testament scriptures that make it very clear that Jesus' present ministry embraces the Gentiles without converting them to Judaism.

Romans 15:9

And that the Gentiles might glorify God for his mercy; as it is written, For this cause I will confess to thee among the Gentiles, and sing unto thy name.

LIVING COMMENTARY

Most scholars believe this is a quotation from Psalm 18:49.

Note 2

Paul was briefly verifying a point that he had already made in this letter to the Romans. In Romans 15:9-12, he quoted four Old Testament scriptures in order to verify that Christ opened up the door of salvation to the Gentiles (Psalm 18:49, Deuteronomy 32:43, Psalm 117:1, and Isaiah 11:10; see also 2 Samuel 22:50 and Matthew 12:21). This was done to make it clear that Gentiles do not have to become Jews in order to be saved. The salvation of Gentiles as Gentiles does not fall into the category of one of those nonessential doctrines (see note 3 at Romans 14:1) discussed in Romans 14, on which we compromise for the sake of our weak brethren.

Romans 15:10

And again he saith, Rejoice, ye Gentiles, with his people.

LIVING COMMENTARY

This is a quotation of part of Deuteronomy 32:43.

Romans 15:11

And again, Praise the Lord, all ye Gentiles; and laud him, all ye people.

LIVING COMMENTARY

This is from Psalm 117:1.

Romans 15:12

And again, Esaias saith, There shall be a root of Jesse, and he that shall rise to reign over the Gentiles; in him shall the Gentiles trust.

LIVING COMMENTARY

This is a quotation from Isaiah 11:10.

Romans 15:13

Now the God of hope fill you with all joy and peace in believing, that ye may abound in hope, through the power of the Holy Ghost.

LIVING COMMENTARY

Hope is a positive imagination (see my notes at Romans 8:24 and 15:4). Therefore, God is the God of vision, or positive imaginations, and He wants to fill us with joy, peace, and faith to produce nothing but positive imaginations. Notice that it takes the power of the Holy Spirit to accomplish this. We can't do this in our own human abilities. So those who are low on hope are not in the power of the Holy Spirit but in the vanity of their flesh. Faith is a noun and believe is a verb. So this is speaking of the acting out of faith. For faith to be put into practice, joy and peace need to be in operation. A person without joy and peace may have faith, but they don't believe. Notice that we are to abound in hope. This is a distinguishing characteristic of those who truly believe. This can be applied to specific situations in our lives. If we truly believe concerning our health, there will be joy, peace, and hope concerning our futures. The same is true with our wealth and with those we are praying for. A lack of these things signals the presence of unbelief.

Romans 15:14

And I myself also am persuaded of you, my brethren, that ye also are full of goodness, filled with all knowledge, able also to admonish one another.

LIVING COMMENTARY

I'm sure these Romans weren't perfect. There were problems in them just as in people today. But Paul was living what he preached. Romans 15:13 says that God is a God of hope. Those who are truly operating in the Holy Spirit will abound in hope, joy, and peace. Paul was using hope (a positive imagination) and seeing the positive side of these believers.

Romans 15:15

Nevertheless, brethren, I have written the more boldly unto you in some sort, as putting you in mind, because of the grace that is given to me of God,

LIVING COMMENTARY

Paul was abounding in hope toward these believers (see my note at Romans 15:14), but he didn't have his head in the sand. He was well aware that there were things that needed to be straightened out, and that's why he wrote this letter. That was what the Lord had called him to do.

Romans 15:16

That I should be the minister of Jesus Christ to the Gentiles, ministering the gospel of God, that the offering up of the Gentiles might be acceptable, being sanctified by the Holy Ghost.

Note 1

We cannot just worship God any way we want to. Our worship has to be sanctified by the Holy Ghost. Until we make Jesus our Lord, the Holy Spirit does not intercede for us. Paul was saying that through his preaching of the Gospel and the Gentiles' reception of salvation, the Holy Spirit was then free to work on their behalf.

Romans 15:17

I have therefore whereof I may glory through Jesus Christ in those things which pertain to God.

Note 2

Paul took the Gospel to the Gentiles, and it granted salvation to those who received it. Therefore, he had quite a bit to boast ("glory") about.

However, he said his boasting was through Christ Jesus, and that clarifies that this was not done in arrogance or pride.

Romans 15:18

For I will not dare to speak of any of those things which Christ hath not wrought by me, to make the Gentiles obedient, by word and deed,

LIVING COMMENTARY

Paul didn't lay claim to things that God accomplished through others. Notice also that Paul used his deeds as well as his words to cause the Gentiles to become obedient to the Gospel. We need more demonstration to go with our words too.

Romans 15:19

Through mighty signs and wonders, by the power of the Spirit of God; so that from Jerusalem, and round about unto Illyricum, I have fully preached the gospel of Christ.

Note 3

Paul was known primarily for his preaching of the Gospel of God's grace (see note 5 at Acts 20:24), but Paul had the miraculous power of God working in him too. Indeed, this should be true of all true ministers of the Gospel (see note 4 at Acts 4:30). Paul struck Elymas, the sorcerer, with blindness, causing the conversion of Sergius Paulus (Acts 13:6-12). In Lystra, Paul healed a man who had been crippled from birth (Acts 14:8-10). In Philippi, Paul cast a spirit of divination out of a girl (Acts 16:16-18), and he was also delivered from prison in that city by a miraculous earthquake (Acts 16:25-26). In Ephesus, the Lord accomplished "special miracles" through Paul by healing and delivering people as they came in contact with handkerchiefs or aprons that Paul had touched (Acts 19:11-12). In Troas, Paul raised Eutychus from the dead (Acts 20:9-12), and while shipwrecked on the island of Melita, Paul miraculously survived a bite from a poisonous snake (Acts 28:3-6). Paul was also delivered from death at the hands of the Romans and Jews many times, including one time when he may actually have been raised from the dead (see note 3 at Acts 14:20). Paul's life, as well as the lives of everyone on his ship, was spared from death at sea through God's intervention (Acts 27:21-26 and 43-44). Paul also wrote to the Corinthians that the signs of an apostle were wrought among them by him (2 Corinthians 12:12), yet there is no record in Acts of a single miracle performed by Paul during his visits to Corinth (Acts 18:1-17 and 20:2-3). Therefore, it can be concluded that there were many miraculous things accomplished by Paul that were not recorded, just as in the case of our Lord Jesus (John 20:30 and 21:25).

Note 4

Ancient Illyricum occupied the territory that is modern-day Albania and Bosnia-Herzegovina, just north of Macedonia where Thessalonica and Berea were located. There is no record of Paul preaching in this area, so it can be supposed that he is referring to ministering up to the border of this province.

Note 5

Some people have interpreted Paul's statement here to mean that he had covered all the area of Asia (see note 3 at Acts 16:6 and note 4 at Acts 19:10), Macedonia (see note 1 at Acts 16:9), and Achaia (see note 11 at Acts 18:12) with the Gospel. The following few verses would lend themselves to that interpretation. However, the immediate context of this verse specifically mentions "mighty signs and wonders, by the power of the Spirit of God." This would lead us to believe that Paul "fully" preaching the Gospel referred to the confirmation of the Word through the demonstration of God's miraculous power (see note 2 at Mark 16:20). Therefore, Paul could be making a distinction between just preaching the Gospel and fully preaching the Gospel. A minister hasn't fully preached the Gospel unless there are accompanying signs and wonders (see note 4 at Acts 4:30). This must be where the phrase "full Gospel" came from.

Romans 15:20

Yea, so have I strived to preach the gospel, not where Christ was named, lest I should build upon another man's foundation:

Note 6

Paul had a burning desire to reach the unreached, yet the greatest legacy that he left us is the collection of his epistles written to those he led to the Lord. This reflected the lifestyle that Paul had that we should have also. Paul didn't just evangelize; he discipled people (see note 5 at Matthew 28:19).

Romans 15:21

But as it is written, To whom he was not spoken of, they shall see: and they that have not heard shall understand.

LIVING COMMENTARY

This is a quotation from Isaiah 52:15. See also Isaiah 65:1.

Romans 15:22

For which cause also I have been much hindered from coming to you.

Note 1

The cause that Paul was referring to was his desire to preach the Gospel to everyone who had not heard. He had wanted to go to Rome, but he felt it was necessary first to preach the Gospel to everyone in the areas he had already been. This is what he referred to in the next verse when he said, "Now having no more place in these parts" (Romans 15:23). He was saying there was no place left in those parts that hasn't heard the Gospel. Therefore, he was ready to depart for new, unreached areas.

Romans 15:23

But now having no more place in these parts, and having a great desire these many years to come unto you;

LIVING COMMENTARY

Psalm 37:4 says the Lord gives us the desires of our hearts. This is how He led Paul to go to Rome. He placed the desire to do so in his heart.

Note 2

In Acts 19:21, Paul purposed in his spirit to visit Rome after he had gone back through Macedonia (see note 1 at Acts 16:9) and Achaia (see note 11 at Acts 18:12). This happened while he was in Ephesus from A.D. 54 to 57 (see note 2 at Acts 18:23). Paul was writing this epistle around A.D. 57 to 58 from Corinth (see Life for Today Study Bible Notes, Introduction to Romans, Date and Place of Writing). Therefore, Paul's "many years" is referring to a two- to three-year period of time.

Romans 15:24

Whensoever I take my journey into Spain, I will come to you: for I trust to see you in my journey, and to be brought on my way thitherward by you, if first I be somewhat filled with your company.

Note 3

Paul mentioned his intention to travel to Spain twice in this chapter (this verse and Romans 15:28). These verses are the only two times in Scripture that this is mentioned. There is no scriptural account that Paul ever made it to Spain. Some have speculated that he went to Spain after his imprisonment in Rome. There are traditions that support that but no facts.

Note 4

Paul was referring to the Romans helping him with his expenses for his planned trip to Spain ("to be brought on my way thitherward by you"). See also Acts 15:3, 1 Corinthians 16:6, 2 Corinthians 1:16, and 3 John 6.

Romans 15:25

But now I go unto Jerusalem to minister unto the saints.

LIVING COMMENTARY

Paul was a minister to the Gentiles (Acts 22:21 and Romans 15:16), yet he was forever longing to minister to the Jews (Romans 9:1-3).

Romans 15:26

For it hath pleased them of Macedonia and Achaia to make a certain contribution for the poor saints which are at Jerusalem.

LIVING COMMENTARY

It is interesting to note there were poor saints at Jerusalem. The church at Jerusalem had liquidated all their assets and lived in a communal style, at least at first (Acts 4:34-35). There wasn't any poverty among them at first. I suspect this was not only motivated by their love for each other but also by their belief that the Lord would be back very soon. However, as the Lord delayed His coming, this communal lifestyle didn't produce wealth. We don't know when, but it was abandoned, and there was poverty in the Jerusalem church.

Note 5

Acts' account of Paul's travels does not give us any details about this collection for the poor saints at Jerusalem. However, Paul did mention it as being the reason he made his last trip to Jerusalem (Acts 24:17), and he wrote about it in his letters to the Corinthians. In 1 Corinthians 16:1-4, Paul gave instructions for the collection for the saints in Jerusalem. In 1 Corinthians 16:1, he said that he gave the same instructions to the churches of Galatia. It is unclear whether he was saying he had also instructed the churches of Galatia to receive an offering for the Jerusalem saints or whether he was simply instructing the Corinthians to receive the collection in the same manner as the Galatians did. At any rate, Paul was only delivering the offerings from the churches of Macedonia and Achaia (this verse) during this trip to Jerusalem. In 2 Corinthians 8:1-5, Paul spoke favorably about the attitude the churches of Macedonia (the churches of Thessalonica and Berea) had toward this offering. He acknowledged that the churches of Achaia (the Corinthian church) had purposed to send an offering a year before the Macedonian churches had (2 Corinthians 8:10 and 9:2). Paul gave the impression that the offering from the Macedonian churches was unsolicited (2 Corinthians 8:4). Paul encouraged the Corinthians to participate generously in this offering, reminding them that they would reap proportionally to how they sowed (2 Corinthians 9:6). He stated clearly that they should not give under compulsion (2 Corinthians 9:7) or try to give what they didn't have (2 Corinthians 8:11-15). He gave them a tremendous promise of God's physical blessing on them if they participated (2 Corinthians 9:8-11). This must have been a relatively large sum of money for Paul to be carrying to Jerusalem. Even though Paul could have demanded these people's trust, since he was the apostle that brought them the Gospel, he made provision for whomever they chose to accompany him to Jerusalem to make sure the money went for what it was intended (2 Corinthians 8:20-21 with 1 Corinthians 16:3). This was a benevolence offering for the poor saints in Jerusalem.

Romans 15:27

It hath pleased them verily; and their debtors they are. For if the Gentiles have been made partakers of their spiritual things, their duty is also to minister unto them in carnal things.

Note 6

Specifically, the carnal things that Paul was referring to here was finances.

Romans 15:28

When therefore I have performed this, and have sealed to them this fruit, I will come by you into Spain.

LIVING COMMENTARY

Notice that this giving to the poor saints in Jerusalem was going to produce fruit to the believers of Macedonia and Achaia (Philippians 4:17). This is Paul's second mention of passing through Rome on his way to Spain (first mention - Romans 15:24), and Paul mentioned that this had been his desire for a long time (Romans 15:23). The Lord leads us by desires (see my notes at Romans 15:23 and Psalm 37:4). It's possible that Paul should never have gone to Jerusalem (see my note at Acts 21:4). He was God's apostle to the Gentiles (Romans 11:13), yet he was ever longing to reach the Jews (Romans 9:1-3).

Romans 15:29

And I am sure that, when I come unto you, I shall come in the fulness of the blessing of the gospel of Christ.

LIVING COMMENTARY

The Greek word "EIDO," which was translated "sure" in this verse, means "properly, to see (literally or figuratively); by implication, (in the perfect tense only) to know" (Strong's Talking Greek & Hebrew Dictionary). Paul saw himself walking in the fullness of the blessing of the Gospel. This is a positive imagination, or hope, as described in my notes at Romans 8:24 and 15:13. Since this is available to all of us through Christ, it is wrong to see ourselves any other way.

Note 7

What a statement! Paul had no doubt that he would be walking in the fullness of God. This reveals that walking in the power of the Holy Spirit is a choice. Some people disagree with this and say that you can't make the blessings of God occur. Their argument is that sometimes blessings happen and other times they don't, based on God's choosing; otherwise, it would be like being able to turn God on and off. The answer to this is that God is always on. We are the ones who are on and off. Anytime we choose life (Deuteronomy 30:19), we can be assured that the life of God that has been given to us through Christ Jesus will flow. The responsibility to stir up the gift that is in us (2 Timothy 1:6) rests on us.

Romans 15:30

Now I beseech you, brethren, for the Lord Jesus Christ's sake, and for the love of the Spirit, that ye strive together with me in your prayers to God for me;

Note 8

This shows how important Paul thought prayer was. Paul begged these believers to intercede on his behalf.

Romans 15:31

That I may be delivered from them that do not believe in Judaea; and that my service which I have for Jerusalem may be accepted of the saints;

LIVING COMMENTARY

Paul specifically asked to be delivered from the unbelieving Jews in Judea. It might look like this prayer wasn't answered. These unbelieving Jews assaulted him, which led to his arrest by the Romans (Acts 21:30- 34). Paul was imprisoned for two years (Acts 24:27) in Caesarea and two more years in Rome (Acts 28:30). This wouldn't have happened if the unbelieving Jews hadn't pressed the matter (Acts 24:1-9 and 27). So, did this prayer not get the positive response Paul wanted, or could the results have been much worse if the Lord hadn't intervened? It's clear they wanted to kill him (Acts 21:31 and 23:12-22). It's also possible that Paul was out of God's will by going to Jerusalem and therefore out of His perfect protection (see my note at Romans 15:28).

Note 9

Paul's prayer request was that he would be delivered from the religious unbelievers in Jerusalem. The answer to this prayer came in a way that many of us would not have liked. Instead of not having any problems, he was assaulted and wound up spending many years in prison. Yet he was delivered from the unbelieving Jews. They tried to kill him three times (Acts 21:31, 23:20-21, and 25:2-3), but the Lord delivered him through the Roman government.

Note 10

Paul knew that trouble was waiting for him in Jerusalem. In Acts 20:22-23, he said he didn't know exactly what would happen to him in Jerusalem but knew it would be bonds and afflictions (see note 4 at Acts 21:4).

Romans 15:32

That I may come unto you with joy by the will of God, and may with you be refreshed.

LIVING COMMENTARY

In the previous verses, Paul had expressed his earnest desire to go to Rome and share the Gospel with them. In Romans 15:30-31, Paul had solicited prayers that he would be delivered from the unbelieving Jews in Judaea so he could come to the believers in Rome with joy. He came to Rome in chains as a Roman prisoner. See my note at Romans 15:31.

Romans 15:33

Now the God of peace be with you all. Amen.

LIVING COMMENTARY

What a wonderful title for our Lord: "the God of peace." Since God is almighty, He could have been whatever He wanted to be. But God is a God of peace. What a blessing to us that this is His nature.

ROMANS

CHAPTER SIXTEEN

Romans 16:1

I commend unto you Phebe our sister, which is a servant of the church which is at Cenchrea:

LIVING COMMENTARY

Vine's Expository Dictionary says that the Greek word "SYNISTAO," which was translated "commend" in this verse, means "'to place together, denotes 'to introduce one person to another, represent as worthy.'" Cenchrea was a port of Corinth (see my note at Acts 18:18).

Note 1

The only mention of Phebe in Scripture is here and in the subscript at Romans 16:27 (found in some Bibles). From these passages, we can see that Phebe was the one who delivered this epistle to the Romans. She had ministered to many, including Paul, and therefore Paul instructed the Romans to assist her in her business in whatever way they could. Because the word "servant" in this verse has also been translated "deacon" in other scriptures (see note 2 at this verse), many believe that Phebe was actually a deaconess of the church in Cenchrea.

Note 2

The Greek word that was translated "servant" here is the word "DIA-KONOS." DIAKONOS comes from the root word "DIAKO," meaning "to run on errands," and specified "an attendant, i.e. (genitive case) a waiter (at table or in other menial duties); specially, a Christian teacher and pastor (technically, a deacon or deaconess)" (Strong's Concordance). This word was used a total of thirty times in the New Testament. It was translated "deacons" three times (Philippians 1:1; 1 Timothy 3:8, and 12), "ministers" six times (1 Corinthians 3:5; 2 Corinthians 3:6, 6:4, 11:15, and 23), "minister" fourteen times (Matthew 20:26; Mark 10:43; Romans 13:4, 15:8; Galatians 2:17; Ephesians 3:7, 6:21; Colossians 1:7, 23, 25, 4:7; 1 Thessalonians 3:2; and 1 Timothy 4:6), "servant" four times (Matthew 23:11, Mark 9:35, John 12:26, and here), and "servants" three times (Matthew 22:13; John 2:5, and John 9). So, it can be said that the dominant use of this word in the New Testament was to specify a minister or deacon. However, out of the six other times this word was translated "servant" or "servants," it was definitely designating a person who performs menial tasks as a slave. Therefore, it cannot be stated emphatically from this verse that Phebe was or was not a deaconess or female minister. History supplies us with information that there were female ministers "in the churches of Bithynia [see note 5 at Acts 16:7] as early as A.D. 100, for Pliny, in his celebrated letter to the emperor Trajan regarding the Christians, reports having examined 'two old women' of the Christian community 'who were called ministers'" ("A Dictionary of the Bible" by John D. Davis, brackets mine).

Romans 16:2

> *That ye receive her in the Lord, as becometh saints, and that ye assist her in whatsoever business she hath need of you: for she hath been a succourer of many, and of myself also.*

> ## LIVING COMMENTARY
>
> This assistance Paul was encouraging included, but wasn't limited to, financial assistance.

Note 3

One definition of the word "for" is "because; since" (American Heritage Dictionary). Paul was saying that the reason they should assist Phebe is because she had assisted others, including Paul. This illustrates the law of reaping what you sow (Galatians 6:7 and Luke 6:38). Some people become offended when they do not receive assistance from others, yet they have never helped anyone. That is not what Paul was advocating here. Phebe had earned their help. Salvation is by grace, but respect and help from others has to be earned.

Romans 16:3

Greet Priscilla and Aquila my helpers in Christ Jesus:

> ## LIVING COMMENTARY
>
> See my note on Priscilla and Aquila at Acts 18:2.

Romans 16:4

Who have for my life laid down their own necks: unto whom not only I give thanks, but also all the churches of the Gentiles.

Note 4

Paul did not elaborate on, nor do the Scriptures reveal, a specific instance where Priscilla and Aquila "laid down their own necks" for Paul's sake. It is possible they were some of the disciples who restrained Paul from entering into the theater in Ephesus during the uproar caused by Demetrius (Acts 19:28-31).

Romans 16:5

Likewise greet the church that is in their house. Salute my wellbeloved Epaenetus, who is the firstfruits of Achaia unto Christ.

LIVING COMMENTARY

Priscilla and Aquila had a church in their house in Rome (see my note on Priscilla and Aquila at Acts 18:2). The early church met in homes until Constantine's conversion to Christianity in the 300s. The church flourished in these home meetings.

Note 5

This is the only mention of Epaenetus in Scripture. From this reference, we can see that Epaenetus was loved very much by Paul. He was Paul's first convert in Achaia.

Romans 16:6

Greet Mary, who bestowed much labour on us.

Note 6

There are a number of Marys mentioned in Scripture, implying that it was a common name. There is no reason to believe that this Mary in Rome is the same as some other Mary mentioned in Scripture. This woman had bestowed much labor on Paul and his companions.

Romans 16:7

Salute Andronicus and Junia, my kinsmen, and my fellowprisoners, who are of note among the apostles, who also were in Christ before me.

Note 7

The name Andronicus means "man of victory" (Strong's Concordance). This is the only mention of Andronicus in Scripture. He and Junia were two of six relatives (see note 9 at this verse) Paul mentioned in this chapter. Andronicus had been imprisoned, presumably for his faith in Christ. Paul said that he was "of note" among the apostles. That probably means Andronicus and Junia were well known, even to the apostles. Andronicus and Junia were Christians before Paul's conversion. It is very possible that they witnessed to Paul and this may have been part of the "pricks" Paul was fighting against at his conversion (see note 6 at Acts 9:5). Since Junia (see note 8 at this verse) was a feminine name, it is possible that Andronicus and Junia were married.

Note 8

This is the only mention of Junia in Scripture. The fact that Andronicus and Junia were both imprisoned, both in Christ before Paul, and both Paul's relatives suggests that they were close, possibly man and wife.

They were both "of note" among the apostles, probably meaning that they were well known, even to the apostles.

Junia and Andronicus were apparently living in Rome.

Note 9

The Greek word used for "kinsmen" here is "SUGGENES" and means "a relative (by blood); by extension, a fellow countryman" (Strong's Concordance). In Romans 9:3, Paul used this word to refer to all of the Jews as his kinsmen. Therefore, it is not certain whether Paul was using this word to denote blood relatives or fellow Jews. The fact that more of these people were Jews than what Paul designated by the term "kinsmen" would suggest that he was speaking of blood relatives. There are six (depending on how Romans 16:21 is interpreted) kinsmen of Paul's referred to in this chapter: Andronicus and Junia (this verse); Herodion (Romans 16:11); and Lucius, Jason, and Sosipater (Romans 16:21). It is possible that Tertius (Romans 16:22) was the one speaking in Romans 16:21, and therefore Lucius, Jason, and Sosipater would be his kinsmen (see note 4 at Romans 16:21).

Romans 16:8

Greet Amplias my beloved in the Lord.

Note 10

This is the only time Amplias is mentioned in Scripture. He was a Christian in Rome to whom Paul sent greetings. His name came from the Latin word meaning "enlarged" (Strong's Concordance).

Note 11

The Greek word that was translated "beloved" here is "AGAPETOS," the adjective form of "AGAPE" (see note 3 at Romans 12:10). It is signifying the type of love that God has. Paul said that Amplias was "beloved in the Lord," meaning this was God's love being expressed through Paul.

Romans 16:9

Salute Urbane, our helper in Christ, and Stachys my beloved.

Note 12

The name Urbane means "of the city" (Strong's Concordance). This was the only mention of Urbane in Scripture. He had been a companion in work ("helper" - Greek "SUNERGOS" - "a co-laborer, i.e. coadjutor" [Strong's Concordance]) with Paul.

Note 13

The name Stachys means "a head of grain" (Strong's Concordance). This is the only mention of Stachys in Scripture.

Romans 16:10

Salute Apelles approved in Christ. Salute them which are of Aristobulus' household.

Note 14

This is the only mention of Apelles in Scripture.

Note 15

According to Strong's Concordance, the name Aristobulus means "best counselling." This is the only mention of Aristobulus in Scripture.

Romans 16:11

Salute Herodion my kinsman. Greet them that be of the household of Narcissus, which are in the Lord.

Note 16

The name Herodion came from the Greek word "HERODES" meaning "heroic" (Strong's Concordance). This was the name of a number of kings of Palestine (see note 3 at Luke 3:1), and it is possible that Herodion was named after one of the kings named Herod. If so, that would most likely make Herodion a Gentile, since it would be very unusual for a Jew to name a child in honor of Herod. Herodion was the third person Paul mentioned in this chapter as being his kinsman (see note 9 at Romans 16:7). If Herodion was a Gentile, as his name could imply, then Paul would have been referring to him as a brother in the Lord and not a natural blood relative.

Note 17

The name Narcissus came from the flower narcissus, or the daffodil. This is the only mention of Narcissus in Scripture.

Note 18

The phrase, "in the Lord," refers to the members of Narcissus' household who had been born again through faith in Christ. This is a very appropriate and descriptive phrase since all believers are in Christ Jesus (2 Corinthians 5:17 and Colossians 2:10).

Romans 16:12

Salute Tryphena and Tryphosa, who labour in the Lord. Salute the beloved Persis, which laboured much in the Lord.

Note 19

Tryphena ("luxurious") and Tryphosa ("luxuriating") (Strong's Concordance) were women at Rome that Paul saluted and commended for their labor in the Lord.

Note 20

The name Persis means "a Persian woman" (Strong's Concordance). She was a Christian in Rome whom Paul greeted. Paul mentioned that she labored much in the Lord. This is the only mention of Persis in Scripture.

Romans 16:13

Salute Rufus chosen in the Lord, and his mother and mine.

Note 21

According to Strong's Concordance, the name Rufus means "red." The name Rufus is mentioned twice in Scripture (Mark 15:21 and here). It is unclear whether both of these instances refer to the same Rufus. If so, then this Rufus to whom Paul sent greetings in Rome would have been the son of Simon of Cyrene, the man who was compelled to bear the cross of Jesus. Paul also sent greetings to the mother of Rufus (see note 22 at this verse).

Note 22

Paul greeted the mother of Rufus and called her his own mother. It is unclear whether this is figurative or literal. Most commentators suspect this was a figurative statement, as is the case elsewhere in Scripture (Matthew 12:49-50, Mark 3:35, John 19:27, and 1 Timothy 5:2).

Romans 16:14

> Salute Asyncritus, Phlegon, Hermas, Patrobas, Hermes, and the brethren which are with them.

Note 23

Asyncritus ("incomparable"), Phlegon ("blazing"), Hermas (probably from "Hermes, the name of the messenger of the Greek deities"), Patrobas ("father's life"), and Hermes ("the name of the messenger of the Greek deities") (Strong's Concordance) were Christians in Rome to whom Paul sent greetings. This is the only mention of these individuals in Scripture.

Romans 16:15

> Salute Philologus, and Julia, Nereus, and his sister, and Olympas, and all the saints which are with them.

Note 24

The name Philologus means "fond of words, i.e. talkative" (Strong's Concordance). The wording of this verse suggests that Philologus was the husband of Julia (see note 25 at this verse). This is the only mention of Philologus in Scripture.

Note 25

The name Julia was the feminine form of the Latin "Julius," as in Julius Caesar. Because of the wording of this verse, many people believe that Julia was the wife of Philologus (see note 24 at this verse). This is the only mention of Julia in Scripture.

Note 26

The name Nereus came from Greek mythology. Nereus was a sea god who lived in the Aegean Sea. This was the name of a Christian in Rome to whom Paul sent greetings. Paul also greeted Nereus' sister, who is not named in this verse. This is the only mention of Nereus in Scripture.

Note 27

The name Olympas came from the word meaning "heaven-descended" (Strong's Concordance). This was the name of a Christian in Rome whom Paul greeted. This is the only mention of Olympas in Scripture.

Note 28

This is the second consecutive scripture in which Paul greeted a group of people and the brethren or saints that were with them. This was probably referring to a local group of believers who regularly met in the households of these people, and that would make those who were mentioned in these verses leaders of those local bodies of believers.

Romans 16:16

Salute one another with an holy kiss. The churches of Christ salute you.

Note 29

This is one of five times in Scripture where we are exhorted to greet other believers with a holy kiss, or a kiss of charity (see also 1 Corinthians 16:20, 2 Corinthians 13:12, 1 Thessalonians 5:26, and 1 Peter 5:14). The culture of Paul's day used a kiss as a greeting, just as we still see in various other cultures today. However, Paul's repeated use of this custom in his instructions to the believers would suggest that he advocated it as a Christian custom. It is certain that Christians have more reason to greet one another with a kiss than anyone else. It needs to be noted that in each reference to this, there is a specific mention of this being a holy kiss, or kiss of charity. That qualifies the manner in which this is to be done. This certainly is not an opportunity for people to exercise their lusts. This should be motivated only by the holiest Christian love for fellow believers. If this kiss of charity is misunderstood or not wanted by the person receiving it, then it would certainly be inappropriate to give it.

Romans 16:17

Now I beseech you, brethren, mark them which cause divisions and offences contrary to the doctrine which ye have learned; and avoid them.

Note 1

This is one of many times that Paul made a very clear statement about withdrawing from individuals who are causing problems in the church (1 Corinthians 5:9-11; Philippians 3:17; 2 Thessalonians 3:6, 14-15; 1 Timothy 6:3-5; 2 Timothy 2:16-17, 3:5; 1 John 2:19; and Titus 3:9-10). We also have an example of Paul separating the true believers from the false and meeting in a separate place in Acts 19:9. These are scriptural precedents for separation based on doctrine. However, Paul did not say to avoid contact with people who simply had different doctrine. He said to avoid those who caused division and offenses over doctrine. Some people have doctrines that disagree with the Word, but they aren't disagreeable. These people can be loved and restored, but those who are causing dissension over doctrine are to be treated as contaminated and infectious. One example of this that Paul used in this epistle was the matter of observing dietary laws. Paul made it clear that there was nothing wrong with any food (see note 12 at Romans 14:14), but it would be sin for people to eat certain foods if they weren't eating them in faith (Romans 14:23). Therefore, there can be differences of doctrines, but Paul told those that were strong in grace to bear with those who were not.

However, if the weak brethren became contentious over their doctrine of abstinence from certain meats and began to condemn others (see note 3 at Romans 14:1), Paul would say to mark those people and avoid them. The first thing Paul said to do was to mark these people. The Greek word that was translated "mark" here is the word "SKOPEO," and it means "to take aim at (spy), i.e. (figuratively) regard" (Strong's Concordance). In modern-day terms, we'd say we should "keep an eye" on these people. They are not to be trusted and should not be given the freedom to move about freely among the believers and spread infection. The way we choose who is to be marked is based on the doctrine of God's Word. There are those who are indifferent to or don't believe the

Word of God, but they aren't out to oppose it. Those, we simply love and continue to share the Word with, praying for their eyes to be opened. However, those who actively seek to subvert others from following the doctrine of God's Word are the ones to mark. Paul gave some characteristics of these people in Romans 16:18. Marking these individuals falls into the category of church discipline and should be done consistently with all those instructions (see note 5 at Matthew 18:17).

Romans 16:18

For they that are such serve not our Lord Jesus Christ, but their own belly; and by good words and fair speeches deceive the hearts of the simple.

Note 2

In this verse, Paul gave us some characteristics of the people he said to mark (Romans 16:17). These people are not truly serving the Lord Jesus Christ; they are serving themselves. That's what the terminology "their own belly" means. This same description was used in the parallel account Paul gave on this same subject (Philippians 3:17-19). There, Paul said that their god is their belly. This is saying that their motive is not the selfless motive of love for God and others, but rather, they are motivated by a love for themselves. This is always at the root of all division (see note 6 at Mark 15:10 and note 4 at Luke 10:20). Philippians 3:19 gives the further explanation that these people glory in their shame and mind earthly things. Paul said in this verse that these individuals use good words and fair speeches and deceive the hearts of the simple. This means that they flatter people (2 Timothy 4:3) and appeal to the same selfish desires that they themselves have, to draw people after themselves (Acts 20:30).

Note 3

Paul said that the simple are those of us who are deceived by these sowers of strife. If we will quit being simple, we won't be deceived. What did Paul mean by "simple"? The Greek word that was translated "simple" in this verse is "AKAKOS." It was only used twice in the New Testament, here and in Hebrews 7:26. In Hebrews 7:26, it was translated "harmless," meaning "without guile" or "fraud, harmless; free from guilt" (Thayer's Lexicon). In this verse, the meaning of this word is "fearing no evil from others, distrusting no one" (Thayer's Lexicon). This is describing those whom today we would call gullible (Proverbs 14:15). Only those who lack discernment between good and evil will fall prey to this deceit. How do we quit being simple or gullible? It's through God's Word. Many scriptures promise that God's Word will cause the simple to start being wise (Psalms 19:7, 119:130; and Proverbs 1:4). A good understanding of God's Word is the greatest defense against deception (John 8:32 and 17:17). The English word "simple" is only used twice in the New Testament (here and Romans 16:19, see note 4 at Romans 16:19).

Romans 16:19

For your obedience is come abroad unto all men. I am glad therefore on your behalf: but yet I would have you wise unto that which is good, and simple concerning evil.

LIVING COMMENTARY

Second Timothy 3:15 says the holy scriptures make us wise unto salvation. Therefore, Paul's exhortation to be wise concerning that which is good is an exhortation for us to stay focused on the truths of God's Word. The Greek word SOPHOS, which was translated "wise" in this verse means "clear." Focusing on God's Word brings clarity of what is good. The Lord wants us "simple" concerning evil. Simple here means "unmixed" or "innocent." We are not to mix or have the knowledge of evil. Evil in this verse means "worthless...depraved...or injurious." We shouldn't focus on things that injure us. Lord, help me to live this verse!

Note 4

This is the second and final time that the English word "simple" was used in the New Testament. The first time was in the previous verse (Romans 16:18). However, this one English word came from two different Greek words. The Greek word that was used in Romans 16:18 was "AKAKOS" (see note 3 at that verse), while the Greek word that was used in this verse is "AKERAIOS," meaning "(a) 'unmixed, pure,' as wines or metals, (b) of the mind, 'without admixture of evil, free from guile, innocent, simple'" (Thayer's Lexicon).

Therefore, when Paul presented being simple in Romans 16:18 as something that is not good, and simple in Romans 16:19 as something that is good, he was speaking of two different things. Romans 16:18 is speaking against being gullible, while Romans 16:19 is speaking in favor of being pure, focused only on things that are good (see note 5 at this verse).

Note 5

This is a wonderful key that the Lord is giving us for living the Christian life, yet very few people use it. It goes contrary to the modern thought that all knowledge is good, even the knowledge of evil. Satan used Eve's desire to know about evil to entice her to sin (Genesis

3:5-6). All that she knew about was good, but Satan convinced her that she would be better off if she knew about evil. That definitely was not the case. God never intended for us to know about evil. That's the reason He forbade Adam and Eve to eat of the Tree of the Knowledge of Good and Evil. We cannot be tempted with things that we don't think about (see notes 7 and 9 at Romans 12:2, note 10 at Romans 8:4, and notes 11-12 at Romans 8:5). Therefore, if we don't think about evil things, we will not be tempted with them. Of course, since the Fall, evil is in the world, and there needs to be knowledge about evil so we can avoid its pitfalls. Paul said, "We are not ignorant of his devices" (2 Corinthians 2:11). Notice that Paul said we should be simple, not ignorant. However, most of us are indulging in a knowledge of evil that is far beyond what Paul was advocating. Paul also said, "For it is a shame even to speak of those things which are done of them in secret" (Ephesians 5:12). Yet many Christians feel it is necessary and beneficial to plumb the depths of the moral debauchery in our world today. That is not so. We don't have to know all about Satanism and what its followers are doing in order to avoid that pitfall and help those who have already fallen in it. If we are seeking God with our whole heart and thinking on all the good He has to offer, we will never fall prey to Satanism. We will also have the wisdom of God to deliver anyone who has become possessed by that spirit. The best defense is a good offense. Bank tellers don't become astute at recognizing counterfeit money by studying counterfeit bills. It would be impossible to school them on all the possible variations they could encounter. Instead, they become so familiar with the genuine article that they are able to recognize a fake. Likewise, Christians should be wise concerning that which is good, and simple (unmixed, separated from—see note 4 at this verse) concerning evil. Undue attention to what Satan is doing will actually give the enemy inroads into our lives.

Romans 16:20

And the God of peace shall bruise Satan under your feet shortly.
The grace of our Lord Jesus Christ be with you. Amen.

LIVING COMMENTARY

The Lord told Adam and Eve that the seed of the woman
(Jesus) would bruise the serpent's head (see my note at
Genesis 3:15). This was fulfilled, at least in part, by Jesus'
first advent and resurrection. But this verse might be
speaking of a future fulfillment of this, too, where the
devil is cast into the lake of fire (Revelation 20:10). It's
also possible that every time we triumph over the devil,
we are bruising Satan. So, this might be speaking of their
immediate victory in their specific situation, or maybe
the future time at the end of the world and the eternal
punishment of the devil.

Note 6

The word "amen" does not mean "the end," as so many people use it in
prayer. It means "properly, firm, i.e. (figuratively) trustworthy; adverbi-
ally, surely (often as interjection, so be it)" (Strong's Concordance). It
was used seventy-eight times in the Bible; fifty-one of those times were
in the New Testament.

Romans 16:21

Timotheus my workfellow, and Lucius, and Jason, and Sosipater,
my kinsmen, salute you.

Note 1

The name Lucius means "illuminative" (Strong's Concordance). This name is used twice in Scripture (here and Acts 13:1). He was referred to as a kinsman of the Apostle Paul (see note 9 at Romans 16:7), or possibly Tertius (see note 4 at this verse). It is unclear whether this is the same Lucius that was mentioned in Acts 13:1. If so, Lucius would have been a long-time associate of Paul, and he would either have been a prophet or a teacher. Some people suspect that this Lucius is the Luke who traveled with the Apostle Paul (see note 2 at Acts 16:10) and wrote the books of Luke and Acts (see Life for Today Study Bible Notes, Introduction to Acts, Authorship).

Note 2

The name Jason means "about to cure" (Strong's Concordance). Jason was a kinsman (see note 9 at Romans 16:7) of the Apostle Paul or possibly Tertius (see note 4 at this verse). The name Jason is used five times in Scripture. Four of these times are from an account in Acts 17 (Acts 17:5-7 and Acts 17:9). It is not certain that the Jason mentioned here was the same as the Jason mentioned in Acts 17, but he probably was. If this was the same Jason as the Jason of Acts 17, then this Jason had been an acquaintance of Paul since Paul first went to Thessalonica (Acts 17:1). This would make it hard to understand Jason as being a kinsman of Paul in the sense of a blood relative. This must be referring to these men as being brothers in the Lord, or possibly, as Tertius' relatives (see note 4 at this verse). Jason apparently took Paul and his companions into his household. Because of this, the unbelieving Jews assaulted the house of Jason, and when they didn't find Paul, they took Jason into custody.

Note 3

The name Sosipater means "of a safe father" (Strong's Concordance). He was called a kinsman of Paul, or possibly it was Tertius who referred to him as a kinsman (see note 4 at this verse). Most scholars believe that Sosipater is the same man as Sopater of Acts 20:4. If so, this would mean that he was from Berea and more than likely a convert of Paul's missionary work there (see note 3 at Acts 20:4).

Note 4

In note 9 at Romans 16:7, the word "kinsman" was defined and its normal usage discussed. However, this verse seems to present a problem with the word "kinsman" denoting either a blood relative or a fellow countryman. There are quite a few scriptures where Paul wrote of Timotheus, and nowhere else is it implied that Timothy was related to Paul (see note 1 at Acts 16:1). Therefore, most scholars exclude Timothy and believe that Lucius, Jason, and Sosipater are the ones being referred to as kinsmen. However, if these men were the same men as mentioned in Acts (see notes 1-3 at this verse), then it would appear that they were converts of the Apostle Paul during his second missionary journey. This would make it doubtful that they were blood relatives as the primary usage of the word "kinsman" would imply. This could mean that these men were kinsmen in the sense that they were fellow countrymen. So that would mean they were of Jewish descent, living in these Gentile cities. There is also the possibility that Paul was referring to them as kinsmen in the sense that they were brothers in Christ. There is also the possibility that Paul had ceased his comments in the previous verse and that Tertius, the writer of Romans (Romans 16:22), was speaking of these men as his kinsmen.

Note 5

Whether these men were Paul's kinsmen or Tertius' kinsmen, they were definitely Paul's converts and companions in the ministry. This gives us some insight into Paul's methods. If these men were the same men as listed in the book of Acts, then they were born again during Paul's second missionary journey (see note 1 at Acts 18:22). This means that these men were converted around A.D. 52, and Paul was writing this letter to the Romans around A.D. 57 to 58 (see Life for Today Study Bible Notes, Introduction to Romans, Date and Place of Writing). That means Paul had discipled these men for approximately five years. Therefore, we have an example of how long it took for Timothy to progress into a position of leadership. Paul was the one who wrote that a novice should not be given a position of authority (1 Timothy 3:6). Timothy was to be left in charge of the church at Ephesus (1 Timothy 1:3) a very short time after Paul's writing of this letter as he traveled toward Jerusalem. Some scholars speculate that the church at Ephesus could have had as many as 100,000 members.

Romans 16:22

I Tertius, who wrote this epistle, salute you in the Lord.

Note 6

The name Tertius is of Latin origin and means "third" (Strong's Concordance). This is the only mention of Tertius in Scripture. He actually wrote the book of Romans from the Apostle Paul's dictation.

Romans 16:23

Gaius mine host, and of the whole church, saluteth you. Erastus the chamberlain of the city saluteth you, and Quartus a brother.

Note 7

The name Gaius was a common Roman name. This name is used five times in Scripture (Acts 19:29, 20:4; here; 1 Corinthians 1:14; and 3 John 1) and refers to at least three different men. Acts 19:29 refers to Gaius as being a man of Macedonia (see note 1 at Acts 16:9), while Acts 20:4 refers to a Gaius who was of Derbe (see note 5 at Acts 14:6), a city of Asia (see note 3 at Acts 16:6). It is probable that the Gaius referred to here was the same man that Paul mentioned in 1 Corinthians 1:14, since the book of Romans was written from Corinth (see Life for Today Study Bible Notes, Introduction to Romans, Date and Place of Writing). This would make Gaius one of the few people in Corinth that Paul actually baptized. This verse says that Gaius was not only Paul's host, but also host of the whole church, implying that he had a house church meeting in his residence.

The Apostle John addressed the epistle of 3 John to Gaius. Some speculate that this man was the same Gaius that Paul was referring to here.

Note 8

The name Erastus is mentioned three times in Scripture (Acts 19:22, this verse, and 2 Timothy 4:20). Erastus means "beloved" (Strong's Concordance). Most scholars agree that this was the same Erastus that Paul sent with Timothy into Macedonia (see note 1 at Acts 16:9) while Paul remained in Ephesus (see note 3 at Acts 18:19). Paul later wrote to Timothy that Erastus abode in Corinth (2 Timothy 4:20), while this verse reveals that he was the chamberlain of that city (see note 9 at this verse).

Note 9

The word "chamberlain" is only used six times in the Bible (2 Kings 23:11; Esther 2:3, 14-15; Acts 12:20; and here). Of the two times this word is used in the New Testament, Acts 12:20 uses "chamberlain" in the sense of an eunuch who keeps the king's bedchamber, and in this verse, it was referring to Erastus being the treasurer of the city of Corinth.

Note 10

The name Quartus means "fourth" (Strong's Concordance). This is the only mention of Quartus in Scripture. He was a Christian brother in Corinth who sent greetings to the saints in Rome.

Romans 16:24

The grace of our Lord Jesus Christ be with you all. Amen.

LIVING COMMENTARY

Praise God that the judgment, or wrath, of our God isn't what Paul was invoking here. Praise God, all the wrath of God was placed on Jesus (see my note at John 12:32). Paul was blessing us with the grace of God. Hallelujah! Sadly, many pastors and churches today aren't blessing their people with the grace of God. They are still living under the Old Covenant and releasing the wrath of God.

Romans 16:25

Now to him that is of power to stablish you according to my gospel, and the preaching of Jesus Christ, according to the revelation of the mystery, which was kept secret since the world began,

LIVING COMMENTARY

Paul was claiming divine authority and inspiration for the Gospel he preached (see my notes at Galatians 1:8-9). He was certain this was how the Lord would establish these believers. Preachers today should be as certain of their message.

Romans 16:26

But now is made manifest, and by the scriptures of the prophets, according to the commandment of the everlasting God, made known to all nations for the obedience of faith:

LIVING COMMENTARY

This verse is a continuation of the sentence started in Romans 16:25. That verse spoke of the Lord establishing the believers through the Gospel Paul preached, which had been a mystery, kept secret until Paul manifested it. And here, this verse says this establishing of the believers also comes through the scriptures of all the prophets. Paul put his revelation on par with the Old Testament scriptures. Peter did the same thing (2 Peter 3:15-16). This reveals that Paul knew his writings were Scripture or inspired writings equal to OT Scripture. Obedience isn't a word that grace people today use very often. That's because obedience is typically associated with keeping the precepts of the OT Law. We have been delivered from the Law (Romans 7:6) and no longer have to obey it in order to be accepted by God (Ephesians 1:6). But obedience is still important; we just don't have to obey the Law. Rather, we have to be obedient to the faith. This is speaking of being born again (see my note at John 3:3), or made righteous (see my note at 2 Corinthians 5:21), through faith in what Jesus did for us. Obedience to the faith doesn't earn us anything from God but rather appropriates what Jesus has provided for us through grace (see my note at Ephesians 2:8).

Romans 16:27

To God only wise, be glory through Jesus Christ for ever. Amen.

LIVING COMMENTARY

It's offensive to many to say that only God is wise, but it's true. All true and accurate wisdom comes from God (Colossians 2:3). The wisdom of this world is foolishness to God (1 Corinthians 3:19) and will come to nothing (1 Corinthians 2:6). Many fools (Psalms 14:1 and 53:1) in our modern day have been exalted by people to positions of honor for their intellect, but there is no wisdom or counsel or understanding against the Lord (Proverbs 21:30). The subscript at the end of this verse does not appear in all Bibles. Most scholars believe this was added later by a scribe. The subscript says, "Written to the Romans from Corinthus, [and sent by Phebe servant of the church at Cenchrea]."

Note 11

This subscript was probably not a part of Paul's original letter to the Romans. A scribe added it at a later date. However, it does seem to be accurate and is therefore retained.

About the Author

ANDREW WOMMACK'S life was forever changed the moment he encountered the supernatural love of God on March 23, 1968. As a renowned Bible teacher and author, Andrew has made it his mission to change the way the world sees God.

Andrew's vision is to go as far and deep with the Gospel as possible. His message goes far through the *Gospel Truth* television program, which is available to nearly half the world's population. The message goes deep through discipleship at Charis Bible College, headquartered in Woodland Park, Colorado. Founded in 1994, Charis has campuses across the United States and around the globe.

Andrew also has an extensive library of teaching materials in print, audio, and video—most of which can be accessed for free from his website: **awmi.net**.

Andrew's LIVING COMMENTARY BIBLE SOFTWARE

Andrew Wommack's *Living Commentary* Bible study software is a user-friendly, downloadable program. It's like reading the Bible with Andrew at your side, sharing his revelation with you verse by verse.

Main features:

- Access to Windows, Mac, and web versions
- Andrew Wommack's notes on over 25,000 Scriptures and counting
- 11 Bible versions, 5 commentaries, 3 concordances, and 2 dictionaries
- Maps and charts
- User notes
- Enhanced text selection and copying
- Commentaries and charts
- Scripture and note reveal functionalities
- "Living" (i.e., constantly updated)
- Quick navigation
- Robust search capabilities
- Automatic software updates
- Mobile phone and tablet support for web version
- Screen reader support for visually impaired users (Windows version)
- Bonus material

Whether you're new to studying the Bible or a seasoned Bible scholar, you'll gain a deeper revelation of the Word from a grace-and-faith perspective.

Purchase Andrew's *Living Commentary* today at **awmi.net/living**, and grow in the Word with Andrew.

Item code: 8350

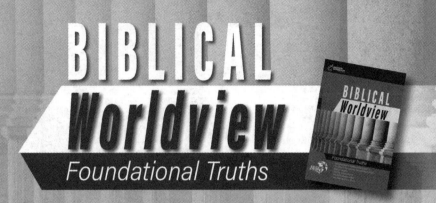

BIBLICAL *Worldview*
Foundational Truths

Defend your faith with confidence.

Our worldview is the filter through which we process life, and as Christians, it should be based on the unchanging Word of God—not popular culture.

Biblical Worldview: Foundational Truths is designed to be used for either individual or group study and includes:

- ♦ **Twelve online video lessons** covering the following topics:
  - How Important Is a Biblical Worldview?
  - The Bible Is the Inspired, Accurate Word of God
  - Biblical Creationism (Creation vs. Evolution)
  - The True Nature of God
  - The Fallen Nature of Man
  - Your New Identity in Christ

- ♦ **A workbook** that helps learners take a deeper dive into the twelve lessons

- ♦ **A USB** that contains the twelve lessons in audio format

- ♦ **Printable PDFs** of each of the twelve lessons—perfect for group study!

Order this essential teaching today at **awmi.net/store** or call **719-635-1111**!

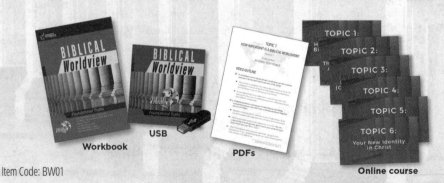

Workbook   USB   PDFs   Online course

Item Code: BW01

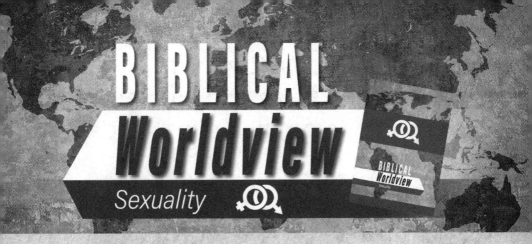

BIBLICAL *Worldview*
Sexuality

What does God say about Sex? Marriage? Homosexuality? Transgenderism? Adultery?

When answering questions about sexuality, believers should base their responses on the uncompromised Word of God—not popular culture.

Biblical Worldview: Sexuality is designed to be used for either individual or group study and includes:

♦ **Twelve online video lessons** covering the following topics:
  • The Need for a Biblical Worldview on Sexuality
  • The Purpose of Marriage
  • The Covenant of Marriage
  • Adultery, Divorce, and Remarriage
  • Sexual Purity
  • The Real Agenda
  • Homosexuality
  • Transgenderism
  • Tolerance and Love
♦ **A workbook** that helps learners take a deeper dive into the twelve lessons
♦ **A USB** that contains the twelve lessons in audio format
♦ **Printable PDFs** of each of the twelve lessons—perfect for group study!

Order this essential teaching today at **awmi.net/store** or call **719-635-1111**!

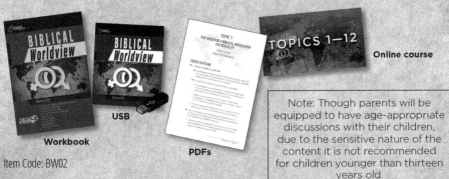

Online course

Workbook

USB

PDFs

Item Code: BW02

Note: Though parents will be equipped to have age-appropriate discussions with their children, due to the sensitive nature of the content it is not recommended for children younger than thirteen years old.

Your peace doesn't have to ebb and flow with the tides of circumstance. Build your life on the solid foundation of the Word.

We offer over 200,000 hours of FREE Bible-based teachings on **awmi.net**.

Visit our website for teachings, videos, testimonies, and other resources that will encourage you with truth for any situation and help you learn God's plan for relationships, finances, faith, and more.

"I was lost deep in the world. . . . I started seeking the truth, and through AWM's resources, I have been set free . . . including receiving miracles of finances when everything seemed impossible. I am at peace with myself. I thank AWM for sharing the truth, which has freed me to understand God."

— David M.

Be empowered to live the victorious life God intended for you! Visit **awmi.net** to access our library of free resources.

Teaching God's unconditional love and grace.

Contact Us

We'd love to hear from you!
Reach out to us at any of our offices near you.

AWM Offices

Andrew Wommack Ministries USA
Headquarters – Woodland Park, CO
Website: awmi.net
Email: info@awmi.net

Andrew Wommack Ministries Australia
Website: awmaust.net.au
Email: info@awmaust.net.au

Andrew Wommack Ministries Canada
Website: awmc.ca
Email: info@awmc.ca

Andrew Wommack Ministries France
Website: awmi.fr
Email: info@awmi.fr

Andrew Wommack Ministries Germany
Website: andrewwommack.de
Email: info@andrewwommack.de

Andrew Wommack Ministries Hong Kong
Website: cbchk.hk
Email: info.hk@awmcharis.com

Andrew Wommack Ministries Hungary
Website: awme.hu
Email: hungary@awme.net

Andrew Wommack Ministries Indonesia
Website: awmindonesia.net
Email: awmindonesia@gmail.com

Andrew Wommack Ministries India
Website: awmindia.net
Email: info@awmindia.net

Andrew Wommack Ministries Italy
Website: awme.it
Email: info@awme.it

Andrew Wommack Ministries Netherlands
Website: andrewwommack.nl
Email: info.nl@awmcharis.com

Andrew Wommack Ministries Poland
Website: awmpolska.com
Email: awmpolska@zyciesozo.com

Andrew Wommack Ministries Russia
Website: cbtcrussia.ru
Email: info@cbtcrussia.ru

Andrew Wommack Ministries South Africa
Website: awmsa.net
Email: enquiries@awmsa.net

Andrew Wommack Ministries Uganda
Website: awmuganda.net
Email: awm.uga@awmcharis.com

Andrew Wommack Ministries United Kingdom
Website: awme.net
Email: enquiries@awme.net

Andrew Wommack Ministries Zimbabwe
Website: awmzim.net
Email: enquiries@awmzim.net

For a more comprehensive list of all of
our offices, visit **awmi.net/contact-us.**

Connect with us on social media.

CONTACT INFORMATION

Andrew Wommack Ministries Inc.

PO Box 3333

Colorado Springs CO 80934-3333

Email: info@awmi.net

Helpline: 719-635-1111

Helpline Hours: Monday through Friday,
twenty-four hours a day (MT)

awmi.net